PRAISE FOR

The Problem with Men

"Read this if you feel like you have made too many mistakes to become something amazing."

—Shana Pryor, PhD, psychology fellow, LT, MSC, USN, Naval Hospital Okinawa, Japan

"Epic story of overcoming setbacks and achieving success. Amazed at how much detail Dr. Levant remembers going back to his early childhood."

—Martin H. Belsky, JD, dean and professor emeritus of law, the University of Akron

"Tells the remarkable story of a life of activism, research, and social contribution by an eminent psychologist and founder of the psychology of men, offering some life-lessons in resilience for all of us."

—Joseph H. Pleck, PhD, professor emeritus of human development and family studies at the University of Illinois at Urbana-Champaign

"This is an important narrative about interrupting the family cycle of violence and abuse. Trauma is too often passed down from father to son and then on to the next generation until someone like Ronald Levant gains the information and courage needed to end it."

> —Christopher Kilmartin, PhD, independent consultant, professor emeritus of psychology, University of Mary Washington

"This book is a must read for those who would like to understand the life of one of the most influential, if not the most influential person in the study of the modern American man. It is of particular value and inspiration for those who have struggled to overcome adversity and hardships in life."

> —Michael Andronico, PhD, private practice, Bridgewater, NJ, past president of American Psychological Association Divisions 49 and 51.

"Dr. Levant weaves a compelling and brutally honest narrative of childhood trauma, grit, and resiliency. This book speaks to the traumas that so many young men experience from their fathers and bullies, the mental health conditions that men struggle with in silence, and the way those experiences can shape our lives. Every chapter has useful life lessons stemming from a lifetime of personal growth and psychological knowledge."

> —Ryon C. McDermott, PhD, professor of Clinical and Counseling Psychology, University of South Alabama, past president of the Society for the Psychology of Men and Masculinities, Division 51 of the American Psychological Association

"This book is a gift. I found myself so moved, and so deeply engaged, that I have just finished reading the entire book in one sitting. In lovingly and honestly capturing his own journey, Ron Levant brings us fully into the so-often unacknowledged prison we have imposed upon generations of men. He then beautifully illuminates the turning points that can create a pathway to living a full emotional life—some serendipitous, some powered by gritty determination, some thoughtfully constructed step-by-step, and many accompanied by loving friends, family, and colleagues. Both for my work as a psychologist and for my own intimate life, I'm grateful."

—**Patricia Papernow, EdD, psychologist, internationally recognized expert on "blended families"**

"This is a painfully honest and moving book. A memoir of life redemption that shows that even when everything seems lost, it is possible to not only recover but also create a 'new' version of oneself. And that new person that rose from the ashes has created a body of work that contributes significantly to the lives of others. Levant's work on fathers and the psychology of men is well known as a groundbreaking contribution to the field of psychology. This book is a tribute to his journey both personally and professionally. The short 'Take Aways' at the end of each chapter invite the reader to reflect and renew themselves, providing another contribution to the lives of his readers."

—**Oliva M. Espin, PhD, professor emerita, Department of Women's Studies, San Diego State University, author of** *My Native Land Is Memory: Stories of a Cuban Childhood*

"A searing testimony to the transformation of childhood wounds into an agent for healing. From Ronald Levant's vantage as an eminent psychologist specializing in men and masculinity, he leads us from his abusive childhood through his unsettled youth and young adulthood and into mature adulthood with an accomplished professional life whose roots were planted firmly in his past. We all carry baggage, but not all of us unpack the baggage, rearrange the suitcase, and give it to others who are walking similar paths. In his life's work, Ronald Levant does."

—**Lyn Barrett, author of** *Crazy: Reclaiming Life from the Shadow of Traumatic Memory* **and founder of Dissociative Writers, Inc.**

"Too often successful and distinguished colleagues keep their private life stories, failures, and challenges top secret so that others will only see them in their best light and are directed to their successes while hiding their struggles. In *The Problem with Men: Insights on Overcoming a Traumatic Childhood from a World-Renowned Psychologist*, Dr. Ron Levant turns this approach on its head and offers a compelling narrative of his life story with all of the challenges, failures, and poor decisions, as well as the joys and triumphs. It is a compelling, brutally honest, and important read that might be especially helpful for those who need some hope as they journey through their own challenged life story."

—Thomas G. Plante, PhD, ABPP, Augustin Cardinal Bea, SJ, University Professor, Santa Clara University, and emeritus adjunct professor of psychiatry and behavioral sciences, Stanford University School of Medicine, author of *Living Ethically in an Unethical World* and *Spiritually Informed Therapy*

"A fascinating glimpse into how personal experiences can unexpectedly result in extraordinary insight into the dynamics that have adversely impacted the lives of many individuals, especially unknowingly vulnerable men. Constantly driven to understand why he keeps making 'highly destructive decisions,' the author's scientific self ultimately discovers why so many men have been drawn to similarly unhappy relationships. His clinical self then sets out on an exciting quest to systematically address this national tragedy."

—Pat DeLeon, PhD, MPH, JD, former American Psychological Association president

"Through his remarkable and raw life story, full of extreme twists and adversities, Dr. Ronald Levant does the thing he has promulgated through his decades of seminal masculinities scholarship. He peels back the layers of his complex self, including his lowest of moments and his stupendous highs, with openness, emotional vulnerability, and compassion—the very traits he believes all boys and men can attain (and deserve)."

> —Christopher S. Reigeluth, PhD, associate professor at Oregon Health & Science University, author of *The Masculinity Workbook for Teens: Discover What Being a Guy Means to You*

"The vulnerability and openness displayed by Dr. Levant in this book make for a raw and refreshing read. It broadens one's perspective on life and the inherent challenges we all face. It provides insight on the value of resilience and finding purpose in order to wade our way through the toughest of times to a more positive existence."

> —Ray Stukes, Jr., author of *The Self-Centered Perspective: Using Self-Mastery, the Power of Introspection, and Choice to Balance Life's Ups and Downs*

"Dr. Levant's bravery in sharing the darker parts of his life, combined with his insights from decades as an expert on masculinity, give voice to the inner struggle that many men face. This is a must-read for any man who ever felt he needed to do, or be, things he didn't want."

> —Eric R. McCurdy, PhD, assistant professor of psychology, Keene State College

The Problem with Men:
Insights on Overcoming a Traumatic Childhood from a World-Renowned Psychologist
by Dr. Ronald F. Levant
with Alisa Bowman

© Copyright 2024 Dr. Ronald F. Levant

ISBN 979-8-88824-432-6

All rights reserved. No part of this publication may be reproduced, stored in a retrieval system, or transmitted in any form or by any means—electronic, mechanical, photocopy, recording, or any other—except for brief quotations in printed reviews, without the prior written permission of the author.

Published by
köehlerbooks™
3705 Shore Drive
Virginia Beach, VA 23455
800-435-4811
www.koehlerbooks.com

The Problem with Men

Insights on Overcoming a Traumatic Childhood from a World-Renowned Psychologist

DR. RONALD F. LEVANT
with Alisa Bowman

VIRGINIA BEACH
CAPE CHARLES

For anyone who has ever experienced confusion and or consternation by my behavior.

CONTENTS

Preface 5

Chapter 1: A Scared Boy Learns How to Fight 7

Chapter 2: Expulsion and Redemption 30

Chapter 3: Saved by Math 44

Chapter 4: The Making of an Activist 54

Chapter 5: Students for a Democratic Society at a Medical School? 78

Chapter 6: "Wear a Flower in Your Hair" 97

Chapter 7: The Evil Dr. Goopcough 107

Chapter 8: Journey into the Darkest Part of My Soul ... 124

Chapter 9: Psychology and Psychedelics 144

Chapter 10: An Imposter Earns a Doctorate 168

Chapter 11: My First Professorship 197

Chapter 12: Fathers: The Forgotten Parent 226

Chapter 13: From Research to Practice
in the Psychology of Men ... 241

Chapter 14: My Dad Dies ... 258

Chapter 15: Hitting My Stride ... 267

Chapter 16: My APA Presidency ... 280

Chapter 17: The Best Part of Me ... 286

Afterword ... 293

Acknowledgements ... 294

PREFACE

You may not know my name, but you probably know my work. I have devoted most of my professional career to understanding the reasons why some men are so problematic—unable to describe how they feel, neglecting their health, and committing savage acts of violence when their manhood is questioned.

Each month, tens of thousands of people search Google to understand the phrase "toxic masculinity." While I don't personally use that term (preferring "traditional masculine norms"), it is based, in part, on my research and on the professional reference books which I cowrote and coedited. I played a leading role in the development of the subfield of psychology that studies the topic and in the creation of the American Psychological Association's division on the psychology of men and masculinity.

However, if you knew me at any point in my childhood—marked by trauma and abuse and later in adolescence by juvenile delinquency—you would not have predicted that I would wind up being the person that I am. Someone with my past rarely rises to the top of a profession, earns stature as one of the top 2 percent of all scientists worldwide, appears on *Oprah* and *20/20*, gains a big spread in *People* magazine, serves as president of a professional association with 133,000 members, develops 21 psychological scales and measures, and publishes more than 300 peer-reviewed studies and 20 books—one earning the William James Book Award from the American Psychological Association.

My hope in telling my tale in this book is to inspire and guide people who may have suffered as I did.

This has not been an easy book to write. First and foremost, there is the very nature of memory itself—unstable, reconstructive. I found myself wishing my memory were more like a hard drive on a computer, but sadly it more closely resembles the attic in my garage.

In some cases, certain details were lost entirely. With others, I had to logically deduce what might have happened. Whenever possible, I've checked my memory against the historical record (if available) or the memories of other family members. I should acknowledge that I changed some names to avoid embarrassing some people from my past.

As challenging as remembering was for me, the hardest part was being as honest as I could be. There was a continuing struggle between my desire to tell the truth and my desire to paint myself in a favorable light. And here I must acknowledge Oliva Espin, PhD. Oliva was a colleague at my first academic job at Boston University dating back to the mid-1970s, and we have remained friends ever since. More recently, Oliva has published her memoir, *My Native Land is Memory: Stories of a Cuban Childhood.* As I was about to embark on writing this memoir, I asked her for advice. Her response: be as honest as you can possibly be, even if it hurts. Her words were a guiding light, and I have acknowledged aspects of my life here that in the past I had preferred to stay hidden. And I am glad that I did. Shining light on shameful secrets reduces their power.

One more point, a trigger warning of sorts. In this book I describe my sexual experiences, beginning with my precocious sexuality as a teen, to my experiences of casual sex in the late '60's. As a teenager, I was motivated by a desire to conform to the traditional expectations of males to be sexual, and back in the '60s I believed that I was participating in the era's ethos of free love. Casual sex wasn't my preference, which was to be in a committed relationship. Although the sex was always consensual, I am aware that these accounts might be triggering for some people, particularly trauma survivors, so if that is the case with you, you may prefer to skip those parts.

CHAPTER 1

A Scared Boy Learns How to Fight

(1942–1955)

any successful people credit their parents for shaping them into who they are today. In that respect, my father deserves at least some recognition.

Had he not terrorized me for most of the first thirteen years of my life, I doubt I would have become an internationally recognized psychologist, partly due to my burning desire to learn what made men like my father such despicable humans.

My story starts with my father.

His story began generations earlier, with a legendary ancestor named Wolf Tomashinskii. Wolf, my great-great uncle, lived in Eastern Europe early in the 20th century. According to family lore, Wolf stood just five feet tall and was just as wide—and mean as hell! Once, the legend goes, he punched a horse in the head, knocking the animal out cold.

Much like family heirlooms, this brutality was passed down through the generations. Some people escaped the "Curse of Wolf." Others were born mercurial. One moment they would seem content. Seconds later, they would explode.

The Tomashinskii's eventually emigrated to Canada, shortening the last name to Thompson. Sarah Thompson, my paternal grandmother, was not physically violent, but the family's mean streak showed up in other ways. She used words as weapons, and they could hurt you as deeply as a man's tight fist. We children knew to stay out of her way.

In contrast, Grandpa Charlie, who worked as a cobbler, was a sweet and gentle man who deferred most decisions to his wife. He had grown up in the city of Minsk, in Belarus. His father, Yisroel Gilk, was devoutly religious and spent most of his days at the synagogue *davening* in prayer rather than working to support his family. To cover the family's expenses, Great Grandpa Yisroel indentured Charlie to work for a cruel man who beat him so severely that he lost his hearing in one ear. Following this incident, Charlie disavowed religion. As a young adult, he emigrated to Winnipeg, Canada, where he changed his last name to Gould. There he met and married Sarah and raised his children nonreligiously.

Of the four children born to Grandpa Charlie and Grandma Sarah, my father—and, to a lesser degree, his older brother George, took after Wolf. A high roller in the furniture business, Uncle George was periodically rich and periodically poor. He was married to Irene, who was blond, very pretty, and a visual artist. They had no children of their own, so when he was wealthy, he would buy us kids all kinds of nice things. But Uncle George and my father were like oil and fire, occasionally bringing family gatherings to a loud, abrupt end. In contrast, their younger brother Arwin took after Grandpa Charlie. He was kind, funny, and soothing to have around. Their sister, Rose, died in her twenties and I never knew her.

◆ ◆ ◆

My father was a tough, barrel-chested guy with a hair-trigger temper, who dropped out of school after the eighth grade to go to work during the Great Depression. He was belligerent, swore repeatedly, and farted loudly—often in the presence of family and friends.

Near the start of World War II, my father escaped the Canadian draft by changing his name from Hamie Gould to Harry Levant, borrowing the name of one of his cousins by marriage. Then he traveled south by train, crossed the border, kept going, and eventually settled in Los Angeles.

It was here in Los Angeles that, one fateful night, he met a petite, dark-haired beauty named Wilma Adler, whom everyone referred to as Billie. She had once dreamed of becoming a professional dancer and, with great longing, kept her unworn dancing shoes in pristine condition. Shy and retiring, Billie glowed with sweetness. Everyone liked her, partly because she was willing to put her needs and wishes on hold if they conflicted with those around her.

She was immediately smitten, and he likewise. They married within months in 1941 and I was born the next year. Soon after, my father enlisted in the United States Navy, and he was off to war to help defeat the Japanese and the Nazis.

He served as a sailor in the Construction Battalion ("Seabees"), which was tasked to build anything, anywhere, under any conditions, using the motto, *We Build, We Fight*. Among the highest-paid members of the military, the Seabees built more than four hundred bases throughout the Americas and beyond. My father trained as a pressman and was tasked to print materials for propaganda drops. He served on both the USS *Hector* and the USS *Prometheus*. He occasionally traveled home for shore leave, visiting me and my mother before returning to active duty.

Mother and I lived at Camp Peary, a naval base in Virginia, and then later at the home of my maternal grandparents, Sol and Edith Adler in St. Paul, Minnesota.

My maternal great grandparents, Bubie Tonnie (Tanya) and Zaydee Louis Labovitch (seated). The boy on the far left is my uncle Joe Baker. My grandmother Edith is right next to him, and my grandfather Sol is on the right end. The three small children are Eugene (the boy), Marjorie (the older girl), and Wilma (the younger girl). I can't identify the man in between my grandma and grandpa.

Sol, who always had a twinkle in his eye, owned a haberdashery making uniforms for students who attended military academies in the Twin Cities, Minnesota metropolitan area. Edith, who loved to bake for her grandsons—pies, cakes, cookies, all in abundant quantities—was a large woman who was exceptionally sweet and kind.

One morning, my mother dragged a playpen to my grandparents' yellowing front yard in St. Paul. She gently lowered me down, leaving for a moment to retrieve something from the house. When she returned, the playpen was still there, but I was gone.

Family members poured from the house, setting off in different directions and yelling my name. Finally, my mother's brother Allan found me at a nearby construction site. There I sat with a small pail and shovel, digging dirt as I watched large earthmovers amass piles of their own. Uncle Allen never breathed a word about where I had been. My mother was so happy to have me back in her arms that she didn't dare to ask.

Soon my father arrived home for shore leave, and it was likely during this trip that my younger brother Lowell came into the picture. During one of these visits, I had a toilet training accident and missed the potty. According to Uncle Allan, my father flew into a rage, closed his fists, and pounded my tiny body. Grandpa Sol screamed as he pulled him off me: "Don't use your fists!"

These first few years were the highlight of my childhood, mainly because my mother was the sweetest, most loving caregiver a boy could want. It also was because my father was seldom around. I only saw him a few times a year, and for a week or so at a time.

While it's hard for me to explain it now, back then I yearned for my father's presence. Whenever men arrived at the door, I unbuttoned their shirts and inspected their chests. If I didn't find thick curls, I turned to my mother and said, "Not Daddy."

◆ ◆ ◆

I was three years old when the war ended and my dad returned home for good, landing in Los Angeles. So it came to pass that, one cold and snowy day, my grandfather drove my mother, Lowell, and me to the train station. Thinking that my father had never seen snow, I packed my pockets with snow and settled into my seat—excitedly rubbing my hands over the cold hard lumps. Dad was going to love this! He was going to be so surprised!

But soon my thighs grew wet. The lumps shrank, then disappeared, and I sat in soaked pants for the rest of that first day of the trip.

Three days later, when we arrived in California, my father was standing on the platform waiting to greet us. I dropped my suitcase, sprinted toward him, and leapt into his arms.

My dad used his military experience as a pressman to land a job at a printing company in Southern California. We lived in an apartment as he saved up money for a down payment on a home. The GI Bill promised low-interest mortgages to war veterans like him. Back then, with so many vets in the market for homes, cookie-cutter houses sprouted up like crabgrass—especially in Southern California, where my dad wanted us to live. For $5,000 he found a 1,187 square foot three bedroom, two bath home located on a semi-cul-de-sac with a street that backed up to the Los Angeles River. It was a steal.

Young families like ours, with multiple children, seemed to live in every house. This was, after all, the postwar Baby Boom. My street became a playground each afternoon, with spontaneous baseball and touch football games. It seemed idyllic—or, at least, it should have been.

My mother was not pleased. The house was in South Gate, and she knew what that meant. With the closest synagogue in an adjacent city, Huntington Park, we would be one of the few Jewish families in a sea of Goyim.

I'm sure she said something about it, as her religion still meant something to her. Unlike my father, my mother was somewhat observant, attended synagogue on major Jewish holidays, and had every intention of raising her boys to one day attend Hebrew school and be initiated into the Jewish community with a bar mitzvah.

Still, as was her nature, she deferred to my father's judgment.

◆ ◆ ◆

During that first week, I explored the neighborhood on foot with my mother occasionally glancing out the window to check on me. Minutes later I found two other boys, a dark-haired boy named

Dougie and a blond named Tommy. Soon we were inside a tent in Dougie's backyard.

"Let's all tell what we are," said Dougie, puffing out his chest with pride. "I'll start. I'm Protestant."

"Oh," said Tommy confidently, "I'm Catholic."

They focused their eyes on me. I wasn't sure what I was supposed to say. Being five years old, sometimes I'd pretend I was a rhinoceros, but somehow instinctively I knew that wasn't what they were looking for.

"Come on, Ronnie, what are you?" asked Dougie.

"Um, I'm Jewish," I finally responded, still very confused.

First, there was laughter. "Jewish!" they blurted between chuckles. "He's Jewish!"

What was so funny? They kept laughing. Was being Jewish bad? Dougie got the first punch in. Tommy got the second. Instinctively I curled into a ball, their fists pummeling my arms and legs.

"You kike!" they yelled. "Dirty kike!"

I squirmed away, pushed my way out of the tent, and raced home, wiping tears as I ran. I flung open the front door and raced through the house for my mother. The story poured out in spurts and gasps, with me pausing to wipe my nose on my sleeve. She wrapped me in her arms.

"We'll talk about it when your father gets home, okay?" said mother. "Why don't you stay inside and play?"

I did try to do what she suggested for a little while, but eventually my yearning to explore overcame my fear. I peeked out the front door, looking left toward their homes and didn't see either Dougie or Tommy. I proceeded down the driveway, then down the sidewalk, passing one house, then another, and careful to note the direction I was headed to find my way back home.

I was heading east when I heard a ping. A sharp pain emanated from my leg.

Tommy and a much older boy were standing on a porch across

the street. A BB rifle rested against the teen's shoulder, Tommy grinning behind him, and the gun's barrel pointed toward me.

"You shot me," I yelled, my palm against my thigh. "What are you doing? Why did you shoot me?"

They ran into the house, their laughter ringing in my ears, and I trudged home with the feeling of confusion mixed with anger and fear. Nothing like this had ever happened before. What was wrong with being Jewish? Why did they hate me so much? Hadn't my father just fought the Nazis to liberate the Jews? This didn't make any sense.

◆ ◆ ◆

Usually, when my father got home, we all sat down to dinner within minutes. But that evening he and I walked over to Tommy's house, which was just a few doors down. Mr. Gallagher answered.

"We just moved into the house two doors down," my father said, "and I'm hoping that you can help me understand something. Today your son beat up my son."

Mr. Gallagher crossed his arms. "Oh, did he?"

My father continued, "Then your nephew shot him in the leg with a BB gun. What's going on here?"

Mr. Gallagher sighed and advanced toward my father.

Sensing danger, I raced back home, my heart throbbing in my throat. I tore into the entryway, and then to the kitchen, rooting around in drawers until I found what I was looking for: a knife. My heart pounding, I sprinted down the block to save my father.

The two men were in the driveway, speaking quietly.

"We're sorry this happened," Mr. Gallagher said, shaking my father's hand. "We'll take care of it. I'll deal with them."

My father glanced in my direction.

"What are you holding? Go home and put the knife away," he snapped.

Minutes later, my father returned home, we sat down to dinner, and no one mentioned a word about what had transpired.

◆ ◆ ◆

This unleashed an extended chapter in my life in which I would be repeatedly ambushed by various gangs of boys, one of whom would always yell, "There's the kike. Let's get him."

Although I eventually made a few friends in the neighborhood, they ran off whenever these attacks occurred, leaving me to take the beating alone. Yet, despite these dangers, as the months ticked by, I managed to settle into a rhythm.

Each afternoon I rode my bike home from school, changed into play clothes, and raced back outside to see what fun I could find. I was loud, rambunctious, and always up for whatever action might be happening. Conversely, Lowell was my opposite. Shy, like my mother, and limited by his asthma, Lowell frequently stayed in his room and played quietly with his toys. He and I lived parallel lives, rarely interacting with one another even when in the same room.

Always on the alert to avoid the parts of the neighborhood where the bullies lurked, I rode my bike everywhere—to elementary school, to the Boy Scouts Lodge in South Gate Park, and later to junior high school. There was no fear of theft back then, and so I never even owned a bike lock. One route to Tweedy Elementary school took me through an abandoned industrial section, which was probably a toxic brownfield. The other route was on a busy street, Atlantic Avenue, and took me past a candy store, which seemed to have been designed for kids like me. There was a vast assortment of penny candies. I particularly liked the wax candies: wax lips, wax cigarettes, little wax tubes filled with juice. The proprietor was a gentle older man. I loved that store.

◆ ◆ ◆

Days passed. Then weeks. Then months. Then a year. Finances were tight. My parents were saving money to purchase a print shop. Therefore, they made sure to return the glass milk bottles for the nickel deposits, outfitted us in the cheapest clothes, and met Lowell's and my requests for the slightest of luxury items—Levi's, model airplane kits, Lincoln Logs—with the same answer, "We can't afford it." Thankfully our uncle George, my father's oldest brother, showered us and our cousins with expensive gifts, including my prized possession: a Grundig Majestic short-wave radio.

The more my father tried to attain his dream of becoming a small business owner, the more family life revolved around his needs. Dinner was served at 4:30 because my father started work early and came home early. My mother never served chicken because when he was a boy my father had seen a decapitated, still-running hen at a butcher's shop.

To him, noise was as irritating as a swarm of mosquitoes. He was subjected to the din of heavy machinery all day, he said, so during dinner, he wanted "QUIET." If my mother fussed over me, asking if I wanted more meat or potatoes, he protested, "No, he's had enough." On other occasions he was terse, shouting, "Shut up, Billie!"

I was a spirited kid—loud, exuberant, boisterous at times, everything my father didn't like. One day, I raced through the kitchen and accidentally kicked one of the empty milk bottles, which hit the wall, shards of glass flying everywhere.

As my mother and I cleaned up the mess, fear swirled in my stomach. My father was not going to be happy about this.

Several hours later he arrived home, and within minutes he noticed the milk bottle's absence. Hushed voices followed between him and mother.

"Ronnie," he said finally, "I told you not to do this." With his hand on my shoulder, he led me to his bedroom.

"Pull down your pants," he said.

I did as I was told.

"And your underwear too. Now, put your hands on the dresser."

"But. . ." I stammered.

"Just do it, Ronnie."

There was a searing pain as the strap connected with my skin. Again, and again, and again.

"May this be a lesson," he said, leaving me there in the bedroom, my skin burning. What unnerved me the most was not the punishment, but how calmly he had delivered it.

◆ ◆ ◆

Desperate to fit in by conforming to the fashion choices of my peers, I had to have Levi's, not some cheap jeans from Woolworths. So, by age eight, I discovered ways to make my own money: mowing lawns, selling stamps to other kids who had collections, and assembling intricate balsa wood model airplanes from kits, and then selling them to kids who didn't have the patience or skills to build their own.

One evening, just before putting the finishing touches on one of these planes, I flipped on the short-wave radio Uncle George had given me. To avoid irritating my father, I closed my door and turned the volume down to a barely audible vibration. Then I fiddled with the dial until I found the Johnny Otis Show out of Memphis. I sat, quietly humming along to rhythm and blues while simultaneously gluing delicate wood pieces.

An hour went by. Then another. I crouched over the plane as I worked, using tweezers, small dabs of Testors model glue, and expert precision to affix each piece.

There. It was done. I still needed to put on the "skin"—thin tissue paper—but the structure was complete. I stood on my bed, reached up, and hung the plane on the wall high above my bed, so that nothing could accidentally fall on top of it. I lay on the bed for a while, gazing up at it, admiring my work. It had a thirty-six-inch wingspan, but it didn't weigh more than a few ounces.

I had spent so much time on the model that I had nearly forgotten to do my homework. I sat at my desk, pulled out my math worksheet, and flipped off the radio so I could concentrate. The next moment I felt the walls shake.

"Damn it, Ronnie!"

My pupils widened, and my body clenched into itself. There were footsteps—loud ones, and my door flew open. I gripped my pencil tightly, barely breathing. Without even looking at me, my father stomped straight over to my bed and seized the fragile airplane. He yanked it down and pressed his palms together. The plane crumpled.

My entire face was rigid. I fought to contain my tears.

His eyes were wild with rage. He tossed the fragments of the plane aside, spun toward my dresser and the Grundig Majestic short-wave radio. Gripping the radio tightly with both hands, he faced me squarely. He cranked his arms back. I hit the floor just before the radio crashed through the bay window.

He turned and walked out of my room without saying a word.

Stunned, I peered out the broken window. Below, on the dirt, were the pieces of what used to be my prized possession. Fury engulfed my chest, burning away my tears.

I hated him with every cell of my body.

I flew out of my room and searched for my mother, terrified I'd find him instead. She was in the kitchen, and the words spilled out of me between angry gasps. How the radio was destroyed, how the plane was destroyed.

"I didn't do anything! I swear. I didn't do anything," I protested. She pulled me toward her and wrapped her arms around me.

"You'll be okay," she soothed, stroking my back, my head, my face. "You're going to be okay." Her warm cheek next to mine, she whispered, "I'll save some money and we'll get you a new model kit."

"I don't want a new model kit!"

Quietly, calmly she warned, "Don't upset your father. He's trying to buy a print shop. He's got a lot on his mind."

My parents, younger brother, and me. It doesn't take a psychologist to recognize a depressed boy.

◆ ◆ ◆

A friend, Billy Barbarich, lived down the street, at the corner of Ledgewood Road and Adella Avenue. A frequent participant in the games on our street, he was a little younger than me and not very smart but still a reliable buddy. My two other friends at the time were Jimmy Neighbors and Chris Hartman. Jimmy was my age, in the same grade at school, and lived on Almira Road, which was the next street over, so that houses on Almira backed up to houses on my street, Ledgewood Road. He was part of a group led by an older boy, Bruce Baker, all of whom lived on Almira Road and with whom I would occasionally take hikes on the bank of the Los Angeles River. Chris lived with his mother and stepfather (his father was killed in WWII) in a different neighborhood close to Tweedy Elementary School. His stepfather owned a small airfield in Long Beach along with several small planes and gave flying lessons.

Chris' stepdad was a kind father who knew the skies like a sailor knows the seas. Occasionally he'd take us up in his small twin-engine Piper Cub and fly us around, pointing out landmarks, which was a real thrill. As we got older, he'd let us fly with his supervision. He would talk me through the controls, what to push and what to pull when, and how to hold the plane steady if the wind hit the wings in a certain way. It reminded me of a complicated car, and with all the freedom associated with it. When it was time to land, he became very serious but never raised his voice. Nor did he ever hit Chris, as far as I knew. I wondered what that was like.

One bright sunny day, Billy and I rode our bikes to South Gate Park. After parking them against a tree, we wandered in search of fun. Mere steps later, I heard the phrase that had become a dreaded refrain during my years in South Gate: "There's the kike."

My stomach churned when I saw the group of boys, hanging out on a picnic table. "Hey kike," one of them said, "Come over here and fight."

Knowing what was coming my way, I turned toward Billy to hand him my sunglasses.

A boy threw his arm around my neck and yanked me down. His fist connected with my eye and then my nose. He kneed me in the stomach. As the air left my lungs with a gasp, warm blood oozed over my lips. My mouth tasted like iron. When he wound up for another blow, I pushed up on his arm and crouched down escaping the headlock. Then I ran toward my bike and peddled home. Billy and my sunglasses were already long gone.

Soon afterward, I joined the local YMCA and signed up for boxing lessons.

I hadn't told Uncle George I'd been getting beat up, but he seemed to sense the potential need. During family get-togethers, he got down on his knees, lifted his palms, and told me to punch as hard as I could. He also taught my cousin Diane how to make a fist "with the thumb on the outside," he counseled. For my birthday that year, he bought me a set of weights with a bench, barbell, and a box of weight plates. I also bought a speed punching bag and installed it in the garage. I would wail on it, imagining the faces of my tormentors.

My arms soon went from skinny twigs to firm and muscled. My entire body seemed broader, firmer, and stronger—and I had learned how to throw a punch.

◆ ◆ ◆

As I rode my bike through the abandoned industrial site on my way to school, one of my many tormentors challenged me to a fight. He didn't know about the boxing lessons. He didn't know about weightlifting, nor about my newly acquired muscles. I walked right up to him and positioned myself in a boxing stance. His friends laughed at what they assumed was my folly.

My first punch bloodied his nose. The next one doubled him over in pain. The third one knocked him to the ground.

I stood over him, ready for more, but the fight had gone out of him.

"I give up," he pleaded from the pavement. "I give up."

As I rode home, my confidence swelled. I could defend myself. The fear of getting jumped was finally gone.

Meanwhile, life at home remained precarious. My father always seemed angry around me, and I frequently was under a cloud of suspicion. He was never warm or kind. As I cut the grass, he watched as if his presence were needed for me to get even the simplest of jobs correct. If I didn't put a rake back where he wanted it, I heard about it. If three blades of grass poked toward the sidewalk, I was cornered and disparaged. If I didn't remove every single piece of debris, I got chewed out.

I was used to the constant criticism. It rolled off my back like pool water. However, his sudden mood shifts terrorized me. One moment he would be quietly reorganizing tools in the garage, and the next he'd be screaming and throwing things—usually in my direction, which left me always on my guard. The only time I felt relaxed was when my father was away from home.

◆ ◆ ◆

That year, during Hanukkah, we made the twenty-minute drive to Uncle Arwin's and Aunt Merle's house in Long Beach. Their three toddlers—Rhoda, Diane, and Anita—were seven, ten, and twelve years my junior, but we loved seeing them. My grandparents Charlie and Sarah were there, too, and Uncle George and Aunt Irene showered all of us with gifts. Also present were our cousins from the Goldstein side of the family[1]. I was especially smitten with my cousin Fagey, who was close to my age, sharp-witted, and cute as a button.

The adults played cribbage while we kids stayed busy with basketball, tag, and other outdoor games.

---

1 The Goldsteins were first cousins. Their ancestral name was also Gilk, and when my father's family changed our name to Gould, they changed theirs to Goldstein.

Just before dinner, someone suggested that we do the "numbers thing." We kids gathered with Uncle George, working together to write out a long set of arithmetical operations.

"Okay," I said, "3426 times 7892, minus 4518, plus 9012, divided by 3719."

Fagey feverishly worked to solve the problem, her pencil skittering across the paper while my father worked the numbers in his head. I peeked over her shoulder as she worked, rooting for her to win. *Please*, I thought, *put him in his place. Don't let him win.*

Fagey had just finished multiplying the first two numbers, writing 27,037,992 on the paper and readied herself for the subtraction. I glanced at my father, who sat there grinning. *No*, I thought, *he can't have figured it out already. Come on, Fagey. You can do this!* While the addition and subtraction came quickly, the hardest part was the division. "You can do it," I whispered.

"I've got it!" my father called out. "7,137.10372. Got it."

I couldn't bear his smugness and walked out of the room without congratulating him.

◆ ◆ ◆

I worked as a dishwasher at a restaurant owned by one of the few Jews who lived in South Gate. I was not yet of age, so I was paid "under the table." Unlike my father, Mr. Cohen was kind, understanding, and nurturing. Even when I broke a dish, he told me to toss it in the trash and not to worry about it. My later employers would have made me pay for it. My father? He would have reached for his strap.

As I scrubbed pots, I imagined my mother leaving my father. Then she'd meet and marry Mr. Cohen. In this fantasy, Mr. Cohen encouraged me, helped me with homework, offered advice, and seemed happy to have me around.

The fantasy followed me home and to and from school. One morning, with my dad already at work, I casually mentioned to mom,

"You know my boss Mr. Cohen? He's Jewish, and a very nice guy."

"No," she said. "Stop that."

◆ ◆ ◆

One day in late autumn, we piled into my dad's Chrysler to travel the two hours to Palm Springs where Uncle George and Aunt Irene had recently moved. With all the windows rolled up, my father puffed on his cigar. Just as he did during our dinners at home, he forbade any talking. To entertain myself, I studied the license plates of the other vehicles—keeping a mental count of the ones from out of state.

We met everyone at a steak house. At first, the atmosphere was jovial. The waitress took our orders, the adults chatted about their lives, and we kids held our own conversations. After a while the waitress walked over, balancing a huge tray on her shoulder. She placed Uncle George's steak in front of him, then my father's, and continued to work her way around the table.

My father looked at his steak, and then at Uncle George's plate. His eyebrows knitted together.

Every muscle in my body tensed up. Bile rose in my throat. Everything around me seemed in slow motion, as if I was observing our table from a distance. There I sat, my hands folded in my lap, my back straight as an arrow, and my eyes and ears fixed directly on my father.

He glared at Uncle George.

Then he erupted.

"Yours is bigger, George. Why is yours bigger?"

I could almost see the words traveling from my father's mouth into George's ears, and then to his brain as George tried to figure out what my father was talking about. Uncle George's mouth had just started to open when my father abruptly stood.

"George set this up," he screamed. "George did this! George called ahead to make sure I got a small steak, and he got a big one!"

The restaurant patrons and staff all went silent.

"Let's go, Billie!" my father demanded.

He yanked my mother out of her seat. Lowell and I quickly gathered our belongings, leaving behind our plates of food. Soon we were back in my father's car and on our way home. Absolute silence prevailed. Once home, mother pulled some leftovers from the fridge and the family—as was customary, ate in silence.

◆ ◆ ◆

Days later (according to my daughter, to whom my mother told this story many years later), my mother dug through her closet. In the back of her wardrobe, she found what she was looking for: the brown leather heels she had once worn to dances. She packed them in a bag, along with some clothes and a few photos. She lingered by the front door, glancing at the drab walls that held so much misery. She sighed. Then, she was gone.

She walked several blocks to the bus stop, sat on a bench, and folded her hands over her purse. Her mind flooded with thoughts, she grimly stared at the pavement, barely noticing other people who were waiting for the bus to arrive.

When it came, they climbed aboard. She remained on the bench—in a fog, trembling.

Another bus came.

She didn't move.

Then another.

"Lady," the driver called out, "are ya getting on or what?"

She waved him away. As the bus pulled back onto the street, she stood and turned toward our street, staring into the distance as if it held important answers. Then she trudged home, unpacked her bag, and put her dancing shoes back where she had found them.

◆ ◆ ◆

In the junior high school cafeteria, a cute freckle-faced redhead caught my attention. Her laugh was infectious, and her slightly boyish body tantalized me. Soon Bobbie and I were hanging out together after school.

One afternoon, with her mother out babysitting, Bobbie led me to her bedroom. She closed the door, faced me, looked me in the eyes, and removed her shirt, then her pants, and then mine. Grabbing my hands, she pulled me to the bed. We made love. Me, for the first time. I was thirteen.

I couldn't get enough of her after that. Whenever her mother was away, I quickly showed up and into Bobbie's bed we went.

These escapades were complicated by the fact that my father allowed me to go out only one night per weekend. He also demanded that I tell him the week before whether I planned to be out on the following Friday or Saturday. That meant Bobbie needed to find all sorts of ways to stealthily ask her mother about her plans for the coming week since I needed the intel to put in my request with my father.

Nevertheless, I did it—and without complaint. Week after tedious week. Still, I felt it well worth it to have those evenings with Bobbie.

One Saturday evening, as I headed for the front door looking forward to Bobbie and her bed, my father yelled "Where the hell do you think you are going?"

I froze.

"To Bobbie's," I stammered. "I told you last week." I wanted to add, "like I always do," but held back.

"No, you didn't," he shouted, moving between me and the door. "You cannot go anywhere without first telling me about it."

Why was he like this? I had done every stupid thing the man wanted me to do, and still he badgered me.

"I'm sick of your stupid arbitrary rules!" I yelled.

My first punch knocked the cigarette out of his mouth. He

looked startled. Scared. Unable to defend himself.

I hit him again even harder. He crumpled to the carpet.

I sat on his chest, hitting his face repeatedly. Blood oozed from his nose and mouth. After unleashing years' worth of pent-up frustration, I stood, walked out the front door and ran to Bobbie's house. My knuckles were bright red, and my hands ached. My father had not landed a single punch.

When I arrived at Bobbie's, I found her seventeen-year-old sister and, as luck would have it, her sister's boyfriend, and his friend. One of them had a car, and I had a plan. If I could cajole them to drive me to Texas, where my friend Gary Hansen had recently moved, I could escape my father's tyranny. These were desperate plans lacking in forethought. I could not imagine going back home after beating up my dad. Even more strangely, I find it hard to understand how I, a thirteen-year-old boy, could persuade a sixteen- and a seventeen-year-old to drive me to Texas, but that is exactly what I managed to do.

We left that evening and drove the 1300 miles over two days. Somewhere along the desolate desert roads, the car acted up. By the time it limped and spurted into a filling station in Eastland, the transmission was done. Now miles from home with a car that didn't run, the two older boys looked scared. One asked, "What should we do?"

I slid out of the passenger seat, rooted around in my pocket for some spare change, and strode to the payphone. Gary answered. He sounded glad to hear from me. It seemed like he missed his South Gate friends.

Soon a station wagon pulled into the station. Inside was Gary and a prim, stone-faced woman whom I assumed was his mother. I pulled out my wallet. Inside was a five dollar bill a neighbor had recently given to me for cutting their grass.

"Here," I told the boy who owned the car. "I'm sorry. I'm sorry this happened."

He took the money and mumbled, "Yeah, okay, thanks."

Then I climbed into Gary's mother's station wagon, with only the clothes on my body and an empty wallet as my sole possessions.

For three nights, I slept on Gary's bedroom floor. His mother set out a plate for me at meals, made pleasantries, but one thing very clear: I was not to stay for long. She didn't want to get involved in another family's drama.

"My mom said you can probably get work at this farm," Gary said, "and stay at a rooming house nearby. That is, if you, um, don't go home."

"I am not going home," I said.

Days later I showed up for work. Someone handed me a pitchfork. I rammed it into a bale of hay, then hoisted it onto a palette. Again and again, I jabbed and lifted. Sweat soaked through my Levi's. My back ached. My palms chafed. I didn't stop. Again, and again. Jab, hoist. Jab, hoist. Nothing was going to send me home. Nothing.

The days passed. My palms blistered, then bled, and then hardened into rough calluses. My back screamed in pain.

More time passed. My eyes and throat burned. My voice turned gravely and hoarse. Exhaustion weighed down every cell in my body.

At first the cough seemed insignificant, nothing to worry about.

One week down. Then two. The cough worsened, keeping me up at night. Another week down. The coughing fits turned violent, leaving me gasping for air. My mouth tasted metallic, my throat raw and on fire.

Pushing through a wall of exhaustion, I limped to the gas station where I'd left the two boys and their broken-down car and called home.

"Hello," she answered.

"Mom," I croaked. "Mom."

She sent me a bus ticket.

TAKEAWAYS

When some people hear the story of my first thirteen years, they ask how I could have gotten through it. Now, almost seven decades later, as I look back on it all, the words of the famed child psychologist Uri Bronfenbrenner come to mind. He once wrote, "In order to develop normally, a child requires progressively more complex joint activity with one or more adults who have an irrational emotional relationship with the child. Somebody's got to be crazy about that kid. That's number one. First, last, and always."

My mother? She was crazy about me. Had she not been, I doubt I would have become who I am today. As a result of her love, I came to believe in myself. Rather than thinking that I deserved the abuse I received, as many abused children do, I felt it was unjust. For example, I called out my father's demands as "arbitrary."

Even more consequential, my belief in myself helped me to develop a trait that stood me in good stead throughout my difficult childhood: Grit. Defined as perseverance and passion for long-term goals, grit enabled me to learn how to defend myself against the neighborhood bullies and later, my father. Furthermore, grit was what got me through day after day of backbreaking work stacking hay. Yet, there was also a heavy dose of trauma from the abuse I received from my dad and the neighborhood bigots and bullies, which, as you will soon see, played an outsized role in my teenage years.

Readers, when you were a child, did you have an adult in your life who was crazy about you? It doesn't have to be a parent. It can be an older sibling, an aunt or uncle, or even a teacher or coach. If so, it can be helpful to recall what you can remember about this person and how they affected your life.

CHAPTER 2

Expulsion and Redemption

(1955–1960)

Bobbie was no longer speaking with me. I'd been gone too long, she said. Plus, she was livid that I had talked her sister's boyfriend into taking a long road trip only to abandon him when his car broke down. In my better moments I had to admit that she did have a point.

My father and I settled into a tense, yet violence-free existence. He claimed that he had let me win that fight, but I knew better. His body was soft and flabby, while mine was firm and muscular. I finally was stronger than he was, and we both knew it.

Feeling adrift, I yearned for acceptance. To fit in with those who had once blackened my eyes and bloodied my nose, I hid my intelligence. It was not cool to be smart. When my mother asked where I had been, I'd say, "We was at the beach," until it didn't sound practiced. Sometimes a group of us from my street would hang out in Billy Barbarich's garage. There we'd spend hours flipping through Billy's father's collection of dirty magazines, comparing centerfolds, and trying to one-up each other with lies about what we had done with girls.

◆ ◆ ◆

My last year in junior high I ran for yell leader with another student, Stan ("the Man") Jordan. We created a comedic skit for our campaign speech, and it was very well received. To our delight, our fellow students elected us. They had noticed us, and it felt good. While it was fun getting the fans all worked up, I also saw how the kids who were active in sports glided through the school hallways. Crowds went wild for them, and they had no trouble fitting in. I was in great shape, I reasoned, and throwing a ball couldn't be all that different from throwing a punch. I knew I could take a hit.

During my first year in high school, I started running track, doing gymnastics, and playing junior varsity football. They didn't call us jocks back then. I was an athlete—far from being an elite one, but good enough to participate. That became my social currency.

More darkly, I was also a budding delinquent, engaging in a range of bad behaviors.

While I was still friendly with the neighborhood boys—Billy, Chris, and Jimmy—my social circle enlarged. I joined the Gents, a Hi-Y (YMCA) boys club, that later I helped to turn into a car club. We designed metal plaques advertising our name, along with a depiction of a top hat and a cane and displayed them in the back windows of our cars. Mine was a 1941 Ford Coupe.

It was the only car in the junkyard that ran. My mother bought it for me with my life savings of $35, and then drove it home. A friend helped me overhaul the engine, replace the rings, grind the valves, clean the cams, and boil out the carburetor. Of course, I had to modify the look. I altered the front springs, so the car set at a sharp angle, with the front end very low to the ground, and got "Tuck and Roll" Naugahyde upholstery done cheaply in Tijuana, Mexico. I had a pair of crocheted dice hanging from the rear-view mirror and painted the car metallic cocoa at an Earl Scheib-type DIY car painting company. Another talented friend hand-painted pin-striping along the side with the car's name: *Cocoa Coupe*.

All that work on the Cocoa Coupe took a long time, while I was becoming desperate for the independence it promised. I had my learner's permit, and my mother had taught me how to drive in her pea green 1953 Plymouth sedan. It was a sturdy car, perfectly suited for my mom.

Several days before, I'd made a secret copy of her key. It now burned a hole in my pocket as I anxiously awaited the quiet tap-tap-tap of a knuckle against my bedroom window.

"What took you so long?" I whispered.

Billy rolled his eyes. "Had to wait till my mother fell asleep."

"I'll meet you at the back door," I said.

We crept through the dark along the driveway to the garage. I slid my fingers under one side, Billy the other, and together we slowly lifted the door until it was wide open. There sat the Plymouth, waiting.

My parents had yet to catch on to the routine. I was starting to care less and less. I slid into the driver's seat, pressed the clutch, and shifted it into neutral. When I gave the thumbs-up, Billy pushed the front of the car as I manned the steering down our long driveway, and all the way to the street.

I took the key from my pocket, and we were off. At the first red light we pulled up next to a Chevy Bel-Air.

Billy nodded. I gave the engine a few good revs and waited for a response.

The two guys in the Chevy hollered out the window and revved back.

When the light turned green, I popped the clutch and smashed the accelerator, gripping the wheel tight as tires squealed through the night.

I smoothly worked the gears through stop signs and near-misses. We were neck-and-neck for blocks, until eventually the Chevy slowed and turned, and we drove on. There was always another stoplight, another car, another race.

Hours later, still in the pitch black, we pushed the car back up the driveway and into the gaping mouth of the garage. Then I slipped back through the back door and into my bedroom.

◆ ◆ ◆

Stealing my mom's car was a short-lived necessity. Soon the Cocoa Coupe was ready, and by the time I turned sixteen, I had also discovered alcohol.

One night, two dozen of us were in the living room of one of my new friends in the Gents, girls and guys all paired off. There was making out, heavy petting, and drinking. Only one of those was new to me, and I did not know how to handle it.

Between make out sessions, the guys would retire to the bathroom to relate the night, play-by-play.

I couldn't stand without swaying so I slumped against the cold tile floor. I'd been drunk before, but never hammered.

"I got under her bra," Jimmy said, grinning. High-fives were distributed.

"You wish," I tried to say, but neither my mouth nor my brain cooperated.

"Ron, you okay?"

This was a new feeling. Where I had been laughing and joking ten minutes earlier, I felt nauseous, and my head was swimming.

The Gents loaded me into the back seat of my car where I curled into a ball.

"My father," I said, muffled, face down in the vinyl.

"We know," Billy said.

They frog-marched me up to my front door and rang the bell.

Mother answered. Behind her, my father loomed, and it took one look for her to know what had happened.

"We'll take it from here," she said. Then the boys were gone.

After getting me to bed, she stood in my doorway with arms folded and her mouth in a thin rigid line. It was the kind of expression that radiated disappointment, even with my eyes closed. The shame was hot.

"You're grounded for a month."

One whole month without my new friends. That was like being condemned to the seventh circle of hell.

◆ ◆ ◆

It did not take long for trouble to find me again.

Just off Ocean Boulevard in Long Beach was the Pike, where amusement park rides, live music, movie theaters, food stalls, and arcades blared and beckoned along the boardwalk. A novel horseshoe-shaped roadway called the Rainbow Pier arced out into the Pacific before returning to the shore. Parents and their children came from all over to spend their days basking in the California sun, riding the Cyclone Racer and stuffing their bellies with cotton candy.

Or, at least, that was how it used to be. That family-friendly veneer had been tarnished by seedier elements that crept in during the post-World War II years. Navy sailors stationed in Long Beach did not much care for salt-water taffy or the Ferris wheel. Their tastes were more suited toward the dodgy carnival barkers, freak shows, open-front liquor stores, and prostitution dens. From the shooting galleries popped the sounds of real .22s. Dingy tattoo parlors offered bold colorful stylings unusual to general American society. As the clientele of the Pike changed, these businesses flourished as sailors used their visits to enjoy a bit of bawdy shoreside fun in port before returning to the sea. It was an ideal place for wayward teenagers seeking an afternoon of adventure at the beach.

Chris Hartman and I loitered on the boardwalk outside the liquor store until Chris pointed and said, "That guy."

"You sure?" He was walking toward us, clad in swim trunks and a dirty tank top.

"On my mother."

"Hey mister," I said, approaching. "Could you get something for us? I'll give you five bucks, and you can keep the change."

No questions asked and one cheap bottle of fortified wine later,

Chris and I sat on the beach watching the waves roll in as we passed the Thunderbird back and forth.

"We should get going," Chris said.

I held up the bottle. Though I'd had more than my fair share, there was still wine to be drunk.

He shook his head. "I have to drive."

"Let's box," I said.

Chris frowned. "What? No. We need to go."

I took another long swig. "Why? Are you afraid of me?" I asked.

"No, you're drunk," Chris said.

I shoved his shoulder. "Come on," I urged.

"Push me again and I'm leaving."

I did.

I finished the bottle myself; then, alone and prickling with anger and with no way home, I stumbled around on the Pike. Round incandescent bulbs were strung back and forth across the boardwalk among the roofs of businesses—so many that it earned the nickname "The Walk of a Thousand Lights." During the day they were a nuisance, obscuring the beautiful cloudless sky, activated only when necessary, and otherwise useless.

Just up the street from the liquor store, where we had obtained the wine, was an empty storefront with a peeling exterior and large, dusty showroom windows.

In the dim reflection I could see myself, fists up in a boxer's stance.

The first jab crunched against the double-paned glass.

With each punch, the cracks connected, then spread outward from the sunken point of impact. Shards rained down around me. Jagged edges of windowpane ripped through my skin. Blood ran down my knuckles and wrists.

Alarms blared.

The cops provided first aid, arrested and booked me, called my father, and threw me in the drunk tank.

I don't remember what was said when he picked me up that

night. What I do remember is his solid, burning silence as I examined my bandaged hands, some scars of which are still visible today.

I was a fucking mess.

◆ ◆ ◆

Like in those old movies that depicted the passage of time by showing pages of a paper calendar fluttering away, years flew by.

I was now halfway through the eleventh grade. The further I advanced in school, the more it seemed like a waste of time. So, I talked a few friends into a scheme. We would attend school through second period when attendance was taken. After getting marked "present," a half-dozen of us would come up with various excuses to leave class. Then we would sneak out the closest door and steal away to our cars, where we had stashed our swim trunks and towels. From there, it was off to Long Beach.

We bodysurfed and sunned ourselves on the sand. It was there that I met Cheryl, a cute brunette with a shapely body who lived in Torrance—a thirty-minute drive from where I lived. We exchanged telephone numbers.

After several hours of sun, surf, and fun, we headed to the bathhouse, showered, and changed back into our school clothes before piling back into our cars. By the time we returned for seventh-period gym, it looked as if we had never left.

Two days later I phoned Cheryl.

That weekend, not wanting my parents to know where I was headed, I left the Cocoa Coupe parked in its usual spot and walked the few blocks to Atlantic Avenue, a major thoroughfare. It was far enough away that I was sure my mother wouldn't drive by and spot me. I turned to face traffic, stuck my thumb out, and waited for someone to stop.

One car approached. A woman was inside, who glanced my way before looking straight ahead as if she had never seen me. It went on like this, one car after another, until a light blue pickup pulled over. A middle-aged man leaned over, opened the passenger door, and said, "Want a lift?"

I climbed in.

"Where are you headed?" he asked.

"Torrance," I said.

"I'm on my way to Gardena, so I can get you a little more than halfway."

So it went, me hitching a ride from one stranger and then another before eventually I arrived in Torrance.

The entire escapade lasted several hours, but it was worth it because Cheryl was waiting. We walked the beach and talked about school, friends, cars, our parents.

As the sun set, she said, "I'd better get home. My mom will start to worry."

That was my cue to hike over to the main drag, stick my thumb out, and reverse the trip. It seemed only men were willing to stop for a teenage boy, and they all seemed lonely. Each driver peppered me with questions, "Where are you going? Why are you going there? Where are you from? What do you do?"

The second car dropped me at an intersection in an isolated area with open fields and oil wells on both sides, but no streetlights. One of the roads was not even paved. Squinting, I tried to see through the darkness and into the distance. Was there even a house around here within walking distance? Where was I?

I stood for several minutes, then an hour. My legs grew stiff. My lower back ached. Not a single car had come down the road.

By the second hour, I grew desperate. My mother was probably getting worried.

Finally, I saw headlights. Please, I prayed. Please stop.

Thankfully it did. By the time the last car dropped me off a couple blocks from home, it was nearing eleven o'clock. My mother looked relieved when she saw me, and rather than yell at me she seemed exasperated and too tired to put up a fight. Neither of us said anything.

◆ ◆ ◆

For the better part of the semester, my friends and I spent a good chunk of the school day at the beach. Sometimes Cheryl joined us. Other times, she didn't.

It seemed that the plan was foolproof.

One day, like every other time before, I snuck back into school and made my way to the boys' locker room. I changed into my gym clothes, lined up for gymnastics practice with the rest of the gym team, and then the coach pulled me aside and told me to go to the principal's office.

When I opened the door, I saw my mother. Her fingers were tightly wound around the handles of the purse in her lap. On her face was that ever-present expression of hard disappointment.

They expelled me. It was the last few months of my junior year.

"Jewish people don't behave like this," my mother exclaimed.

She blamed my expulsion on the influence of the goyim and repeated her perennial demand that we move to a Jewish neighborhood. To my surprise, my father capitulated. Soon, we relocated to West Hollywood, to a Jewish enclave called the "Borscht Belt" which was located near the La Brea Tar Pits.

◆ ◆ ◆

West Hollywood during the late 1950s was a very hip place, with remnants of the beat generation still around. There were coffee houses, where people gathered in the evening to recite poetry and play bongo drums, and a jazz club where I saw musicians like Les McCann and Eddie Harris. Out the Pacific Coast Highway toward Malibu there was a very cool coffee house called Positano, situated high up on a hill. Patrons would park near the highway and wait for a VW microbus, which would ferry them up the hill to the coffee house to listen to jazz and beat poetry while sipping espresso.

I attended Fairfax High School, which was said by everyone at the time to be "98.6 percent Jewish." How they could capture a fluctuating statistic with such precision escaped me. At Fairfax, the academic level was high, and most students went on to college at one of the two best universities in Southern California—UCLA or the private University of Southern California. Conversely, the athletic level was low. Accordingly, I did poorly academically but was inappropriately elevated to the varsity football team.

At South Gate High I was on the junior varsity team and played on the offensive line as right guard. That worked because I was 5'9 and 150 pounds, on the track team, and reasonably fast. Hence, I could get out quickly and make holes for running backs by blocking the line-backers.

At Fairfax, on the varsity team, opposing guards were twice my size. Right before my first game, I remember thinking, "These guys are enormous." It didn't matter how fast I was. I never stood a chance. At one of the first snaps, I was hit so hard that I was laid out on the field unconscious and had to be removed on a stretcher.

I awoke in a daze.

My head throbbed. The light burned, as if filled with tiny razor blades, and I heard a constant beeping sound that was very loud. If only someone would make it stop.

My mother came into focus. She was next to my bed, looking tense and worried. Wait? Whose bed was this? As I glanced around the room, it slowly dawned on me that I was not in my bedroom. As more of the room came into focus, I realized it was an emergency room.

Rarely did my parents take us to doctors. They were too expensive for my family, who had scrimped and saved to buy a printing shop. This must be serious.

Eventually a doctor appeared. My mother nodded as the doctor talked. His words seemed jumbled together. I could barely figure out where one stopped and the next began. Then, one word came through loud and clear. Concussion.

My football career was over.

◆ ◆ ◆

I was very lonely at Fairfax High. It was not easy to break in and make friends. Like many high schools, Fairfax was very cliquish and many of the students had known each other since elementary school.

Besides, what had made me fit in at South Gate made me stand out in a not-good way at Fairfax. I was a working-class kid among the upper middle class. That "we was out at the beach" earned me strange looks from my peers. They wore much nicer clothes, and on my first day of school I was frozen out by every kid I tried to talk to. I ended up eating lunch alone.

For a time, I would drive my Cocoa Coupe to South Gate on the weekends to hang out with my old friends, but soon that petered out. Even after several rounds of replacement plugs, a new muffler, and countless other parts and upkeep, the old girl started to show her age. Eventually I sold the Coupe for a measly $135. Thankfully, my mother was now working as a part-time bookkeeper, a development that brought in extra money along with her financial independence. To drive to and from work, she upgraded to a newer car and kept her old green Plymouth for me. Compared to the Coupe, it was an embarrassing step down to say the least, but I was glad to have it.

I got a part-time job at the Farmers Market, a magnificent mega produce store, with many independent booths charging very high prices for their luscious strawberries. I learned something about the produce trade while working at a booth that specialized in showy fruits. It set me up well to work at the local grocery store in the produce department, where Mr. Rabin—the manager, hired me as his assistant.

He also was the father of Carrie, whom I had first noticed while walking the halls between class periods. She was very sociable, making all her friends laugh while making the rounds. I was smitten with her blue eyes that sparkled when she smiled, which was often. She was Jewish too, but not serious about it.

Carrie was a junior while I was a senior, but she was college-bound and spoke very highly of UC Berkeley. "It's the best in the state," she said, which was no exaggeration[2]. Finally, I plucked up the courage to ask Carrie on a date.

I picked her up in the Plymouth, took her to the cinema, and we kissed during the movie and even more in the car. When I dropped her off, I walked her to her front door and my goodnight kiss turned into a hot groping session.

Anyone walking by could have seen us. Her parents could have opened the door at any second, but they didn't. And there I was, on the front porch in the dark, pulling down her pants and performing oral sex on my new girlfriend without a care in the world except for her.

◆ ◆ ◆

Carrie also had a relationship with another guy named Dave. I was resentful of Dave's higher social class, and Carrie often spoke of how sophisticated he was, noting that he wore hundred-dollar suits. Plural. That was a lot of money in the late 1950s, equivalent in purchasing power to over $1,000 today. I was ashamed that I couldn't afford anything close to what Dave had, not to mention jealous, but I said nothing about it to Carrie. Of course, Dave was planning to go to Berkeley.

Carrie shared a bedroom with her grandmother, who would

---

2 On a visit to Berkeley in 2010, I noticed a parking lot with twenty spaces at the Radiation Laboratory, where the Physics Department was housed. Twelve spaces had signs: "Reserved for Nobel Laureate."

periodically be away on a babysitting job, which was how we carried on our sexual relationship. I would go over to her house late at night and tap on her bedroom window, and she would sneak out and let me in through the side door.

One night, I fell asleep in her bed and only awakened when her parents woke up. I had to hide in her cramped clothes closet for hours until I could pretend to have just dropped over.

My earlier escapades sneaking in and out of my house prepared me well for these trysts. By this time, I had stopped caring if my parents knew where I was. My mother understood I was out at all hours of the night, and sometimes failed to come home at all.

On my graduation night, Carrie and I decided that we would celebrate by staying overnight in a hotel. We felt so grown-up checking in, not to mention having an entire private room to indulge our teenage libidos. But when I drove her home the next morning, Mr. Rabin was waiting for us. We had checked out of the hotel way too late, and he came outside when he heard my car approach. We were *so* busted.

I never saw her again. Mr. Rabin abruptly moved his family to some unknown location, and no one knew where they had gone. Many attempts over the years to learn her whereabouts proved fruitless.

Needless to say, I lost my job.

TAKEAWAYS

Looking back on my teenage self, my delinquency resulted from a combination of acceptance-seeking and poor judgment. While acceptance-seeking is normal for most teens, poor judgment is not. It was the result of delayed psychological development due to my trauma history.

A recent study determined that children who had been physically assaulted had four times the risk for subsequent mental disorders as compared to children who hadn't been assaulted. I do know that the violence that I suffered as a boy inured me to the very real risks that I took—in using alcohol, in precocious sexuality, in drag racing, and in violating all kinds of rules and laws. Together these factors caused me to go completely off the rails. Luckily, my mom was still in my camp, looking out for my best interests, and believing that I had a better future than I had ever imagined for myself. Had she not engineered the move to West Hollywood, I doubt that my life would have turned out as it did. I never thought about college or my future when we lived in South Gate, but now I was among other kids who were quite serious about college.

For readers who might have gone down the delinquency path in their teenage years and want to understand why, think about the role of trauma in your life. Were you abused by a parent? Were you bullied in school? Parental abuse and school-yard bullying is unfortunately more frequent than we would like to think. The good news is that there are effective psychotherapeutic treatments for adults who suffered trauma during childhood.

CHAPTER 3

Saved by Math

(1960–1961)

Working-class kids were like fish propelled forward by a river's current, moving only in the direction our upbringing allowed. No one asked, "What do you want to be when you grow up?" We already knew the answer. Our flow of life led to only two destinations: a job at one of the local factories or a career with the armed forces. Only a few had higher aspirations—for a trade like electrician or plumber.

In 1960, the country was at peace. The Korean war was long over. Though the evening news warned about issues in Vietnam, it would still be several years before US soldiers traveled there to fight and die.

This relative safety allowed boys like us to sound more confident than we were. On one of my visits to South Gate, the following dialogue occurred.

"If I join up, I'm going to be a Marine," Billy Barbarich boasted one day as we tinkered on our cars.

"Me, too," said Chris Hartman, as he flexed his biceps to prove it. "They're the toughest. They're the ones who captured Iwo Jima during World War II. Whenever there's a war, the Marines go in first, and basic training is *brutal*. My uncle told me you have to be able to do forty pushups in two minutes to qualify."

Billy rolled himself out from under his Ford and assumed a perfect plank position on the oil-stained concrete.

"One of you guys time me, okay?"

Chris kept an eye on his wristwatch while counting out loud, as Billy ground out pushup after pushup.

"Time!" Chris shouted. "thirty-four. So close, Barbarich."

"My dad was in the Seabees. That's like the wimp battalion compared to the Marines," I said.

"I bet you can't wait to get away from your dad," Billy smirked, popping up and jabbing me lightly on the shoulder with his dirty fist.

"You know it," I said. "I'll take boot camp and a shaved head over living at home any day."

Did I *really* want to be a Marine? Did it matter? The Marines were where boys became men. That was enough for me.

Meanwhile back at home, Robert Klein knocked on my front door.

I knew him from track. A lanky, studious kid with thick glasses, he was one of the few at Fairfax who had invited me to sit with him during lunch.

"Hey, Bobby," I said, "What's going on?"

"I'm headed to Los Angeles City College to take the admission test," he said. "Wanna tag along?"

With his hands in his pockets, Bobby shifted his weight from one foot to another.

"Why me?" I asked.

He shrugged. "I'm kinda freaked out about it. It's college, you know? It will determine the rest of my life. Having a pal there might, I don't know, make me feel less freaked."

I had two choices. I could sit there in an exam room with a bunch of nerds and bored out of my skull or hang in the house alone, hoping and praying my father didn't show up unexpectedly.

"All right," I said. "Let's go."

Soon he and I were in an auditorium, pencils in our hands, test booklets in front of us.

I could have merely waited until Bobby finished. Still, the test was in front of me, and I had nothing better to do.

So, I started reading questions and filling in circles. There were some math problems and general information questions like: What is the capital of Minnesota?

It was all easier than I expected. As I darkened the last oval, I felt confident I'd gotten them all correct.

We handed in our booklets, filed into a gym, and climbed onto the bleachers. On the basketball court stood several City College instructors.

"Engineering can open doors," one of them said. "It's a growing profession. More companies need engineers than ever before. This career can lift you into a comfortable middle-class life."

"Don't let the math scare you," another cautioned. "That's what we're here for—we can help you learn."

No one had encouraged me before, not like this. The instructors seemed so earnest, so kind, and so easy to be around. They didn't know me, but they seemed to already believe in me.

I could see myself here, learning, taking classes, growing, becoming something different, something more.

When we left the building, I was enrolled in six classes: Introduction to Engineering, Engineering Drawing 1, US History to 1865, Trigonometry, Health Education, and Physical Education. In a few short hours, I'd gone from envisioning myself as a marine to being a future engineer. In 1960, tuition was free to state residents in all higher education institutions in California, including the University of California system, the California State College system, and all community colleges. There were nominal fees that I could handle.

Engineering Drawing vexed me. Once on paper, the lines couldn't be erased, and mine were jagged, scratchy, and sloppy. Each mistake forced me to start over with a new sheet. My back ached from hunching over the drafting table for hours. I gripped the pencil so tightly that it took a long time for my cramped hands to unfurl. I couldn't imagine myself doing it any longer than one semester. Looking back on it now,

I should have realized that drawing was not my strong suit. After all, I had earned D's in handwriting in elementary school.

In contrast, math enchanted me.

As I worked on trig problem sets, my attention narrowed. The rest of the world vanished. It was just me, my pencil, and the problems. Working the problem sets felt so natural, so calming, so intuitive. Minutes and then hours would slip by as I worked.

I always got them right, and I couldn't get enough of them.

Partway through that first semester, my trig instructor pulled me aside.

"You've got a knack for this," he said. "What are your plans? Do you have any interest in getting a four-year degree?"

"I dunno," I replied. "I haven't thought about it."

"Well, I think you should—think about that, that is," he said, gently squeezing my shoulder. "You have what it takes. You're the cream of the crop."

An unfamiliar emotion swelled throughout my chest. With my book bag slung over my shoulder, I strode down the hall, out of the building, and to my car with purpose, pride, and direction. Until now, the only thing I'd been good at was getting into trouble. The praise was very appealing, dare I say addicting? Whatever it was, I wanted more of it.

◆ ◆ ◆

In addition to noise, my father hated disorder.

Each dining room chair had to be pushed in, lined up, and flush with the table. If we weren't sitting down to a meal, the table must be clutter-free. Nothing could be on top of it, not ever, not even for a moment.

It was the same with every room in the house.

He wanted things lined up, tidy, and in their place, all according to his complex set of rules about what did and did not belong where.

Even though he and I rarely spoke, the quiet and order made the small house feel stuffy, more like a hospital than a home.

Thankfully, these days, he wasn't around much.

He worked full days, nearly every day. After closing time there were printing presses to clean, books to keep, and an endless number of things for him to organize to perfection. My mother kept the food warm, not bringing it to the table until she heard him walk through the front door, often long after 5 p.m.

Now it was only 3:30. He wouldn't be home for hours.

I spread my papers over the dining room table. It was so much easier to work problem sets here than on the tiny desk in the bedroom.

My focus narrowed. Mathematical operations filled my mind. My anxieties vanished. It was just me, the math, and the quiet ticking of the living room clock.

I was deep into a problem set when I heard the front door open and then close. The sound seemed so far away, almost as if it came from someone's home down the street.

My thoughts wrapped around the problems, clinging to them, not wanting to let go.

It was probably my mother. Who else could it be?

Hunched over my work, I scribbled the various functions of angles onto the paper—sine, cosine, tangent—not bothering to look up.

She'd know I was concentrating. She wouldn't expect me to stop to say hello.

"Get that mess off the table," he sneered.

I flinched.

He stood at the head of the table, reeking of grease, chemicals, machinery, and cigar smoke. Bloated with irritation, his displeasure filled the air between us. The small room felt even smaller, more cramped, stifling, and suffocating.

Still, the problem remained latched to my mind. I couldn't let it go.

"Give me a few minutes," I mumbled, "Let me finish this..."

My pencil scraped down the page as one side of the table lifted. Papers slid, then tumbled, then fluttered to the floor.

He released the table, its two legs landing with a loud thump.

The floor was covered, papers everywhere, all out of order.

For a moment, my mouth agape, I sat and stared at the papers on the floor, not comprehending what had just transpired.

The clock ticked. One second. Then two. Then there was rage.

I slid my chair out so hard it could have lit a match. "That's it," I said, "I'm outta here! That was the last straw!"

"Whatever," he said as he walked into the kitchen. "Just clean that mess up."

I gathered my papers, brought them to my bedroom, and plotted my escape. Later, when my mother arrived home, I didn't bother to tell her what had transpired. The days of me seeking her comfort were long gone.

It did not escape me that this was reminiscent of an earlier phase in my life when I had run away from home to Texas. The difference was that I was now an adult and could take care of myself. I wasn't running away from home this time.

Days later, I put a deposit down on a furnished studio apartment on Melrose Avenue, within walking distance of City College.

"I can't stand this anymore. I can't live like this anymore," I told my mother as I lugged several boxes of my belongings to the front door. I turned and hugged her.

"I'm sorry," I said, my face buried in her shoulder.

"So am I," she said.

She stroked my hair. "I'm so, so sorry."

◆ ◆ ◆

After dropping my stuff at the apartment, I trudged up and down Melrose Avenue, and beyond, in search of stores with "help wanted" signs in their windows.

I spotted one on the door of a woman's shoe store. Inside, I found the manager.

"Do you have experience?" he asked.

"Yeah," I said with a shrug.

It was a lie. I knew nothing about women's shoes, but I could figure it out. He'd never know.

He gave me a quick tour of the showroom and then the storeroom in the back, pointing out the Mary Janes, kitten heels, flats, and so many different names and styles that I couldn't begin to remember it all.

That was okay. I was a fast learner. I'd catch on.

My first customer was a well-coiffed woman in a pencil skirt and fitted jacket. She handed me a shoe from the display rack. "I'd like to try this on, in size six," she told me.

"I'll be right back," I replied.

In the back, I stared at the shoe—and then at the piles and piles of boxes. Where was it? I pulled a box down and opened it, only to see that it was like the shoe from the showroom, but not exactly. I tried again, and again. Each box contained shoes that were *almost* what she'd asked for, but with slight differences. The strap might be broader or narrower, and the heel thicker or smaller.

I pulled another box from a stack. The shoe inside looked like a match. Maybe? I wasn't sure. It would have to do. She'd never know.

I trotted to the showroom, sat on a stool near her feet, and pulled one of the shoes from the box.

"That's not what I asked for," she sneered. "Don't you have the style that I want?"

"Oh no, ma'am," I said, "I'm so sorry. It's my mistake. I'll be right back."

Back to the storeroom, I went. I came back out, seemingly with shoes that looked like an exact match to me—but were 100 percent wrong as far as she was concerned.

As I searched in the back yet again, the manager appeared.

"What's going on?" he asked. "The customer told me you were taking forever."

A lie started to form. Surely, if I blamed her—on how picky she was—he'd understand.

"You don't have experience, do you?" he asked. "You're certainly not able to do the work."

"I can learn," I stammered.

"You're fired," he told me.

He didn't bother to pay me for my time. Not that I felt that I deserved it.

I had some savings, about two months' worth. It wasn't time to panic, but I needed a job, and I needed it sooner rather than later.

◆ ◆ ◆

I soon found one managing the produce department of a Scandinavian grocery store on Vermont Avenue, not far from the college campus. My prior experience in the produce game stood me in good stead. Managing this produce department meant I had to order the produce, which required me to project sales accurately. I also had to receive the order, check it over, store some items in the walk-in refrigerator, and put some on display. I also had to keep the display fresh by trimming the vegetables, particularly the lettuce.

It soon became my home away from home, and I loved everything about the place. There were such exotic items as knäckebröd in colorful packages, lutefisk in large wooden barrels, and lingonberries in individual boxes. I loved the lingonberries, but the lutefisk—not so much.

The Swensons, the owners, were a middle-aged Swedish couple with thick accents and loving personalities. A large woman with a hearty laugh who always wore a white apron, Mrs. Swenson loved to talk, often distracting me from my tasks. Short and bald, Mr. Swenson reminded me of Elmer Fudd from the *Looney Tunes* cartoons of my childhood. A penny pincher, he strode over whenever Mrs. Hansen had cornered me in a conversation.

"So, Ron," he'd say in his thick Swedish accent, "are you going to sharge me for this little bit of conversation?"

"No, Mr. Swenson," I always answered. "I'm not. I'm just talking to Mrs. Swenson."

In the evenings, I would often go to a coffee house on Melrose Ave, across from the college, order an espresso and listen to jazz and poetry. Sometimes I'd stop in to see my mother, always when my father wasn't home. During those visits, she was in constant motion, pulling food from the fridge and asking whether I was hungry. When it was time to leave, she often handed me a casserole or a plate of brownies.

By the end of my first semester, I was earning decent grades, loving work, paying my rent and other bills, and enjoying my social life in the evenings. In the second semester I took my first calculus course, and then a second course in calculus the next semester, along with my first physics course. I soon reached the end of what City College could offer.

I applied to only one four-year school, Berkeley. As I said earlier, Berkeley was much more than just a four-year college. It was far and away the best university in California, and one of the best in the country. Secretly, I hoped to reunite with Carrie, my old high school girlfriend. That's where she'd said she was headed before she and her family had disappeared. Miracle of miracles, I was accepted.

TAKEAWAYS

This was clearly the turning point in my life. Thank you, Bobby Klein, for inviting me to accompany you to the LACC admission test! And thank you, my trig and calc instructors, who provided such wonderful encouragement! I no longer remember your names, but I remain very grateful for your support, which enabled me to believe that I could succeed in college.

To readers who may be struggling as I once was, I would suggest seeking people in your life who can offer the kind of encouragement I received. They can be relatives or friends, or anyone who sees your better angels, and is willing to tell you that they do. Encouragement can do wonders, as it did for me. One study found that teacher encouragement increased students' self-efficacy and motivated them to improve their performance[3]. I am so grateful for the encouragement that I received that I recently endowed a scholarship at LACC for psychology students.

---

3 Tuckman, B. W. & Sexton, T. L. (1991). The effect of teacher encouragement on student self-efficacy and motivation for self-regulated performance. *Journal of Social Behavior and Personality*, 6 (1), 137

CHAPTER 4

The Making of an Activist

(1961–1965)

By the fall of 1961, I had stepped off the path of juvenile delinquency. Three semesters at City College had transformed me. I'd applied myself to my studies, done well, and earned respect and encouragement from my professors. In the absence of my father's looming negativity, I felt unstoppable.

I now had a purpose, and I wanted nothing less than *the best* of everything for myself. I'd earned it.

It was with this sense of entitlement and overconfidence that I loaded my belongings into my mother's 1953 Plymouth and drove the 350 miles from Los Angeles to the University of California at Berkeley.

Berkeley was the best in the state for many disciplines. It, however, was the best in the world for just one: physics. During the early 1960s, more Nobel laureates emerged from Berkeley than from any other academic campus in the world. One of the few state schools with a cyclotron and radiation laboratory, Berkeley's physics professors and labs were second to none.

So, of course, physics had to be my major.

During orientation, I learned that the best students joined the Greek system. Given that most of Berkeley's fraternities refused to invite Jewish men to join their ranks, I was left with only two choices: the Jewish fraternities Zeta Beta Tau (ZBT), called the

"Zebes," or Sigma Alpha Mu (ΣAM), also known as the "Sammies." Of the two, ZBT was considered the better one, so naturally that's where I pledged.

Within days of arriving, I moved into the fraternity house and into a dorm room I shared with five other pledges: Jim Gidlow, Jules Greenstein, Jim Harris, Dave Hoffman, and Steve Scheinman.

Not having been around educated people much, I only knew about three topics: cars, sports, and girls. Unlike myself, however, most of the ZBT brothers had grown up in homes where at least one parent (often both) had been to college. They read newspapers, followed world events, and seemed very knowledgeable about so many things. I admired their sophistication and wanted to become more like them.

Many were majoring in history, and they often talked about the courses they were taking, the best professors, and the relevance of history to our rapidly changing world. They seemed so enthusiastic that I wondered: Maybe I'd made a mistake majoring in physics. Should I change my major?

◆ ◆ ◆

On the first day of classes, I packed up my massive textbooks and trudged across Berkeley's vast campus as I made my way to Calculus 3 and then Elementary German. Hours later, my brain fried, the fraternity house beckoned with its promise of a soft bed and a night of decent rest.

When I opened the front door, the pledge master was waiting. He handed me a mop and barked, "Report to duty, Levant!"

That was code for "jump." Any model pledge knows how you're supposed to respond.

"Let me just—" I said, as I started to remove my book bag.

"You talking back, pledge?" the pledge master yelled.

"No, no, I just—" I only wanted to put my book bag in the room that I shared with the five other pledges. Was that too much to ask?

"I think it's time for the paddle," he yelled. "Hey, brothers, we've got a pledge who needs some discipline. Gather round!"

From all over the house, brothers hooted and hollered. Cold fear took root in my gut. They stomped down the hall as the pledge master grabbed my arm and yanked me forward. Soon we were in a cavernous room. The brothers stood in a neat line against the wall. A six-foot-long paddle hung on hooks, just above their heads.

"Take off your pants, Levant," the pledge master shouted.

"What? Why?"

"Off with the pants!"

"Off with the pants!" the brothers chanted. "Off with the pants!"

They crowded in, forming a circle around me. The other pledges looked shrunken, afraid, as if rolling their shoulders forward and staring at the floor would turn them invisible.

I slowly unbuttoned my jeans.

I knew too well what was coming. I'd driven hundreds of miles to escape this.

Yet, here I was, yet again, surrounded by bullies who barked orders, who looked down on me, and who expected nothing less than complete subservience.

"Faster pledge! What's taking you so long?"

The desire to fight—to unleash my pent-up rage—swirled. My muscles tensed like coiled cobras. I clenched my fists until they shook.

You signed up for this, I reminded myself. *This is what it takes to be the best. Just do it. It's no big deal. You can take it. You've taken it before.*

Resigned, I shimmied out of my Levi's, then my underwear.

My sweaty palms pressed into the cool wall. I grit my teeth. The brothers gathered behind me, making comments about my skinny ass.

I felt the familiar sting of a hard object smacking against my bare skin.

One by one, they took turns. My skin stung, then burned, then felt as if I'd spent hours sitting in the coals of a bonfire. I endured, each time hoping it was the last.

They left me alone, naked, and bruised—inside and out.

For the rest of the day, I mopped floors, scrubbed crud from the fridge, and bleached toilet bowls. All the while, the pledge master inspected my work, finding insignificant flaws with everything I had done, and often making me start over. "You missed a spot! What's wrong with you, pledge? Scrub harder!"

My fingers raw, my muscles aching, my rear end sore, I finished my last task around 8 p.m., retrieved my book bag from the entryway, and settled onto a couch to do my homework, shifting my body weight to the side to avoid putting pressure on my sore bottom.

"What's wrong with you, Levant?" the pledge master asked. "Put that away. It's time to paaarteee!" On came thumping music and out came the keg.

Someone handed me a beer.

"Chug! Chug! Chug!"

I did as I was told.

Again, and again, and again.

The floor tilted. People came in and out of focus. A wave of nausea arose from my stomach. Then everything I'd eaten that day was on the floor.

The pledge master hooked his arm around my neck.

"Clean it up, Levant."

I fell into bed around three in the morning, so tired and sick that I barely noticed the snoring and farting sounds erupting from the other pledges in the room.

I woke to a waterfall.

What was happening? I felt around with my hands.

My pajamas were soaked. My bed was soaked.

There were men laughing and shouting. My brothers.

I jumped out of bed.

"Get him," someone yelled.

Something hit me. There was a sting, then an eruption. Water. Lots and lots of water.

"What? What!" I stammered. Nothing made sense. The other pledges were yelling, too.

More things hit me—in my torso, my shoulders, my crotch, my face. More stinging. More water. So much water.

The room came into focus. Colorful remnants of water balloons were strewn everywhere. I, along with the other pledges, looked as if we'd awoken from a nap in a full bathtub. Our brothers were laughing.

Still in a haze, I pulled the drenched sheets from the mattress and put them in the clothes dryer, then dragged the mattress to the lawn to dry.

It was now 5 a.m. What had I gotten myself into?

In my underwear, my rear end bruised, I curled up on the floor and fell into a fitful sleep.

◆ ◆ ◆

On this went, day after day, night after night. Each night I fell into bed exhausted. My hands stung from the disinfectant used to clean the house. My eyes burned from lack of sleep. Even my lungs were tired.

I carried my resignation on my back, its weight growing heavier and more unbearable with each passing day. "Just get to the end of the semester," I told myself. "You made a commitment. Just see this through. You've invested too much to quit now."

One week down. Two weeks. Three. A month. A month and a half. Two.

Exhaustion became my constant companion. The long walk between classes, once merely challenging, was now a slog. The glands in my throat were tender, hard, swollen. I could barely swallow.

Midsemester, during dinner, brothers Don Bell and Jerry Levinson got into it, each calling the other names, one storming away in a huff.

The tiff picked up steam over several days, with each brother gaining allies. The fraternity became a house divided. We were either on Team Don or Team Jerry. Allying with one meant becoming enemies with the other. The air was full of tension, of brothers loudly arguing over the slightest of things. It felt as if the ground was constantly shifting. I never knew what to say. Given my ever-present exhaustion, I usually opted for the easiest solution: silence.

Then everything boiled over. Brothers piled into the living room floor, punching, kicking, holding each other in various wrestling moves.

One brother ushered us pledges away from the melee. In another room, we sat in silence, the loud yelling, thumping, and grunting paralyzing us. I couldn't believe it. Here I'd made it halfway through. I'd invested so much time. I'd put up with so much—and now the fraternity was embroiled in a civil war.

About an hour later, the house grew quiet.

A brother led us back to the living room, where everyone was laughing, smiling, and looking proud of themselves.

There was no blood, no black eyes, no broken noses. In my experience, none of this was congruous with the aftermath of a real fight, let along the brawl that had shaken the foundation of the frat house.

Instead, everything seemed normal, as if the fight had never happened.

It had all been a ruse.

They'd play-acted the whole thing—not only the big fist fight, but the entire weeks-long argument.

"Let this be a lesson to you," the pledge master told us. "Of the importance of brother unity."

I went through the motions of laughing, high fiving, telling them how convincing they'd been. Yet, inside, I felt no unity. I felt about as close to them as I felt to my father.

The following week, too exhausted to lift my head and with the chills that left me constantly trembling, I checked myself into student health services. I had mononucleosis. It would be weeks before I felt better.

By the end of the semester, I became a brother at ZBT.

I also landed on probation, with a 1.62 grade point average.

Just months before, I'd been on an uphill swing, turning my life around—and now this. Apparently, I wasn't as smart as I'd thought.

◆ ◆ ◆

For spring semester, I signed up for the Psychology of Personal and Social Adjustment. Designed for nonmajors, the course was taught by Alex Sherrifs, a popular professor who connected with students in ways few other professors could. Every single one of the lecture hall's 557 seats were filled, with even more students leaving their names on a sign-up sheet on the off chance someone didn't show up. Like many of my peers, I showed up at his office hours regularly, chatting with him not only about his classes, but also college life. He seemed so engaged, so interested in how I was doing—how all of us were doing.

During his classes, I scanned the room, on the lookout for Carrie, or another woman that I found interesting. Eventually, I spotted a particularly attractive young woman with dark hair, brown eyes, and a curvaceous figure.

The following class, I sat next to her.

After class, as we filed out of the room, I asked, "What'd you think about his point about cognitive dissonance? It seems kind of bogus to me. What do you think?"

"Well it does make a lot of sense to me. Because personally, I don't like being inconsistent. So, if I believe something I want to act consistently with my beliefs."

She blew me away and I craved more of where that came from.

"My name's Ron, by the way," I said, "My next class isn't until three. Want to go over to the Student Union to get some coffee?"

"Joyce," she said, shaking my hand. "Sure. Coffee sounds great."

It quickly became clear that Joyce was more intelligent than any other female I'd ever known. Like so many of my classmates, she'd grown up with educated parents and could talk about a wide range of subjects. I loved listening to her. Like me, she was Jewish. She was also practical, soothing, and down to earth.

A couple days later, we went out for burgers. Afterward, I walked her to the two-bedroom apartment she shared with another woman student. She invited me in. The following morning, I woke to her touch, soothingly stroking my head, my back, my arms. I didn't want to leave. Nor did I want to sleep in the fraternity, ever again.

By the end of Spring semester, I'd pulled my grades up and gotten myself off probation. With plans to move in with Joyce in the fall, I resigned from ZBT. Everything was looking up. For the first time in a long while, I felt hopeful.

For the summer I signed up for a zoology class at City College. It wasn't possible to rent an apartment for just a couple of months. Plus, I needed to save money. So, I moved back into my small childhood bedroom I'd once shared with Lowell. It wasn't ideal, of course, but it was only for a couple of months. Between school and work, I was rarely home. Neither was my father. That made it bearable.

◆ ◆ ◆

That fall, things moved quickly, as they generally do for the young and dumb.

Now that Joyce and I slept next to one another every night, sex came easily and often. Although birth control pills had been approved by the FDA in 1960, they were not yet widely available, and we had no access to them. I sometimes used condoms. Most times I didn't.

I liked Joyce a lot, but I wasn't head over heels, at least not in the way I had felt about Carrie. I loved being around her, of course. I especially loved the sex.

Still, had that fall unfolded just a little differently, Joyce and I might have lived together for a semester, maybe two, perhaps even longer. Eventually, however, one of us would have met someone else. We would have drifted apart. She would have gone one way. I would have gone another. Decades later, we would have remembered one another fondly as "that fling I had while in college."

But we were so reckless.

"I'm late," she told me.

Those two words somehow made everything seem so clear. I liked her, but I didn't love her. Something was missing. The chemistry was just slightly off. She wasn't the *one*. I wasn't in love. I wasn't ready—not for marriage, not for fatherhood, not even to renew the lease we shared. I was just starting to get on my feet, to understand my place in the world, to dream about my future. I wasn't ready for this.

Yet, I was no rat.

I proposed. It was the honorable thing to do.

Several days later, when her period came, the proposal felt too big to take back. She'd already told her parents about it. I'd already told mine. Despite the uncomfortable pit in my stomach, we made plans to marry.

"It will be okay," I told myself, as if I were whistling past the graveyard. "It's going to be okay."

Joyce's parents threw a big Jewish wedding, complete with 250 guests, most of whom I'd never met. We honeymooned in Ensenada, Mexico, an inexpensive beach town close to the US border. By the time we returned, Joyce wasn't just late. She was pregnant.

She went into labor during final exams. I'd been up three nights straight as I crammed for finals. A pot of coffee and adrenaline were likely what kept me alert during the drive to the hospital. After nurses walked Joyce to a delivery room, I slumped into a seat in the waiting area. Several other expectant fathers paced and smoked.

I woke to a hand on my shoulder, shaking me.

"Mr. Levant? Mr. Levant?"

"What? Yes! Yes! What? I'm here!" The words didn't want to come. It was as if my brain had shut down and I'd lost the on switch.

Everything seemed blurry.

"I'm awake. Is everything okay? How's Joyce? Is she okay?"

"Mr. Levant," the nurse said, "She's fine. You have a baby girl. Would you like to meet her?"

She led me to a plate glass window. On the other side was another nurse, holding a tiny being wrapped in a pink blanket. Caren Elizabeth, that's what we'd agreed to name her. She was named after my grandfather Charlie, and my grandmother, Edith, as well as some of Joyce's relatives, following the Jewish tradition of naming children after deceased relatives. The choice to spell her name with a C rather than a K was deliberate: We wanted the word "care" in her name.

"Hi Caren," I said, waving. "Hi honey."

It didn't feel real. A part of me knew that this fragile being was my daughter. Another part of me felt as if I were watching the scene unfold from afar, almost as if it were all happening to someone else.

An uncomfortable feeling crept through my body. My father had taught me what terrible fathers were like. I knew who I didn't want to be. What did good fathers do? It was as if someone had put me in charge of a battalion without teaching me to shoot. Several days later, I drove back to the hospital, walked Joyce and Caren to the car and started my new life as a father.

◆ ◆ ◆

Caren was an easy baby with simple needs: eat, sleep, cuddle, repeat. She didn't cry much. When she did, it wasn't hard to figure out what she wanted.

On top of that, we lived in married student housing. The series of old military Quonset huts on University Avenue had been converted into apartments. Because we were surrounded by other young parents, we formed a baby-sitting coop. Some weekend evenings we'd hold a hootenanny, a folk music get-together popularized by Woody Guthrie and Joan Baez. We'd gather in someone's pad, sit on scratchy couches, and sip wine from Gerber jars as we sang "This Land is Your Land." It was great fun, and the babies and toddlers clapped along with the tambourines and giggled to the sound of the kazoos.

Now with Caren to watch over, however, every part of our lives became highly scheduled. When one of us was working or in class, the other had to be free to care for Caren. Other than the hootenannies, this left little time for me and Joyce to spend time together. Our conversations revolved around our schedules and who was watching Caren.

Thankfully, we both worked at the university bookstore, a flexible job that allowed us to change our work hours as needed.

The walk back to my car from the bookstore took me through Sproul Plaza, a hotbed of campus political activity. Named for the administration building, Sproul Hall, the Plaza occupied the open space between the Hall, the campus' southern entrance, Sather Gate, and the Student Union. About a dozen student activist organizations lined the plaza with tables, handing flyers to anyone walking by. Quite often, a student would climb the steps to Sproul Hall and start pontificating, usually about civil rights or the failings of capitalism. Increasingly, as I listened, I became aware of how messed up our country was.

As I was leaving work to drive home, one of the students offered me a flyer: *CORE: Open Meeting for New Members.*

It was a pitch to join the Congress for Racial Equality, one of the most powerful organizations involved in the civil rights movement.

CORE had earned notoriety for registering Black voters in the South—a seditious exploit according to some at the time. They also helped to organize Martin Luther King Jr.'s March on Washington, which culminated in his "I Have a Dream" speech. CORE's Freedom Riders challenged segregation laws on public transit, strategically positioning themselves on interstate buses only to be met with firebombs and beatings. I admired these brave souls, and wished I could be more like them. Yet, as a student with a job, a wife, and a baby, my free time was scarce.

But maybe?

I pocketed the flyer.

Later, Joyce and I sat at the kitchen table, Caren bouncing on her knee. I nervously pulled the folded CORE paper out of my jeans pocket.

"Maybe we can do something? You know," I said, "Do some good."

It was hard to read her face. She handed Caren to me, then took the flyer. As she read, she said nothing.

"Yes," she finally said, "let's get involved."

One evening later in the week, we left Caren with another couple in the baby-sitting coop and found our way to the CORE meeting at the Student Union. Joyce and I sat in a couple of tan folding chairs off to the side as CORE members welcomed activists to a podium at the front. The room crackled with restless, infectious energy as students from all over campus filed in, clambering over one another to sit with friends.

Once everyone was settled, the room fell silent.

"You may or may not be aware," a CORE leader boomed, as if he were out on the plaza instead of inside the confines of a sparsely furnished conference room, "but Lucky Market refuses to hire Negros."

Thunderous boos erupted from the audience, swallowing the room whole and me and Joyce along with it. We joined in, quietly at first, then more loudly.

The speaker held up his hand.

"The California Fair Employment Practices Act of 1959 says a business can't discriminate based on color, national origin, ancestry, religion, or race," he continued. "That law was passed five years ago. For five years, Lucky Market has openly violated the law with no repercussions. Well, we're saying no more! We're going to do something about it!"

The room again erupted in cheers, whoops, and lightning-sharp whistles.

Lucky Market was about to become regrettably very aware of me and my new friends in the most inconvenient, nonviolent way possible.

"We're going to jam up their checkouts until they agree to hire Negros!" the speaker roared. "Who's with me?"

Hands flew up all around me. I remembered my childhood, the bloody noses, the split lips, my mother pressing towel-wrapped ice against my eye. I thought of the times someone had rubbed my face into the dirt, kicked me in the gut, and screamed, "You dirty kike!" The sheer terror of those years washed over me, coming back in full force. It was electrifying.

My hand shot up.

◆ ◆ ◆

I started in the produce aisle. Without checking prices, I grabbed apples, carrots, lettuce, bell peppers, mushrooms, and strawberries and shoved them into my shopping cart. In the next aisle went several bags of chips. Then came detergent, several pounds of meat and fish, a gallon of ice cream, and some milk.

The haul weighed the cart down. I had to push hard to get it to the register.

The clerk was young. She eyed my cart, then me, glancing at the CORE pin on my lapel. I was dressed in my nice suit jacket and tie, just as we'd planned, looking as respectable as I could. She seemed quiet, resigned, unsure of herself.

Did she know what was about to happen?

I unloaded things onto the platform for her to ring up.

In another checkout lane, there was another student from CORE, with another cart just as full.

Then a third student showed up at the final checkout.

Now commerce from all three lanes had slowed. A line of customers formed in each checkout line, now all occupied by CORE students and their generously full baskets of groceries. Slowly the clerks made their way through the dozens of items.

The clerk ringing me up needed to check a price. She flagged over someone, who took several minutes to fetch the appropriate information. That's what we'd hoped for.

The lines grew longer, snaking their way into the aisles. Other shoppers shifted position, growing more impatient with each passing moment.

The clerk sighed, mumbling "Jesus Christ" under her breath. She needed another price check.

The man behind me huffed and audibly complained.

Finally, she bagged the last item.

"That'll be thirty-three dollars and fifteen cents," she said.

My moment had arrived.

"Well, I'm not paying," I said, "not until Lucky Market agrees to hire Negro employees."

She sighed, walked around to get my cart, and quickly piled the items back into it to be reshelved.

"Earl," she yelled, "can you put these back?"

I stood, not moving, blocking the customers behind me from unloading their baskets.

In the next lane, I overhead the same conversation unfolding, as well as a threat to get the manager.

A big man in an apron strode over.

"What seems to be the problem?" he said. "Why won't you pay?"

"I'm not paying until you agree to hire Negro employees," I said, shifting anxiously from one foot to another.

The big man glanced at me, then to the CORE students who'd entered the other checkout lines at the same time as me. He could see where this was going.

"Get out," he yelled. "All you riffraff. Get. Out!"

I stepped out of line, leaving the mountain of unpaid merchandise to be reshelved. The clerk moved on to the next customer. What she didn't know: behind that impatient, huffing man was a young, well-dressed woman with her own basket full of purchases and CORE pin. As I left Lucky's and hustled back to the campus, I passed other CORE students on their way to take the next shift.

The shop-in lasted ten days. All the while, the store lost money, as some of the meat rotted, ice cream melted, and milk went sour before it could be returned to the refrigerated cases. Shoppers caught on and began taking their business elsewhere. California Governor Edmund G. Brown publicly condemned the shop-ins. That compelled San Francisco mayor John Shelley to intervene, asking CORE leaders to meet with representatives from Lucky stores.

Lucky caved, agreeing to hire Black employees. Not long afterward, that particular Lucky store was permanently closed.

It was amazing, exhilarating—and I wanted more of it.

Meanwhile, back at the CORE office, something new was in the air.

During a meeting, I looked around and noticed that all the women were sitting together. That was odd.

Then one stood, interrupted the speaker, and said, "In CORE the men have written the articles and given the speeches while the women typed the stencils for the mimeograph machine and made the coffee. Well, from now on that will change. The women will write the articles and give the speeches while the men will type the stencils and make the coffee."

I was gobsmacked!

Here we'd been fighting for racial equality, yet women had been left off the table. In our own organization, one that prided itself in treating everyone equally, things were, in fact, not equal at all.

The more I thought about it, the more I saw sexism around me. Women couldn't get credit cards without a man to sign for them. Many of the Ivy League schools—including Yale, Princeton, and Harvard—did not allow women students. Even at Berkeley, people referred to female students as "there for their MRS Degree." They were just as bright as us men, some more so, but they were not taken as seriously.

◆ ◆ ◆

That summer the fight for civil rights grew to a fever pitch.

One thousand volunteers from CORE and many other organizations traveled from all over the nation to register Black voters in Mississippi, which had the lowest percentage of African Americans registered to vote in the nation—a dismal 6.2 percent. Local officials and residents pushed back. The White Citizens' Council, a national group that had formed in the wake of the 1954 Brown vs. Board of Education ruling, along with the Ku Klux Klan, terrorized Black communities and anyone who came to their aid. They beat volunteers and firebombed Black churches and businesses. In late June, a Mississippi police officer and Klansman pulled over a Ford station wagon. Inside were CORE members Andrew Goodman, James Earl Chaney, and Michael Henry Schwerner. The officer booked them for speeding. After being released from jail, the three CORE volunteers disappeared.

It wasn't until August that the FBI uncovered their bodies, buried under a dam at a nearby farm. They had all been shot.

They were all close to my age. When I heard the news, I vowed that I would do whatever I could to make sure that their deaths would not be in vain.

◆ ◆ ◆

That September, I graduated with a Bachelor of Arts degree in history. I had applied to medical school, but didn't get in. Instead, I enrolled in graduate school at Berkeley in history.

I first had to pass the foreign language qualifying examination, which I took in German. The work was deadly boring, with me sitting for hours in a carrel in the basement of the library as I translated German documents into English, writing everything out on three-by-five-inch index cards. Though the experience convinced me that I wasn't cut out for a PhD in history, it afforded me some extra time to throw myself into the fight for civil rights. I was able to edit the Spring 1965 issue of the *Campus CORElator*, the magazine of the Berkeley Campus Chapter of CORE. We published articles by Stokely Carmichael, a leader of the civil rights organization SNCC (Student Nonviolent Coordinating Committee), who later changed his name to Kwame Ture, and Barbara Garson, who would a few years later publish the satirical play *MacBird*, which superimposed the assassination of JFK onto the plot of Shakespeare's *Macbeth*, carrying the implication that Johnson was responsible for the assassination of JFK.

In addition, I worked as director of the UCB Fraternities Food Co-op, a job I got because of my background as a member of ZBT and my experience in the produce trade. I managed the ordering and delivery of groceries to the UCB fraternities who participated in the Co-op. I had a nice office on the second floor of a men's clothing store on Bancroft Way adjacent to the campus, plus it took at most twenty hours per week and netted me $5,000 a year, which would be almost $50,000 in today's dollars. After graduating with a bachelor's degree, Joyce got a full-time job as a social worker. With our combined incomes we were able to buy a new car—a small Fiat 600D, white, with a rear mounted engine—that cost around $1600. These were very good years in our marriage and family.

Around this time, Lowell transferred from UCLA to Berkeley, enrolling in Gary Snyder's poetry workshop. A beat poet, Snyder was a huge deal. He'd done poetry readings alongside Allen Ginsberg. Jack Kerouac had modeled a character, Japhy Ryder, in his 1958 novel *The Dharma Bums* after Snyder. Snyder had recently returned from Japan, where he'd spent eight years studying Zen Buddhism. Lowell's classmates included the writers Will Staple, Eileen Adams, Laura Dunlap, Jim Wehlage, Gene Fowler, Gail Dusenbery, and Hilary Ayers.

He was still quiet, rarely speaking. Yet, I got to know him through his poetry, which, like many poets of the time, pushed back against authority.

◆ ◆ ◆

That fall, after witnessing the unforgettably violent events of Freedom Summer, Berkeley CORE activists were electrified with purpose. In addition to speaking out against racist businesses, we were also campaigning against Proposition 14, which was on California's November ballot. If voted into law, the measure would forbid the legislature from outlawing housing discrimination.

Sproul Plaza was almost never empty. On any given day, hundreds of students gathered to listen to someone hold forth from the administration building steps. As the anti-Prop 14 movement built, however, some people in Berkeley's administration grew nervous. This was especially true of my former psychology professor. According to Dr. Sherrifs, now a vice chancellor, the fight for civil rights was political, and universities should remain neutral. Students could have political opinions, of course, but we needed to share them off campus.

In response, nineteen student organizations from across the political spectrum, calling themselves the United Front, intensified their actions in retaliation for this First Amendment violation. The already numerous tables in Sproul Plaza multiplied. It became the soul of the movement across campus, the hub for all-night vigils and all-day rallies.

In October, CORE member Jack Weinberg drove to campus with a huge old door balanced on the roof of a car. Once he and his companions arrived at the intersection of Telegraph and Bancroft, they carried the door through Sather Gate to Sproul Hall, propped it up on trestles just in front of the steps, and proceeded to distribute information considered political by the university's top brass.

As expected, agitated administrators, not able to leave through the front door, emerged from the side exits of the building along with the university police. Conveniently a rally had already been scheduled for noon, which meant students happened to be pouring into Sproul Plaza just as the authorities confronted Weinberg, who'd come prepared for such a confrontation.

An officer asked him for his identification. He refused to turn it over. Instead, he yelled, "Oh, please Br'er Fox, don' throw me in de briar patch!"

Curious students pressed inward, leaning in to see and hear what was going on.

Weinberg shouted, "We want to see social change in the world in which we live. We want to see this social change because we are human beings who have ideas. We think, we talk, we discuss, and when we're through thinking and talking and discussing, well then, we feel that these things are vacuous unless we then act on the principle that we think, talk, and discuss about. This is as much a part of a university education as anything else."

More police arrived, along with a cruiser.

Weinberg raised his voice.

"We feel that we, as human beings first and students second, must take our stand on every vital issue which faces this nation, and in particular the vital issues of discrimination, of segregation, of poverty, of unemployment; the vital issue of people who aren't getting the decent breaks that they as individuals deserve..."

An officer cuffed him. Another grabbed his arm.

"Come with us please," one of them said.

Weinberg went limp, flopping toward the pavement. This was an essential part of nonviolent civil rights protest—don't do the cops' work for them.

The officers bent forward, struggling to carry Weinberg's full weight. It took five of them, each with a limb and one supporting his body. They barked at the crowd to move as they shuffled through the swarming students, carrying a smugly satisfied Weinberg between them.

"Take all of us," students shouted. "Take all of us!"

Finally, the officers lugged Weinberg's limp body into the back seat of the car.

Students closed in on the vehicle.

Someone yelled "Sit down! Sit down!"

In seconds, everyone was on the ground.

Now hundreds of students sat many rows deep on the Plaza in every direction. The cruiser was surrounded, and it couldn't move without running over the whole lot of them.

An hour went by.

One student let the air out of one of the cop car's tires. Someone else shoved an apple in the tailpipe. Yet another dumped lemonade into the gas tank. Jack grinned from the back seat.

CORE member Mario Savio, having recently returned from Mississippi, jumped onto the roof. I clocked out of the bookstore and walked through the Plaza just as he started to speak. Savio took the microphone and orated the speech of his lifetime, every word spat from his lips like steel shards.

"There's a time when the operation of the machine becomes so odious, makes you so sick at heart, that you can't take part! You can't even passively take part! And you've got to put your bodies upon the gears and upon the wheels... upon the levers, upon all the apparatus, and you've got to make it stop! And you've got to indicate to the people who run it, to the people who own it, that unless you're free, the machine will be prevented from working at all!"

There were so many of us, sitting everywhere, inside Sproul Hall, outside the hall, on the steps, everywhere.

I noticed Lowell and moved to sit with him. For a while Joyce joined us. But, given arrests were likely, she left. We both couldn't end up in jail together. Who would care for Caren?

For hours, Lowell and I sat, quietly talking about a range of topics.

Around three in the morning the police gave a final warning. "If you leave now, you won't be arrested."

Feeling nervous, and not wanting to leave Joyce to take care of Caren alone, I stood.

"Hey," I said, "I'm getting out of here."

"I'm staying," Lowell said.

"Good luck," I said.

I walked several steps. Then I looked back. He seemed so resolved.

It took the police twelve hours to arrest Lowell and close to eight hundred students.

◆ ◆ ◆

After his release, Lowell and I took the long route to Oxnard to visit our parents.

Rather than take the freeways, which would have gotten us there in about eight to ten hours, I pulled onto US Highway 1, the coastal highway. We drove for about an hour before Lowell suggested a detour. "There's a great little town around here," he said.

Fluent in Spanish, he chatted easily with the Mexican American residents, finding us an authentic Mexican restaurant for dinner. Later, we drove to the beach and unrolled our sleeping bags. There, under the stars, Lowell pulled out a joint. We took turns taking drags and enjoying the beauty all around us.

And so it went, driving a little each day, then stopping at a small town and sleeping on the beach. A trip that could have been done in one long day took us nearly a week.

When we returned to Berkeley in January, the new acting chancellor, Martin Meyerson, established new rules for political activity. He designated Sproul Plaza as an open discussion area during certain hours of the day. The fight was over.

Student life returned to normal.

Lowell, however, still had to stand trial, along with hundreds of others. The trial unfolded in a huge auditorium and dragged on for days and then weeks. As lawyers argued his cause, Lowell became dispirited. Why was it so hard to do the right thing? Why were the powers that be so against equality?

January came and went. So did February.

By March, Lowell and others were told to enter pleas.

The legal proceedings were still lurching forward when Gary Snyder, Lowell's poetry professor, organized The Berkeley Poetry Conference of 1965. The roster consisted of: Robin Blaser, Robert Creeley, Ed Dorn, Richard Duerden, Robert Duncan, Allen Ginsberg, Joanne Kyger, Ron Loewinsohn, Charles Olson, Gary Snyder, Jack Spicer, George Stanley, Lew Welch, Ken Irby, Jim Koller, David Schaff, and John Wieners.

The conference was immensely popular, and soon grew too big for the allocated space and time. People participated in any way they could. Some even perched on ledges adjacent to the open windows of California Hall to listen to the "Revolution." Lowell found a spot on a narrow ledge.

Due to the popularity of the conference, an extra day, July 25, was added so that the growing crowds could hear from the young poets from the Bay Area. Among them: Lowell, who read seven poems. This one was particularly well-received.

To a Fog-Covered Moist Carpet of Precarious Rivers, Pussy-Brambles, Eucalyptus, Moss, and Cow-Dung—Dead and Alive, Uneven and Unordered, Just East of Tilden, With a Fence Around It
By Lowell A. Levant

You move in the gazes that turn intent
    from the side, toward me,
in the smile that pulls in smoke
    and in the deliberate long puffs,
in the delicate exact turn of the breasts
    with the hand to the chin
    and to the back of the car seat
   that served as a couch,
with the forearms to the calves,
in the blinks, the fingertips, the strolls,
    and the statue of liberty pose to the West,
in the urge and in the way
to soar within the flesh –
    that ride on the witch's carpet:
ambiguous and sneaky
complicated and useless
requiring order but demanding that it not be form,
for even the best shoes wear out,
while bare footprints on the shifting sands last forever –
Finally, you move in the unpracticed purrs
in my tense, tired lap, so that I may realize
you alone.

Soon after the conference, sentencing of the FSM defendants began. Lowell was charged with "failure to disperse." He pled *nolo contendere* ("I do not wish to contest the charge") and was sentenced to probation.

Any respect for Berkeley was gone. Lowell wanted nothing to do with the institution. After one year, he dropped out and moved home to live with our parents. He never completed his degree and became a truck driver while continuing to write poetry.

As for me, I applied to medical school again, and this time was accepted at the University of California San Francisco School of Medicine.

TAKEAWAYS

Attending Berkeley during those tumultuous years was a rare privilege, allowing me to witness and participate in some of the most important political struggles of that historical period. Yet again, it was the grit developed during childhood that likely allowed me to succeed. What else could have gotten me through the horrors of life as a fraternity pledge or helped me to face the challenges of early fatherhood or enabled me to get off academic probation?

What I didn't know at the time but do know now: I would emerge from my Berkeley years forever changed—and for the better. My involvement in the civil rights movement and my introduction to feminism centered my point of view in the pursuit of social justice and would influence my decisions for decades to come.

To readers, what is your point of view, and what informs it? Considering this question can help you have an examined life.

CHAPTER 5

Students for a Democratic Society at a Medical School?

(1965–1967)

As we moved into the two-bedroom flat in San Francisco, the city where Joyce had grown up, I couldn't help but feel smug. Throughout my life, my dad had told me that I didn't do anything right—that I'd never be as perfect as he was. *Well, Dad,* I thought, *you're the one with the eighth-grade education. I'm the med student with a diploma from the top public university in California. So... who is more perfect?*

It wasn't just my father that I felt compelled to prove wrong. It was the world, the status quo, and later, the patriarchy. After our successes at Berkeley, I felt powerful. Change was coming, and I was going to help usher it in.

With this overabundance of idealism coupled with first-day jitters, I trudged up Parnassus Hill, past the long rows of double-decker homes, and toward the medical school. Everything about San Francisco seemed different from Berkeley, just across the Bay. There were some obvious downsides: it was cold, foggy, and incredibly hilly. Yet, San Francisco was also magical, what with the cable cars, Golden Gate Park, Fisherman's Wharf, North Beach, and the famed City Lights Book Store. Just a year before, *Life* magazine had pegged San Francisco as "The Gay Capital of America," and fabulous Finocchio's and other venues featured entertainment by female impersonators. I couldn't think of a better place for a pot-smoking, goatee-sporting, radical student to call home.

Out of breath from the climb, I slid into an auditorium seat for first-year orientation. With my nerves on fire, I glanced around the room. My classmates were among the best and brightest of my generation—future internists, pediatricians, surgeons, and whatnot, a few likely to become Nobel laureates. We were quite a homogeneous group, I realized, with most choosing from just two styles of dress. It was either formal jackets and ties or, like me, typical business casual attire. More ominously, most of us shared the same gender identity. Why, out of a class of one hundred students, I wondered, were there only two women?

After the information-packed session, I lingered in the hallway, trying to figure out what to do next. Just a few feet away, two faculty members leaned against a wall as they puffed on cigarettes, flicking the ashes into a nearby tray.

One, a stocky, dough-faced man with short, slicked-back brown hair, asked, "Why did we admit these women? They're just going to get married and have babies."

"Their places could have gone to men, who would have gone on to become doctors," said the other as he took a drag, slowly releasing a plume of smoke.

My idealism plummeted, landing in my stomach like indigestion after a holiday feast. What had I just heard? Had they really said . . . *that?*

I would have never overheard such a conversation in the People's Republic of Berkeley. I was certain of that. Everything suddenly felt wrong, like a bad omen.

The sickening feeling stayed with me as I hiked to the Anatomy Department office to get my lab assignment. A smartly dressed middle-aged woman told me where and when to report. Then she lowered her voice and leaned in so close I could smell her perfume. "Just between us, honey," she whispered, "you really ought to shave.

The people who make scholarship decisions will see you more favorably without that goatee."

She seemed gentle, even caring, as if she'd appointed herself to serve as a surrogate aunt who would watch over me and help me succeed.

Still, as I walked away, my hand stroked my goatee as if touching it would somehow shield it from the powers that be. This facial hair was a lot more than a personal grooming choice. It was part of my identity. It advertised my affiliation with the New Left. She didn't have to say the words for me to catch her drift. At the University of California San Francisco Medical Center (UCSFMC), new lefties weren't welcome. Just outside the building, I lit up a Marlboro to calm the heebie-jeebies swirling throughout my body.

No way was I shaving. That much I was sure of. There would probably be consequences. I knew that. Still, the words of the Bard of Avon came to mind, "To thine own self be true." The status quo would have to learn how to live with Ron the Radical. I'd left the fake version of myself—the scared boy who'd do anything and everything to fit in—back in high school.

◆ ◆ ◆

At 3 p.m. I found my way to the massive Gross Anatomy Lab. It was filled with one hundred students, fifty cadavers, and the sickening stench of formaldehyde and death. As expected, to slow the decomposition process, the room was as cold as an industrial refrigerator. Thankfully, I'd brought a sweater.

At my dissecting table stood Gary Bowman, the young man who would serve as my lab partner for the semester. His fingers lightly drummed the table, his thighs, then the table again. He shifted his weight from one hip to the other. He paced. He was constantly in motion, almost vibrating with energy.

As we shook hands and exchanged pleasantries, I took in his

face, specifically his mustache. My anxiety from earlier drifted away like fog in the afternoon sun. I wasn't the only radical here. Gary and me? We were going to get along fine. Perhaps medical school would turn out okay for me after all.

On our table was the body of a thin older man with white hair and the hallmarks of death and decomposition: sunken chest, loose skin, misshapen muscles, and fingers in contracture.

We started with the axilla (known colloquially as the armpit)—which, oddly, seemed fitting. Thanks to the decomp, much of the man's insides had blended into a monochromatic soup. Identifying specific arteries and veins was like trying to isolate one specific chunk of potato in a vat of clam chowder.

To add to my stress, our professor wandered around the room as we worked. With a stern look and piercing eyes, he periodically whipped out his forceps, grabbed a piece of flesh, and asked, loud enough for the whole room to hear, "What is that?" I prayed that he wouldn't come to our table.[4]

◆ ◆ ◆

Gary and I spent two hours a day, five days a week with our cadaver, taking turns slicing into its flesh and poking around its interior in search of various muscles, tendons, nerves, veins, and arteries.

It provided plenty of time to get to know one another. Like me, Gary was Jewish and married. As I'd suspected, he'd also gone to Berkeley and was interested in the New Left. Unlike me, he rode a motorcycle and played the guitar.

We quickly became close friends and collaborators, frequently meeting outside of class. He shared my need to push back against the medical school's conservatism. We wondered: could we form a New Left student political organization? Would students find the

---

[4] This professor, also a thoracic surgeon at San Francisco General Hospital, was later found to be a fraud with no medical training.

time for such a thing? Were there enough of us radicals around to get anything accomplished?

Gary learned that the New Left organization, Students for a Democratic Society (SDS), had started an initiative in 1965 titled "Radicals in the Professions." We contacted a staff member at SDS, who helped us figure out how to set up an affiliated student organization. We called it the Medical Center Committee for Independent Political Action (CIPA) and registered it with the administration, as was required.

Not long after completing these steps, my home phone rang.

"Is this Ron Levant?" a woman asked.

Her voice was soft yet tired, as if she'd been fighting a losing battle for decades.

"Speaking," I said.

"You're with the Medical Center Committee for Independent Political Action. Is that correct?"

"Yes, that's me," I answered quizzically. Gary and I had just formed the group weeks before. How had this woman found us?

"I'm Peggy McGivern," she said, "a public health nurse in Delano. I run the National Farm Workers Association Clinic here."

"Okay," I said, still confused.

"I'm trying to care for the migrant farm workers down here," she went on. "We have a severe outbreak of coccidiomycosis. Maybe you've heard of it? It's also known as Valley Fever."

"I think so," I said, "Maybe."

"It's a fungal infection. The grape workers pick it up when they're working in the fields. It's in the soil. As they work, the spores become airborne. They inhale them, and then they bloom in their lungs, making them very sick. They become too tired to work and sometimes develop pneumonia, sidelining them for weeks. If they can't work, they don't get paid. It's financially catastrophic for them."

"Oh," I said, "I see." Compassion for the farm workers swelled. Still, I had no idea what she thought I could do about it. Delano was four hours away, and I was a first-year medical student, not yet a doctor.

"It's truly a terrible situation," she said, beleaguered. "I could use your help."

"My help?"

"The closest hospital, in Bakersfield, is a thirty-five-mile drive from here. These farm workers often don't have vehicles, and the hospital seems completely uninterested in sending personnel here," she said. "I'm their only hope. It's just me here, on call, twenty-four hours a day. There's an antifungal available to treat this, but we don't have enough of it to go around. . ."

She trailed off. There was a long silence.

"I tried to get the California Department of Public Health to do more," she continued, each word sounding like a sigh. "If only they would deploy medical teams to treat the workers where they live and work, I think we'd be able to get ahead of this."

Again, there was a long silence.

Then she asked, "Do you think your student organization could organize medical personnel to travel to Delano to help me in my clinic?"

Now it was my turn to create an uncomfortable silence. Should I tell her that our student organization consisted of just two members? Or that we were both first-year medical students?

I hesitated, sensing her desperation. Was she grasping for straws by reaching out to an untested student organization? Mixed with my ambivalence, however, was a powerful sense of injustice. It was clear to me that, were this disease spreading among the inhabitants of Beverly Hills, the Department of Health would be doing more—a whole lot more. The people in power, however, looked upon poor immigrant grape pickers as unimportant (they didn't vote) and expendable. If they died, there were always more immigrants willing to take their place. The workers were being exploited, and that infuriated me.

There was also a selfish component, as I wanted a distraction from the stress of the Gross Anatomy Lab, which was taking a toll. Plus, my rebellious spirit craved a good, juicy antiestablishment campaign.

"Yes," I said, with a confidence that surprised me. "I'll need to run this by the CIPA cochair, of course, but I'm sure we can help."

I raced up Parnassus Hill and to the Gross Lab. I couldn't wait to see Gary.

As usual, he paced in front of our dissection table, drumming his fingers on any surface he could find.

"Man, I need to tell you something. You're not going to believe this," I said as I used a scalpel to slice deeper into our cadaver.

The corpse's insides were the same goopy mess as usual, yet my dissecting hand moved with precision and confidence that I hadn't experienced before.

"So, this nurse called me," I explained, "from Delano. She is with the National Farm Workers Association, which is leading the grape strike—*La Huelga*. You must have heard about Cesar Chavez? Anyway, she wants CIPA to help organize medical personnel to travel to Delano to treat the farm workers with Valley Fever. The local hospital has abandoned these poor people, and we're her only hope. Can you believe it?"

I drew my gaze away from the indistinct tissues of the dead man's body and raised my eyes toward Gary. For just the briefest of moments, he stopped vibrating and fidgeting. He, at first, looked perplexed, then enraged, then delighted.

He strode over, grabbed my shirt, pulled me upright, and raised his right palm for a high-five.

"Out of sight, man," he said. "That is far-fucking-out! Let's go do it!"

◆ ◆ ◆

Soon, Gary and I were in his red Mustang convertible and on our way to Delano to get a first-hand look at the situation.

In her crisp white uniform, nurse McGivern met us outside a trailer that had been retrofitted into a clinic. She was thin and haggard as if she'd been working days on end. "Come on in. Let me show you around," she said after greeting us.

It was after hours, and the clinic was empty. We walked through the living area, which served as the intake room, then the dining area, now a dispensary. In the kitchen was the examining room, where she treated the sick. The furniture consisted of metal folding chairs and bargain basement desks. The walls were white and plain. Everything about the place felt sterile and temporary, almost as if they were squatters ready to skedaddle as soon as the authorities discovered them.

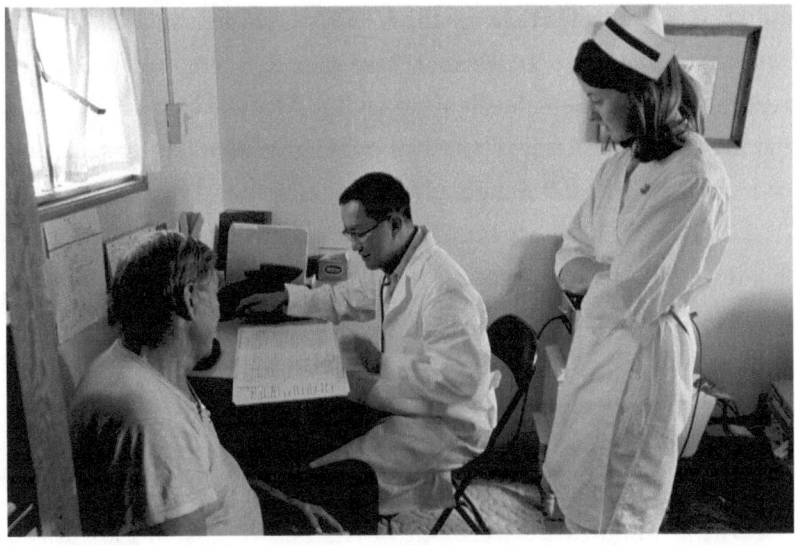

Peggy McGivern and a doctor examining a patient in Delano, CA. 1966. Photographer Emmon Clarke. Courtesy of the Tom and Ethel Bradley Center at California State University, Northridge.

We followed her to a farm the following day to see where the migrants worked and lived. I first noticed the children. There were so many of them milling about on a dirt common area in front of the long row of shacks. Why weren't they in school? The setting was surreal. I'd never seen anything like it.

"They work the fields, too," nurse McGivern said. "Americans love drinking expensive bottles of wine produced by the hard labor of these gentle workers—who not only could never afford just one of those glasses of wine, but also have no money for aspirin, antiseptic, or even Band-Aids. I will never give up on them. Never."

Her determination was contagious.

We plotted a strategy with nurse McGivern, then drove back home.

I threw myself into the initiative as if the world's fate depended on my time and energy. I posted flyers about the effort all over campus and asked students to attend a CIPA meeting about Delano. Gary and I then wrote an article for the UCSFMC student newspaper, the *Synapse*, requesting volunteers to take part in a temporary clinic to treat the farm workers. Students at UCLA Medical Center reprinted that article. Cesar Chavez, the National Farm Workers Association leader, also wrote a letter highlighting our efforts and requesting help.

I didn't have high expectations. I would have been thrilled if ten or twelve students had gotten involved. We set up fifteen folding chairs in the small CIPA office on the evening of our first meeting. Then we waited.

As 7 p.m. neared, students began making their way into the room. At first, it was just one or two. Then a couple more.

Then whole groups of them.

Within minutes we were out of chairs. More than four dozen students filled the room.

Gary extended his arms overhead for a double high-five. "Way to go, man!"

◆ ◆ ◆

Within days a stream started in which dozens of faculty and students from UCSF and UCLA medical centers would travel to the small clinic in Delano. Gary and I took turns going there for several months, with the other staying behind to dissect our cadaver. All the while, Joyce and I became those two proverbial ships that passed one another in the night. I'd arrive home as she was leaving. She returned from her work as I was on my way out. Our conversations revolved around who would watch Caren and whose turn it was to gas up the car.

Over the next few months, Gary, me, and the rest of the developing team worked hard to curtail the epidemic, earning needed publicity that helped to draw even more attention to our fledgling student group. Though we were granted office and meeting space as a recognized student organization, we had yet to elect officers. Gary and I continued to serve informally as the cochairs. Each meeting consisted of reports on the status of the Delano project: how many volunteers were scheduled for a given week, how many patients had been treated, and what the needs were for volunteers, drugs, and supplies for the next week. Then came a free-ranging discussion of what we wanted CIPA to become.

◆ ◆ ◆

As 1966 dawned, so did San Francisco.

The streets of the working-class neighborhood of Haight Ashbury came alive with poets, musicians, dancers, and performance artists, who performed in the streets for donations. Gaunt long-haired hippies increasingly rejected materialism, higher education, and nine-to-five work life, instead choosing to panhandle or perform for money.

Given this growing vibe, it only made sense that Ken Kesey, author of *One Flew Over the Cuckoo's Nest*, and his band called the Merry Pranksters decided to drive their psychedelic bus into town and join forces with the Grateful Dead to put on the festival of a lifetime.

Soon posters for the Trips Festival were plastered everywhere.

"This is the FIRST gathering of its kind anywhere," the poster read.

There would be entertainment by two of the important up-and-coming bands, Big Brother & the Holding Company (before Janis Joplin joined as lead singer) and the Grateful Dead, along with, the poster promised, movies, flowers, open theatre, poetry, liquid projections, nudity, and the acid test. An acid test. A real acid test!

I'd heard that an acid test had been held the month before in San Jose by former Harvard professors Timothy Leary and Richard Alpert. According to people who'd tried it, LSD and psilocybin weren't just drugs, like pot. They sent people on a *trip* that left them forever changed. As people hallucinated swirls, light, shadows, waves, and beauty, the drug loosened and expanded their minds, helping them to connect to something more. Something greater. Afterward, they talked of being liberated in ways they couldn't describe.

My curiosity would not allow me to miss it.

I *had* to be there.

Lowell agreed to drive from Berkeley to join me.

Days later, when we parked near Fisherman's Wharf and walked down to Longshoreman's Hall, we were transported to alternate reality.

Neon flashing lights surrounded us, moving and changing with the beat of the music. Thousands of people swayed with the lights and sounds. Some wore bright, psychedelic colors. Others were nude.

"What do you think?" I asked Lowell, pointing to a cup of LSD-laced Kool-Aid.

He glanced at some of the people shaking, moving, and waving—clearly hallucinating—seeing things that he and I could not.

"How would I be able to drive home?" he wondered.

"You're right. It's not a good idea. Maybe another time?"

"Yeah, maybe another time."

I lit a joint. We passed it back and forth as we swayed to the lights and music.

Hours later, when we left, I felt different.

"That was mind blowing," I told Lowell before walking to my car.

"Let's do it again," he said.

◆ ◆ ◆

By the close of my first year of med school, Joyce and I were drifting apart, as thoughts of CIPA occupied most of my waking moments. The tension in my marriage only intensified when the San Francisco Medical Committee for Human Rights, a prominent local organization, approached CIPA to participate in a project to assess and highlight the unmet healthcare needs of the Black community in the Deep South. My growing commitment to the Civil Rights Movement would not allow me to say no.

Despite the inherent dangers, we recruited five students, one nurse, and two physicians to join "Project South Help." Then, to cover their expenses, we held a benefit dance concert, which we titled "Last Gas Before the Desert," with entertainment provided by one of the new San Francisco rock bands, the Sopwith Camel, and by the SF Mime Troup.

This is one of the flyers we used to advertise the benefit for Project South Help.

Publicity and recognition followed. The *San Francisco Chronicle* ran a story about the effort, with photos of me and Marty Leibowitz, another CIPA member. A report titled "The Untold Story: The Constructive Student. A Special Report to the

Board of Regents of the University of California, October 1966" also contained a write-up on CIPA.

In poured donations as well as letters of encouragement. Clark Kerr, the president of the University of California, reached out. Then we heard from Raymond J. Sontag, PhD, a professor of history with whom I'd become close when I was an undergrad. He sweetly cautioned me to temper my expectations for social change and to not neglect my medical studies.

His warning, though well-intentioned, only emboldened me. With each report and news story, our membership climbed, and I became intoxicated by the idea of truly making a difference.

Thanks to our past successes, I felt invincible, as if I had the energy and smarts to pull off any project that came CIPA's way. Given all the great publicity, offers to collaborate arrived regularly, and my pride allowed me to refuse few of them. When a federation of fifty-seven community organizations in the Mission District asked us to do health organizing among the Mexican American community, I beamed with confidence. They seemed to believe in us.

Perhaps that's why I never thought to ask, "What would this take? Do we have the skills and resources to get it done? What will happen to my marriage if I spend even less time at home? What will happen to my studies?"

Had I considered those questions, I might have realized that no one in CIPA had community organizing experience. Only a few of us spoke Spanish. We didn't know how to do needs assessments, either.

I dealt with this and my other worries and tensions by smoking pot, which had become my way of life. At that time, pot was everywhere and very available. Plus, it made me feel good, sometimes reminding me of Berkeley. Like my facial hair, pot was a part of my identity. It was what made me a hippie and a radical. I clung to it.

Though I didn't seek it out, I also didn't turn down opportunities to try other drugs if they happened to be around. So, when Gary invited me over to try an opioid painkiller he'd swiped from a clinic,

I was at his front door within minutes.

After inserting the syringe through the rubber cap on the vial, Gary pulled on the plunger, drawing the Talwin into the syringe. He then pushed out the air.

"I'll do myself first," he said. "Then I'll do you."

He swabbed his arm, applied a tourniquet, and inserted the needle into his vein.

"Interesting," he said.

"All right, let's get you done," he said as he reached for a new syringe.

A few minutes after the shot, a strange sensation took over the roof of my mouth. "My mouth feels funny," I said.

"Same here," Gary said. "It's like . . . tingles. Lots of tingles."

He flipped on his turntable and put on *Rubber Soul*, a new Beatles album, and selected the second track, "Norwegian Wood." We listened, chatted, and waited with curiosity to see what else this new drug might have in store.

Within a half hour, I was back to normal.

"Eh, it's not doing much for me," I said as I got up to head home. "Next time, steal something better. I don't need to try this stuff again."

He didn't say it, but I assumed Gary felt the same. The drug was a dud.

◆ ◆ ◆

One evening, with my eyes burning and mouth parched, the phone rang. It was late, too late for someone to be calling.

I lifted the handle, put it to my ear, and mumbled, "Hello."

There was a click, then a dial tone.

I placed the handle back on its base. This was becoming a thing, wasn't it? Hadn't someone hung up on me just a few nights before?

I stared at the phone, first with hazy curiosity and then with indignation.

Joyce was having an affair.

That was it. She had to be.

Was there any other explanation?

I shook my head as if it were an Etch a Sketch, and the movement would erase the thought from my mind. I had to be wrong. *Please, I thought, be wrong.* Maybe I was just paranoid. Pot can do that to a person.

Caren was sleeping, but I needed some air. She'd be okay, I thought, for a little while. I'd only be gone for a moment. I just needed to clear my head.

I was mere feet from my front door when I saw him. The man was two doors down. He was wearing an overcoat, with the collar turned up, and a lit cigarette held sideways in his mouth.

I stood still, bent down, and hid behind a bush. Was he watching me? Spying on me? I'd heard about men like this. The CIA was attempting to remove radical students from California universities. It all made perfect sense. They'd heard about CIPA and understood our power. *Of course, this spy was keeping tabs on me. Of course. Wait until I tell Gary about this!*

As the days and weeks passed, I tried to shake off the idea that Joyce was stepping out on me. Yet the evidence was right there, every time I picked up the phone only to hear a click and a dial tone.

Similarly, I told myself that there were plenty of other explanations for the Overcoat Man. Maybe, for example, he lived down the street, and his wife didn't let him smoke indoors. That said, Gary and some of the other CIPA members seemed to think I was onto something, telling me that the dude seemed suspicious. "Keep a diary, and list the times and dates you notice him," they told me.

The man turned up more and more often and in more and more places.

It seemed impossible to interpret it any other way. The CIA had to be after me.

◆ ◆ ◆

My paranoia fueled further radicalization. No longer was I merely fighting for health rights. Now, I was taking a deep dive into Max Schactman's Independent Socialist Committee and obsessed with Marxist ideology, which was several standard deviations to the left of most of the health professions students in CIPA. The Mission District project dragged on, with us making little headway. CIPA meetings devolved into angry recriminations. Group members openly questioned my leadership. Newer members thought they knew better and that my politics were too far left.

When we held our first-ever elections, I ran for president. I'd founded the organization! It seemed I'd earned it, as if I were the organization's rightful leader.

"With Gary, I created this organization," I told the members during my campaign speech. "We've had a lot of success. We know what we're doing. We fight oppression in every form. That's what I intend to do with every cell in my body. You're either with me or against me."

It turned out they were against me. I lost, and a dental student took over the leadership of the organization that Gary and I founded.

◆ ◆ ◆

That January during the Human Be-In in Golden Gate Park, Timothy Leary encouraged us to "Turn on, tune in, and drop out."

"Maybe I should," I told Lowell.

"Should do what?" he asked.

"Drop out. Maybe I should drop out of medical school," I said. "I don't understand the point of any of this anymore."

"You gotta do what you gotta do," he said.

That month, the new CIPA leadership organized the first-ever antiwar rally on a medical school campus. Kindly and despite my differences with the new leadership, they invited me to speak to the crowd. As I took in the health science students and professionals—over one thousand of them—packed into the small plaza, pride swelled inside me. The campus had come a long way in such a short time. No longer were Gary and I just two scruffy radicals up against a set of clean-shaven conservatives. We'd built a movement and changed the campus.

Yet, that sense of pride mingled with a growing paranoia and anger. Stress was my constant companion. My marriage, my studies, and my future all began to crumble.

To regain some clarity, Joyce, Caren, and I joined Gary and his wife Nancy on a camping trip in Big Sur. With the Santa Lucia mountains rising dramatically from the Pacific Ocean, our campsite offered breathtaking views, clean air, chirping birds, and all the serene comforts of nature.

It was the perfect place to unwind.

Early one morning, I snuck off to take a few hits while Joyce, Gary, Nancy, and Caren stayed behind. When I returned, I overheard my name.

Why was Joyce talking about me?

Why were they all talking about me?

I stormed into the tent.

Muscles tense and skin on fire, I screamed, "Why are you talking about me? What is going on?"

"What are you talking about?" Joyce asked. "No one's talking about you."

"You're lying. I heard you! I knew you were having an affair. I knew it!"

My face was inches from hers. Chest tight, heart pounding, the rage wanted out. My focus narrowed. Everyone else disappeared. All that was left was me, Joyce, and the rage inside me.

The rage wanted to destroy. It needed to do something. I was sick of being ignored, underappreciated, and backstabbed.

Fist tight, I swung.

"Man, what's going on?" Gary tackled me from behind. We fell, me squirming, him holding me down, my arms pinned to my sides.

I kicked, writhed, and bucked.

"Stop," Gary screamed. "Ron, stop. Why are you doing this? Stop!"

He was like a mountain lion, too strong for me to topple.

With my cheek against the tent floor, my eyes focused on Caren. Her dumpling of a face was red with terror. Her dark eyes wide, she hid behind Joyce's legs. Tears fell down her tiny cheeks.

Joyce seemed stunned, almost frozen in place, with her palm against her cheek.

What had I done? What was wrong with me?

Slowly, silently, we packed our belongings, got in the car, and drove north to San Francisco. Shame crept into my soul, took up residence, and grew. I'd sworn to myself, repeatedly, that I would never become my father. Yet, here I was, obnoxious, aggressive, and everything I despised.

I couldn't look Joyce in the eye.

Two months later, she and I sat quietly and agreed that the marriage wasn't working. Then we made love, trying to erase the terrible last few months with a positive memory. Soon after, I heard that Joyce was dating someone else.

TAKEAWAYS

In this period, my mental health started to slip away, leading to my marital breakup. The way I understand this was that due to my traumatic childhood, I had a reservoir of rage lying just below the surface, that, when activated, could lead to violence, as when I punched Joyce.

In addition, the cornerstones of my personality were not all properly in place—I had not fully developed into a mature adult. Given my lack of maturity, I allowed the early success of the Delano project to imbue me with a dangerous overconfidence—hubris—the very reason for the downfall of many heroes of Greek mythology. I took on the new Mission Project without fully evaluating whether CIPA had the resources to do what was required. As it became evident that we did not, I sought to escape by becoming ever more radical in my approach, flirting with a fringe group of Marxists who were to the left of Leon Trotsky. This only served to alienate my fellow members of CIPA, leading to my loss in the election for president. Unfortunately, my downward descent had only just begun.

Readers, if you are a trauma survivor and you struggle as I did, please seek psychological help. We have many good treatments for psychological trauma today. The National Register of Health Service Providers in Psychology has a very helpful online directory: https://www.findapsychologist.org/

CHAPTER 6

"Wear a Flower in Your Hair"

(Summer 1967)

As the Vietnam War and the draft picked up steam, the Age of Aquarius dawned. Thousands of young people quit their jobs, packed their scant belongings into their cars, and traveled west to San Francisco in search of a better world. Money and materialism were out. Freedom, love, peace, acceptance, and "make love, not war" were in.

The epicenter of the cultural explosion was the section of San Francisco where Haight and Ashbury streets intersected. Barefoot hippies danced, played flutes, sang, recited poems, and played bongos, all the while spreading joy and happiness. The Diggers—an offshoot of the SF Mime Troupe that had participated in CIPA's benefit dance concert—offered free food. A progressive doctor opened the Haight-Asbury Free Clinic in a storefront, treating anyone regardless of their ability to pay. Huckleberry House served as a refuge for young people without shelter. A Free Store opened its doors, too. I witnessed the following interaction in the Free Store (which resembled a Goodwill store), illustrating the spirit of the time.

Man 1: "How much for this jacket?"
Man 2: "How much do you want to pay?"
Man1: "Two dollars?"
Man 2: "Okay."

Man 1 hands over the money to Man 2 and leaves the store with his jacket.

Man 2: "Anyone want two dollars?"

With so much freely available, anyone could make do in The Haight for quite a long time, no nine-to-five job required. This gave folks plenty of time for artistic expression.

Psychedelic signs were everywhere, featuring highly distorted or surreal visuals and bright colors. Jerry Garcia, Janis Joplin, Grace Slick, and many other soon-to-be-famous artists moved into the neighborhood. Music and the scent of cannabis permeated the air. Free concerts erupted in Golden Gate Park.

The whole scene was mesmerizing, dreamlike, and alive with creativity and novelty.

The rest of the world had war, stress, and hate.

The Haight had its opposite.

It all seemed so real, so tangible, so powerful. I was convinced that the Aquarian vibe would spread—and the entire world would be forever changed for the better. It was right, and it was what the world needed. Eventually, we wouldn't be a counter-culture movement. We'd be the dominant culture.

◆ ◆ ◆

With my marriage to Joyce over, I was now free to pursue other opportunities.

So, when Louise Anderson, an administrator at the medical school, expressed interest, I asked whether she'd like to join me for a walk.

She and I meandered all throughout the Haight, wandering in and out of the stores, coffee shops, and head shops, exploring the side streets, taking in the sights, sounds, and goings on. At one point we walked by Janis Joplin, sitting on her stoop on a side street with a pint of Southern Comfort by her side.

From the H. Salt takeout restaurant, we ordered fish and chips. We carried the malt-vinegar-flavored meal tucked into a funnel of newspaper to the end of Haight Street, where Golden Gate Park began. Then we climbed Hippy Hill and sat. The sun warmed our backs. Pot smoke drifted all around us.

With dark hair and piercing eyes, Louise seemed so sure of herself.

"Look," she told me, "I really like you, so I don't want you to take this the wrong way. Before we get too into each other, you should know that I have no intention of settling down. I like sex, you know? I'll have it with you, if you'll have it with me, but I'll also have it with other people. You'll never be the only one in my life. Do you understand? Free love, baby."

I would have preferred a monogamous relationship. That's just how I was. Yet, I liked that I knew where I stood. Her honesty was refreshing, especially after all those months of suspecting Joyce's infidelity. At least, with Louise, I knew what was likely going to transpire. There were no secrets. Plus, this was the Aquarian Age. Jealousy was what the establishment did. Us hippies? We loved the ones we were with.

Louise and I saw each other a lot after that.

On any given day, we were meandering through the Haight, hanging out or making love at her apartment, or smoking dope on Hippy Hill. Though I remembered what she'd told me about free love, it seemed more like an idea than a reality. Louise and I spent so much time together that I *had* to be the main player in her life—if not the only player. I felt sure of it.

One foggy morning, Louise and I passed a joint back and forth as we talked about a demonstration scheduled for that afternoon at the Civic Center. Her nipples bore their way through her crop top. I caressed the curve of her breast with my hand. We'd already made love once that morning, yet I was ready for more.

She smiled sheepishly. That was unlike her. It was as if she knew something I didn't. Why was she holding back? Why wasn't she reciprocating?

I imagined myself unbuttoning her cut offs, gently resting her on the table, and taking her in the kitchen.

The doorbell interrupted my reverie. Louise rose to answer. Without bothering to first look through the peephole to see who it was, she flung open the door. On the stoop stood a tall Black man.

At first, I was startled. Despite my involvement in the Civil Rights movement, I knew very few Black people. That's how it was back then, due to redlining and whatnot. He was a towering figure, with noticeable muscles. Why was he here? What did he want? I craned my head toward the door to eavesdrop.

Louise wrapped her arms around his neck, hugging him close. Then she grabbed his hand, led him into her apartment, and said, "Ron, this is Carl. Carl? This is Ron."

We exchanged pleasantries, with Carl and Louise shooting each other knowing glances.

"So, about the demonstration later today," I said.

"Oh, honey," Louise said. "Why don't you go to that without me. As it turns out, I'm going to be quite busy today."

She glanced at Carl, and he at her. Clearly. Quite busy. I got the drift. She wanted me gone, and for the next few hours Carl was going to be her main attraction.

"Um," I said awkwardly. "I think I'm going to bounce."

She hugged me, but not in the loving, sexual way she often did with her breasts hungrily pressed into my torso. This hug was short, cursory. It was her way of saying "please leave." "Okay, um," I stammered. Was this really happening? Was she really doing this? It was one thing for her to hook up with men when I wasn't around. But to do it right in front of me? I'd never known anyone that brazen.

"Right," I continued. "Um. Carl? Nice to meet you."

He mumbled something. I'm not sure what. His attention was almost completely focused on Louise. It was as if I was already gone.

"All right then," I said awkwardly. They were no longer paying attention to me. "I'm out."

I closed her front door behind me and set off to the Civic Center. *Don't think about it*, I told myself. At the demonstration, I chatted up several women, in hopes of taking one of them back to my 1959 VW microbus, painted red, and outfitted as a camper, with a bed and miscellaneous cabinets, which I had purchased from my savings after Joyce and I split up (she kept the Fiat). I figured, if Louise was going to love openly and freely, so would I.

◆ ◆ ◆

I couldn't get enough of the Haight and found myself spending more and more time there—sometimes with Louise, sometimes on my own.

I no longer understood the point of medical school. Why had I ever thought that was a good career choice? It all seemed silly now. As Timothy Leary had suggested months before at the Be-In, I decided to drop out of society. I disenrolled, lost my scholarship, and scraped together money to live on by renting rooms in my apartment to a parade of characters.

I was no longer observing the hippies from the outside in.

I'd become one.

Sometimes I slept on a foam mattress in an extremely large walk-in closet in my apartment. Other times, I crashed on the coach of a friend, on the mattress of my microbus, or with Louise or some other woman.

During the days, I roamed the Haight, sometimes volunteering to dish out free soup with the Diggers or calm anxious kids on bad acid trips at the Free Clinic.

◆ ◆ ◆

One rainy afternoon Louise and I walked from one booth to another at an arts and crafts fair in another part of the city—the Richmond District. We met another couple and hit it off. Gina was short and lean, with long dark brown hair and brown eyes. She was very hyper and talked very fast with a lot of hand gestures. Rob was tall and muscular, and obviously hit the gym often. He had a moustache and light brown hair that he wore in a ponytail.

"Wanna come back to my pad?" suggested Louise. It was clear from the sexual energy pouring from her soul exactly what she had in mind.

Back at her place, we congregated over a joint on the living room floor. Clothes came off. She and Gina made out and fondled one another's breasts.

"Come on, honey," Gina said, straddling Louise from behind, her hands cupping each of her breasts. Rob entered Louise, rhythmically moving in and out. Louise seemed so calm, relaxed, almost in another place. Her head lolled to the side. Her eyes rolled upwards.

I lay next to her, watching, uncomfortably hard, close to the action, but left out of the fun.

She panted. She cried out. She moaned. She begged. Her body arched. Her thighs quivered. A bead of sweat dripped down her cheek, onto her chest, and around her breast. Rob grunted. Gina cooed.

Louise screamed and thrashed. I had never seen Louise like this, nor had I ever made her feel like this. The moaning grew more intense. Then all three exploded, falling into one another completely spent. Their breathing slowed.

"That," said Louise, still catching her breath, "was amazing."

"Oh man, so sorry," said Rob, seemingly noticing me for the first time. He tried to stroke my cock, but I demurred. I wasn't into men and eventually went flaccid. All four of us crashed on the floor, covered by multiple blankets.

In the morning, I woke with the lyrics from Crosby, Stills, and

Nash running through my head: "Now witness the quickness with which we get along."

◆ ◆ ◆

While dishing out soup, I noticed the microphone. It was there for bands that occasionally entertained the crowd, but, at that moment, it was idle.

What a great place to have a rally, I thought.

I hopped onto the truck bed, grabbed the mic, and evangelized about the evils of the war in Vietnam. Hippies glanced my way, seemingly confused.

Everyone seemed confused.

Why weren't they gathering around me? Why weren't people raising their fists and or signaling me with peace signs? Why was everyone ignoring me?

I continued to preach.

Emmet Grogan, the founder, and several other Diggers strode over. *Finally*, I thought, *an audience*. Rather than stand and listen, they walked all the way to the truck bed. One of them tied my shoelaces together. Not funny!

I bent to untie my shoes. When I stood, the mic was gone. One of the Diggers had carried it off. The others retreated, leaving me alone. Confused, I looked right, then left. What was going on? Why didn't anyone care about what I had to say? This was important stuff! My message needed to get out! What was wrong with them?

At the time, I was convinced *they* were the problem, the slackers, the sheep, the fakers who weren't as dedicated to ending the war as I was. Later, looking back on it all, I saw things more clearly. What I did that day represented very poor judgment, yet another sign of my worsening psychological health.

◆ ◆ ◆

By July the peaceful Summer of Love vibe was turning sour. Throngs of middle-aged, middle-class tourists clogged Haight Street, their cars coming to a crawl as they gawked at the long-haired hippies who posed for pictures and panhandled. Haight Street had become a chronic traffic jam, and the hippies were becoming resentful, feeling as if the tourists saw them as zoo animals rather than human beings.

One afternoon, as Louise and I wandered from one store to another, we noticed several hippies meandering into the street. They pulled out cameras and snapped photos of the tourists. At first, tourists seemed to appreciate the humor and understand the point: it was rude to gape and stare. A feeling of community developed. Several hundred people gathered to observe, including Louise and me. The Age of Aquarius bloomed all around us.

Then the fun dissipated. Tension grew. Tempers flared. People flipped the bird and cursed.

A squad car blasted its siren. People ran.

Caught up amid the mayhem, Louise and I stood and watched, not knowing where to turn or what to do.

Helmeted riot control officers carrying long batons arrived. They descended onto the crowd, batting people out of their way. People were running, falling, being beaten, and then they were cuffed and thrown into police wagons. It was sickening, maddening, wrong.

Louise strode over to one of the officers.

"What are you doing?" she demanded. Louise was so assertive, and so good at getting her point across. He would see her as a voice of reason, a citizen, someone who mattered, and someone who deserved a say. I was sure of it.

An officer bear hugged her, pinning her arms to her sides. There was a flash of a baton, then a crack, then a helpless, guttural grunt. Louise fell. What had they done?

I raced toward her. An officer jumped onto me as pain shot into my side, arms, and head. My face against the asphalt, a knee in my back, boots battering my ribs.

Is this it, I wondered? *Is this how it ends?* I fixed my gaze on Louise from the ground, several yards away from where she lay. If this was going to be the last image my eyes processed, I wanted her to be in it.

Someone yanked me to my feet. There was a metallic sound as they cuffed my hands. With his palm against my back, an officer pushed me forward and into a van. We arrestees were taken to San Francisco County Jail and put in a large holding tank filled with unkempt dudes sporting prison tattoos and angry expressions.

I tried to avoid eye contact.

Finally, I faced a judge, who told me that I was charged with failure to disperse. After pleading *nolo contendere* ("I do not wish to contest the charge"), I was fined $29. As I left the courthouse, I was happy to be done with the entire horrible incident.

I later learned that Louise's jaw was broken in two places. It would take her months to recover.

Police officers usher me into a paddy wagon. I am in the center. Photo taken by an unknown photographer.

TAKEAWAYS

In a continuation of the theme of being at the place where history was being made, I found myself at the epicenter of the American Counterculture, in the Haight Ashbury district of San Francisco, at the dawning of what some of us earnestly believed was the "the Age of Aquarius." This began as an extraordinarily idealistic period, where many aspects of social life that had been assumed as "the way things are" were being tested and alternatives were being formulated. The common denominator was that, for a short time, many of life's necessities were now free, which was profoundly anticapitalist.

While some aspects of this period were truly wonderful, others were the opposite, such as the police riot that resulted in my arrest. Meanwhile, my mental health continued to deteriorate, leading to my withdrawal from medical school and my increasingly poor judgment.

CHAPTER 7

The Evil Dr. Goopcough

(1967–Fall 1968)

The system was coming down on our heads! The pigs were out of control! We had to do something! Dropping out of society wasn't enough! Ushering in the Aquarian Age wasn't enough! Spreading peace, love, and kindness wasn't enough! Someone had to stop it! Someone had to change it! We could no longer wait! The time for change was now!

As I ranted and raved in the courthouse parking lot, other arrestees gathered, then raised their closed fists in solidarity. Plans hatched. Phone numbers were exchanged. An army was forming.

The revolution was nigh!

From the courthouse, I raced to the bank, withdrew hundreds of dollars, and gave some of the dough to John, one of the arrestees, asking him to rent an apartment that we could use as a basecamp to regroup. He found us a ratty apartment in the Filmore district. The wallpaper was peeling. The place stank of mildew.

Dozens joined the effort, pouring into our base camp, all of them people who'd been arrested on Haight Street.

"What should we do?" I asked. "How should we start the revolution? How can we form a resistance movement to stop the pigs and dismantle this system of oppression?"

Someone yelled, "Let's do a sit-in at police headquarters!"

"Far-out!" and "Right on!" people shouted, all in between drags on a joint.

Before we could organize a plan, however, someone else piped up, "No, let's do a sit-in in the street and stop all traffic and commerce!"

Again, there were high fives and raised fists.

Again, the idea went no further.

It went on like this, with someone mentioning a way to resist the powers that be, all of us getting excited about it, then none of us able to flesh the idea out into an organized plan.

As I grew increasingly agitated by our ineptitude, I glanced at Louise. With an ice pack pressed against her bruised, swollen cheek, she occasionally raised a fist or grunted in unison with the crowd. She didn't need to talk for me to know how she felt. Rage seeped from her pores.

Day after day we ranted and organized. More ideas came and went.

Our ranks thinned.

More time passed.

Each day, fewer revolutionaries showed up.

By the end of the month, only four of us were left: Louise, John, who had become the de facto second-in-command, an attractive young women named Mary, and me.

With her jaw wired shut, Louise was on a liquid diet. But the swelling and bruising had subsided. She could now talk, though she sounded a bit robotic.

"What's your bag?" she asked through her clenched teeth. "Lay it on me."

"I don't know," I said, blowing a plume of smoke from a joint. "I'm just sick of the City. Everything's bumming me out. Everyone gave up. It's all so disheartening. It all feels so dark, so stupid, so pointless. I want to do something. But I don't know what or how. I think the City is the problem. Maybe it's killing my vibe, you know?

Wanna get out of here? Go to the country for a while?"

"Like commune with nature?" she asked, "Out of sight. I can get into that!"

Bless that woman. She was up for anything.

"How about camping?" I asked.

Suddenly animated, she sat up, the sheets falling, exposing her beautiful breasts. She was in no shape for sex these days, not with her still healing jaw, but the woman rarely wore a thread. It was one of the things I loved about her.

Soon we had a map in front of us.

"There," she said, pointing to Guerneville, a small, rustic logging town near the Russian River. "That looks like it's in the middle of fucking nowhere. It's the perfect spot to plan a revolution, don't you think?"

"Out of sight!" I said, "I like it."

"You and the others can live off brown rice while we're there," she continued. "It's supposed to transform your consciousness. That's why the Buddhist monks eat it! You know, it's part of that macrobiotic Zen diet. Each stage gets you closer to enlightenment. Brown rice is the last stage. Let's skip to the end and just blow our fucking minds!"

"Maybe that will help us to stop spinning our wheels and get something fucking done," I said.

Days later, John, Mary, Louise, and I bought a twenty-five-pound bag of brown rice, climbed into my VW microbus, and drove north to the Santa Rosa Highway.

An hour and a half later, after lurching up several steep, twisting roads, we pulled into a remote area. Redwoods towered above, their majesty reflected in the nearby Russian river. I couldn't think of a better location to reimagine the social order. With no rules or social mores to restrain us, we could be completely free. Distracted by everything around me—and especially by Louise's almost constantly nude body—the darkness and disillusionment began to lift.

Each morning we woke to sunlight, the scent of pine, and bird song. On my Coleman stove, we boiled water for rice, along with soup for Louise. Then we hiked, smoked pot, napped, sang, smoked more pot, swam, walked around nude, smoked more pot, ate more rice, and walked along the river. We often sat on the banks of the river, pulled out a joint, passed it around, and chatted about all sorts of ways to change the world for the better.

One day passed into another.

By week's end, no decent ideas had taken hold. I paced around, feeling increasingly irritated. Why couldn't we come up with anything? What was wrong with us? With me?

It was like the famous line from MacBeth. The effort had been "full of sound and fury, signifying nothing."

We returned to the city, and never saw John and Mary again.

◆ ◆ ◆

Much like that proverbial stone, I rolled from one location to another, doing what I felt like, and when I felt like it. I was aimless, purposeless, and increasingly despondent. With no permanent address and no phone that I regularly answered, Joyce and Caren were drifting away from me like seeds from a dandelion pod on a windy day. Joyce wasn't trying to keep Caren in my life, and I wasn't resisting.

Sometimes, as I fell asleep at night, I imagined Caren's sweet, inquisitive face staring hungrily at me as I told her a fantastical story about wicked doctor Goopcough who lived high up on the hill at the medical school.

When had that been? Was it weeks ago? No, gosh, more than a month. Had it been that long?

Joyce had dropped her off that day then glanced around our old apartment, sniffed the stench of stale pot, and visibly recoiled at the sight of one of my tenants.

"I'll be back in an hour," she'd said curtly. Clearly, Joyce hadn't approved of my living situation.

She was right. Caren deserved more than a drifter who lived in a walk-in closet or the back of a microbus.

Still, that day, Caren had faced me with wide eyes, eating up my made-up story as if it were a bowl of ice cream.

"Evil Dr. Goopcough," I said, captivating her. "He wears a white coat, and he carries around a giant stethoscope that allows him to hear the heartbeat of everyone in the city."

She'd crawled onto my lap, then cuddled against my side.

"It's important that we do not get too close to him," I warned. "Because he steals people's hearts."

She put her tiny hand into mine.

"He keeps the hearts in glass jars, where they continue to beat. We can't hear them, but those hearts are crying to be reunited with their loved ones."

"That's scary," she whispered. "Can we help the hearts?"

"No, we can't go up there," I said. "We need to stay safe. To stay safe, we must stay as far away from the hill as we can."

I put my arm around her.

"I'll keep you safe, honey. Don't worry."

"Okay Daddy," she'd said.

The memory washed through me. That day I'd felt like maybe, just maybe, I could give this beautiful young being what she needed in life. I just had to try harder. That was all.

But now, weeks later, as I tossed and turned on the mattress in the back of my microbus, I wondered about that evil doctor. Maybe he wasn't such a fantastical work of fiction after all.

Perhaps that evil doctor was me.

◆ ◆ ◆

To offset my growing sense of inadequacy, I gravitated toward commune culture, hoping that living in harmony with a group of like-minded people could break me free from the despondency and malaise that seemed to drag me down whenever I stayed put for more than a few days.

One evening, Lowell mentioned, "Well, John Staple is in one up in Chico," he said. "Do you remember him? He's Will's brother. You may recall that Will and I were in Gary Snyder's poetry workshop. Why don't you go up there?"

"That's cool," I said. "Think they'll have me?"

"Just ask for John, and tell him I sent you," Lowell said. "But I should warn you. They're fruitarians."

"What the fuck is that?"

"They only eat fruit," he said, "because it's more mind blowing or something."

"Far-out," I said. "I can dig it."

A gaunt man in a T-shirt, dirty long pants, and a piece of rope for a belt answered the door.

"My brother Lowell knows Will Staple," I said. "He's John Staple's brother. I'd like to join your commune."

"You're a friend of John?"

He turned and yelled, "Hey John? Someone's here."

A medium-sized man with thick wavy brown curls, a scraggy beard, gentle face, and serious eyes meandered over.

He recognized me from a get-together at Berkeley, more than a year earlier. "So, you're Lowell's brother?" he said, giving me a warm embrace. "Come in, come in, brother, let me show you around."

He handed me a peach, and then walked me through the two-room apartment where twelve people lived, all of them just as gaunt as the man who'd answered the door.

"This one's free," he said, pointing to one of the mattresses.

He reached out and touched my face. "Dude, you've got some dark circles under your eyes," he said. "A fruit-only diet will do you some good. You'll see. In a week or two, you're going to feel like a new man. There's a whole bushel of peaches in the kitchen. Help yourself if you're hungry."

I figured fruitarian diets had something to do with the dawning of the Age of Aquarius. Everything always did. Maybe, like brown rice, eating fruit served as a door to greater consciousness? I didn't ask questions—and didn't need answers. I was just happy to be there, in a commune, with other like-minded people. Whenever I was surrounded by other hippies, my discontent, disillusionment, and darkness seemed to fade—at least for a while.

For the rest of the day, I did my best to settle in, chatting with a few of the folks who were milling about. The rent in Chico was ridiculously cheap. It didn't take much to come up with it each month. Some of them picked fruit for money. Others stole it as they walked through orchards.

That evening a thin, brown-haired woman showed up.

"You're new," she said, walking straight toward me. "I'm Sue."

"Ron," I said, extending my hand.

"You're a gas," she said, taking my hand and leading me to a mattress in one of the bedrooms. "Want to smoke some grass?"

She looked around, to make sure no one was paying attention. Then she pushed her mattress to the side, lifted the floorboard underneath, and pulled out a plastic bag full of weed.

"Don't tell anyone," she said, motioning to the floor board. "We're supposed to share everything."

She rolled a joint, then lit it. She took a long drag, then passed it to me.

Then she took off her clothes.

I woke next to Sue's nude body and hunger so intense that I wasn't sure a whole bushel of peaches would be enough.

By the end of the week, all I could think about was food. My stomach gnawed at me almost constantly. So did the darkness that I was trying so hard to escape.

"Keep moving," I told myself. "Just keep moving."

"Hey," I told Sue, "I'm gonna head back to the city for a few days. But I'd love to drop acid with you when I get back."

"Groovy," she replied.

I handed her some cash. "Think you can score some while I'm gone?"

"Sure can, honey," she said. "Come on. Let's ball before you go."

A week later I returned. Sue and the acid were nowhere to be found. She'd likely gone somewhere or met someone and gotten distracted. That was the nature of rolling stones like us. We never stayed put.

◆ ◆ ◆

Back in San Francisco, I drifted around, sleeping in my microbus, walk-in closet, or whatever open couch, mattress, or floor space was offered. The fruitarian life wasn't for me. However communal living still intrigued me. I figured I just had to find the right tribe.

While volunteering in the free clinic one warm and sunny afternoon, I got wind of a commune called the Ashram. Like the one in Chico, this commune had a spiritual component. So, after helping a young man come down from a bad acid trip, I walked down a side street, to a triple-decker house with apartments in each floor.

A skinny, long-haired, blond man with a scraggly beard answered the door.

"Hi, I'm Ron," I said, extending my hand. "I heard about your community. I'm seeking an ashram-like environment. I've been seeking for a while. Can I stay here?"

"Sure, come in," he said, leading me to a room near the front of the house. "Sit."

There was a stuffed sofa that had clearly seen better times. The fabric was ripped, and it smelled dank.

Another gaunt young man appeared.

"Father Peter would like to see you."

He led me to another room, where I encountered a bearded man with wild black hair and green eyes.

"Hello brother," Father Peter said, giving me a warm hug. "What are you looking for?"

"Peace," I said. "I've been through hell. I've been arrested. My girlfriend got her jaw broken. I need somewhere to chill out."

"Well, this is the place for you, my friend," he said. "Welcome to our humble community."

Father Peter showed me around, introducing me to a parade of characters, all of them men.

There was Warren, who was dressed head-to-toe in black. With long stringy blond hair and a beard, he seemed emaciated.

Dennis, a thin, tall, clean-shaven man made it immediately clear that he loved men more than he loved women.

"Last night I licked another man's asshole," he proudly declared.

I retracted in horror.

"What?" he asked, parading around me. "It was a clean asshole. I don't eat dirty assholes."

As we finished the introductions, in walked an extremely large man with long dark hair, a shaggy beard, and a huge coat that seemed out of sync with the day's warm weather.

"Ah, wonderful," said Father Peter. "The Angel has fulfilled his destiny. Our bountiful feast has arrived!"

The giant opened his long coat. It was lined with pockets. In each one was a can of crab meat.

"Wait," I asked, startled. "Where did you get all of that?"

"This is our Angel, sent to us from above," said Father Peter. "Praise God and all of his angels! He will send out his angels with a loud trumpet call, and they will gather his elect from the four winds, from one end of heaven to another!"

What was he talking about?

"Is all of that stolen?" I asked.

"There is no thievery in a land of plenty," Father Peter replied.

"There is no yours. There is no mine. Everything is unowned. What's theirs is yours. What's yours is mine. What's mine is yours. What's ours is theirs. This feast is now ours to behold. Oh, what a glorious feast it will be! Gather everyone. Gather. The time to break bread is upon us!"

"Let us pray," Father Peter said. "In the holy language of Aramaic, the language of Jesus."

He began chanting and swaying.

"You prepare a table before me," he boomed. "Baseema! Bab! Yamma! Khoooba! Invite the poor, the crippled, the blind because the war on our souls must come to an end. These are the times where the meek will stand, where the flowers will bloom, where boys will become men, where the enlightenment will unfold, where love is the only truth. Blessed everyone who eats the bread of God. Tama elawna leba yama nara. Hon skeedah. Hayirre! May the Age of Aquarius live on!"

Was I the only one who had no idea what was going on? What was Father Peter saying? Was I too stoned to get his drift?

Someone handed me a can of crab meat and a plastic fork. Uneasily, I took it. I was up for so many things, even illegal things. I was willing to do drugs. I was willing to get arrested if it meant my efforts changed the world for the better.

But steal? It was a line that I didn't want to cross.

Yet, I was so, so hungry. I hadn't eaten all day.

I dug into the can and shoved a clump of meat into my mouth.

◆ ◆ ◆

That evening, we gathered in the dark for a reading.

Warren stood in front, a candle held at his chest. It cast an eerie shadow, illuminating parts of his face. Dressed in all black, the rest of his body seemed to disappear. He was so gaunt and so fair-complected that the light made him appear ethereal—more like a ghost than a human.

"Once upon a midnight dreary," he recited. His voice sounded so creepy. I sat up straight, my nerves tingling.

"While I pondered weak and weary," he continued.

His voice quivered. His hands trembled.

"Open here I flung the shutter," he said, so loudly and piercingly that I startled.

He held my attention throughout the entire reading.

By the end, I felt haunted, and more alive than I'd felt in a long time.

That evening, I slept on a stained mattress that reeked of body odor and urine. In the morning, many of the other members departed to "procure our bountiful sustenance," as Father Peter put it. Some left to panhandle. Others were off to buy piles of the *Haight Ashbury Free Press* and the *Berkeley Barb*, the main underground newspapers, for a nickel each and sell them for a quarter. Still, others, like the Angel, planned to shoplift. Given that I had savings that I could contribute, I spent the day stoned out of my mind, walking the Haight, and then volunteering at the clinic.

Increasingly, as the days passed, I suspected Father Peter wasn't who he said he was.

The man was peculiar. There was no getting around it. Something about the way he looked at me—and everything and everyone—seemed off. His words and phrases were odd, full of flowery, over-the-top expressions and descriptions. As he showed me around, it seemed as if he was playing a role in a production, and I was a member of the cast. It felt more pretend than real.

Was he really speaking Aramaic? Or was he pontificating gibberish? Based on his wrinkles, he was too old to be trusted. Was I the only one who doubted the authenticity of this poser?

Things came to a head toward the end of the week.

We sat in a circle. Father Peter sprinkled a white substance onto the edge of a knife.

Then he leaned toward the knife and snorted.

"Ahh," he explained. "Heavenly manna. We shall all partake!"

The knife was passed around. Warren snorted. Then the Angel. Then Dennis.

The knife passed to me.

"Go on, Ron," Father Peter said. "Your healing awaits."

This was over the line.

"Come on," Father Peter said. "This is a requirement. You must do it to be a true member of the Ashram."

Though I'd yet to drop acid, I considered it a good drug, along with pot. These were the conscious-raising substances of the hippie movement.

But meth? It and smack were what the Hell's Angels did. I didn't want any part of that culture.

"Ron?" Father Peter asked. "Are you with us?"

I stared at the knife. I wasn't comfortable with this. I hadn't signed up for this. I didn't want this.

"Go on, Ron," Father Peter said, more gently this time. "Come. Join us in Paradise."

Just this one time, I thought. *Get it over with.*

I sniffed, as little as possible, just enough to look as if I was playing along.

After a short wait, my nerves constricted. Pressure exploded. My teeth clenched, then ground back and forth. Why was I talking so much? So fast? What the heck was I talking about? Words tumbled out of my mouth. Before one thought ended, another began.

I curled up in the corner. All around me, other Ashram members sat, zoned out, on their rags or cushions.

Please let this end, I thought.

The following day, I left, never to return.

◆ ◆ ◆

By the fall of 1967, hippies were increasingly abandoning the

Haight-Ashbury district, moving to Marin, Berkeley, or Santa Cruz instead. Others simply went home, to Nebraska, Wisconsin, or wherever it was that they had called home before rushing off to California.

Just months before, people had been singing, dancing, blowing kisses. Everyone seemed so full of love. The dawning of the Age of Aquarius seemed possible, so bright, so beautiful.

Now, when I walked on Haight Street, the drug dealers, lined up in front of the stores, whispered "Crank?" or "Smack?" and not "Pot?" or "Acid?" as had been the case a few months earlier. The whole place seemed dirtier. The once-brightly painted store fronts appeared dingy, muted, and past their prime.

Rather than hippies blowing kisses, I more likely encountered groups of Hell's Angels with their hogs parked diagonally in the street.

Beefy and loud, the Angels were easy to spot, what with their unkept beards, matching jackets, and tattoos that advertised their Nazi affiliations. They tended to travel in groups of six or more, and they picked fights with anyone who dared to get in their way. I found them off-putting and threatening. I didn't want to make eye contact. I didn't want to smile. Always on guard, I put my head down and made myself small, trying not to attract their attention. I knew enough to avoid them. I didn't want to be where they were.

I still believed in and wanted to be a part of the Age of Aquarius. Now that my marriage was over and I rarely saw Caren, hippie culture was all I had left. I clung to it, seeing myself as a foot soldier in an important, yet beleaguered cultural revolution. Living in harmony with each other and with nature seemed not only possible, but also needed.

Still, one thing was obvious: the Haight was no longer the epicenter of love. Things had shifted. If I wanted to be a foot soldier, I'd have to seek out new experiences somewhere else.

"What do you think about getting out of here again," I asked Louise as we lounged naked, our bodies intertwined.

"Why don't we board horses?" she suggested.

Neither of us knew anything about the animals, yet the idea took off.

Soon I was withdrawing more money from my savings, using it to pay a month's rent on an empty horse ranch in Sebastopol. It consisted of various structures—pens and barns along with expansive fields. We put an ad in the paper, suggesting people bring us their horses to board. No one took us up on it.

We spent our days walking naked through the tall weeds, smoking weed, watching Susie, my Hungarian sheepdog, also known as a Puli, romp in the tall grasses. We made love, out in the countryside, with the sun warming our bodies.

Occasionally, hippies would come to visit, stay for a day or two, and then leave.

The setting agreed with me. The weather was dry and warm, allowing us to be outdoors most of the time. I loved the sensation of fresh air and sunlight on my skin. I never wanted to wear clothes again. I felt free, relaxed, content, chill.

As days and then weeks passed, however, we grew increasingly desperate. My savings were limited. I wasn't about to pull out even more money to pay for a second month.

We had to find another way.

"I know," said Louise. "Let's pick apples."

We showed up at an orchard, high on Dexedrine, hoping the speed would help us to pick faster. With a basket slung over my shoulder, I propped my ladder against a tree, climbed the rungs, grabbed an apple, and dropped it into the basket.

Grab, drop, grab drop, over and over.

The work was quiet. No one talked.

My arms ached. Sweat soaked through my Levis.

Grab, drop, grab, drop.

Finally, my basket was full. I climbed down the ladder and lugged it over to a huge box. It would take several more baskets to fill the box. To make decent money, we'd each need to fill several boxes.

The day was already half over. How were we both so slow—so bad at this? The other pickers were filling their baskets at twice the rate that Louise and I were doing. What were we doing wrong?

Up another ladder I went. This time I tried to pick at least two apples at a time.

I broke a fingernail. My finger bled.

The ache intensified into pain. My hands quivered. The ladder shifted.

Another basket done.

Up another ladder. More picking. More pain. More fatigue.

On it went. By the day's end, my entire body trembled from fatigue and pain. We'd only earned $30. Even if we did this every day, it wouldn't be enough to make rent.

"I'm sorry honey," I told her, "This was amazing, but I think it's time to head back to the city."

◆ ◆ ◆

Louise moved back into her old apartment with a roommate. I moved back into my large walk-in closet at 1277 3rd Avenue, where a few people had formed a makeshift commune during my absence. Laurie was slight, blond, and pixie-like, and Taylor was a buxom freckle-faced redhead. Jimmy was a thick-set guy with blond hair with a longish beard. He was often in the kitchen cooking up whatever he could scrounge together into a kind of soup—lunch meat, potatoes, ketchup packages stolen from McDonalds, ramen noodles, whatever he could find.

The vibe was so different from what it had been when I'd shared the same space with Joyce and Caren. Oh, Caren, just thinking about her brought pain. I hadn't seen her in weeks. Or was it months? She was probably so big by now.

I knew I should do more, try harder, do something to maintain a presence in her life. At the same time, Joyce clearly needed and wanted space. She was involved with someone else. Plus, she had her parents nearby to help when she needed someone to watch Caren. I was no longer a passing thought.

I wasn't sure Caren should be around me anyway. I was probably a bad influence. Maybe she was better off without me.

One evening, Taylor caught my eye. Soon we were naked, making love in my closet of a bedroom. Everything felt mechanical, as if I were going through the motions. There was no joy, no passion. Even sex couldn't snap me out of my malaise.

The following evening, Laurie crawled into my bed. This was the Age of Aquarius. There was supposed to be no jealousy or possessiveness. True hippies loved the one they're with, right? I welcomed her, hoping and praying that the darkness would lift, even if it was just for a few moments. It didn't.

I woke the following morning to whispering.

When I emerged from my closet, the two women confronted me. "You're such a dog!" Taylor screamed. "How could you? We were just together the other night. I can't believe you'd do this behind my back!"

Now Laurie joined in.

"If I'd known you'd been with Taylor, I would have never slept with you. You should have told me!"

"Dude, you're such an asshole," Jimmy said.

"We don't want you here," another commune member said.

"Get out!"

I gathered my meager belongings and headed for my microbus.

Everything was such bullshit. Yeah, right, there would be no possessiveness or jealousy? It was such a giant steaming load of crap. Why had I believed in all of this balderdash? I'd been so naïve.

They were all a bunch of assholes. Everyone was.

I was.

Just like my father.

I'd tried so hard not to be like him. Yet, here I was, the most hated hippie.

No one liked me.

I was a failure, an asshole. I was never going to be anything in life.

I hated myself, the world, and everyone in it.

The hopeless feeling wrapped its tentacles around every cell, organ, muscle, and extremity. My motivation was gone. The joy was gone. It felt as if it would never come back.

I was completely out of gas, and it seemed as if the closest filling station was on the other side of the world. What was the point? I didn't want to be alive.

I should just walk out in front of a car, I thought.

That's when I knocked on Gary's door.

TAKEAWAYS

Readers may wonder why I titled this chapter "The Evil Dr. Goopcough" rather than "Searching for Communal Living." The reason is that the brief encounter with my daughter recounted herein was so full of love that I have held it in my heart to this day. I know that she did as well. It symbolized what could have been against the backdrop of what in fact was: I was slipping into a psychological whirlpool, desperately seeking a life raft. Grit made me keep trying to find something to hang on to, going from one commune to another, finding only disappointment, and plunging ever deeper into depression. And depression feeds on itself, by preventing the sufferer from being able to actualize their attempts to counteract it. Readers who are in similar circumstances would be well advised to reach out for help, as I finally began to do in seeking out Gary's help.

CHAPTER 8

Journey into the Darkest Part of My Soul

(Winter 1968)

Gary could tell something was off just by looking at me. "Come in, friend," he said. "Come in."

Gently, he led me to the kitchen. Like the one in my apartment across the street, it was a smallish older kitchen, but his was painted light yellow. He rummaged around in a cabinet, and then returned with a joint, which he promptly fired up.

"Here," he said, handing it to me.

I hadn't seen him much during the summer and fall, not since dropping out of medical school. He had thrown a party that I had attended, but how long ago was that? It was a complete blur. My only memory of that evening was more of a feeling than anything else—that of being an outsider. One of the CIPA guys had asked me, "So, what's happening?" Chuckling, I sarcastically replied, "You're asking me?" Clearly, I was too out of it to have any idea what was going on. The guy had laughed nervously, then walked away.

Gary sat across from me, resting his hands over mine. "Lay it on me, Ron."

"I'm such a failure," I told him. "I don't know what's wrong with me. I hate everything, everyone, including myself. The world would be better off without me. I'm scared that I might do something that can't be undone."

"Why don't you stay here, my friend," he said. He was warm,

understanding, gracious—the best friend a person could have. "We'll get you set up, help you out, watch over you, keep you safe, and give you what you need to recover."

He and Nancy embraced me as if I were a beloved child, setting up a cot in their garage.

They checked on me each day, seeing what they could offer, how they could help. Other than that, I can't remember much of this period of my life. One day blurred into the next. Nothing excited me. Nothing interested me. Nothing brought a smile to my face. Just the smallest of efforts felt impossible.

What did depression feel like? For me, it was an unrelenting swirl of despair, despondency, unhappiness, low spirits, and self-directed anger. It is often said that depression is anger turned inward, and that was certainly true for me. I was my harshest critic by far. But most fundamentally, I lost my faith in myself, the very thing that had gotten me through my difficult childhood.

On my worst days, I never got out of bed. On my better ones, I pushed past my inertia. *Come on Ron*, I'd admonish myself. *Open your damn eyes. Why can't you do this simplest of things? What the fuck is wrong with you?*

It took everything I had just to roll over and put my feet on the floor.

Lowell drove to San Francisco to visit. With long hair, a scraggly beard, and a tie-dye shirt, he was flying his freak flag like I'd never seen before. He seemed off, like *really off*. His sentences meandered from one topic to another, with little to no connective tissue between them. I struggled to listen. He just wasn't making sense. All I could gather: he loved acid. LSD was the one topic that kept coming up. Yet, he was higher than anyone I had ever seen, even at the free clinic where I helped hippies come down off bad acid trips. Was he ever *not* high? Was he in even worse shape than I? The mere thought depressed me even more.

With encouragement from Gary and Nancy, I shuffled outdoors

where the air felt heavy, the sky seemed dim, and my negativity followed me wherever I went. At the end of Haight Street, just before Hippy Hill, there was a busy road—Stanyan Street.

Cars whizzed past. Inside there were people with lives—real, meaningful lives. They were on their way to work, or to play. They were happy. They weren't failures.

I groggily watched them for a while, waiting for the right moment to move forward.

What the hell? Why wait? What was the point?

I strode forward toward Hippy Hill, not bothering to look up, wondering how it would feel and what might happen when it was over. I took another step. Then another. Soon. It would happen soon.

There was screeching—so much screeching. The sounds, they were so loud, grating, uncomfortable. Horns blared. The scent of rubber wafted up my nose.

Someone screamed "You stupid motherfucker!"

I took another step.

More squealing. More burnt tires. More motorists shouting obscenities.

Another step.

I refused to look. It will be over soon. It had to be. I hoped for darkness, nothingness, a void, relief.

Cars idled. My back warmed from the heat of an engine.

"What's wrong with him?" someone asked. "Why is he standing there?"

"Who fucking cares? He's an idiot," another person yelled. "Dude, get out of the street!"

Another step, and another.

There was grass under my shoes. Somehow, I had made it to the other side. Somehow. Why was I still here? Why hadn't I died? Why didn't someone put me out of my misery?

I climbed the hill, sat, pulled out a joint, and smoked. It brought me no pleasure. I was a failure at everything, even at ending my life.

Weeks passed. Nothing changed.

I went to bed depressed. I was depressed in my dreams. I woke up depressed. I felt depressed all day and went back to bed. Depression was a cocoon that enveloped my life.

I imagined depression as an existential trap door that I had fallen through, after which it immediately sealed up so that I could not find my way out.

One morning, as I joylessly spooned cereal into my mouth, Gary handed me the phone.

"It's Joyce."

I put the receiver to my ear.

"Hello?"

"Hi Ron," she said. "I'm calling because Steven's moving back to New York."

"Oh," I replied, with no emotion. "Okay."

Why did she think I cared about what Steven did? She had left me for him, and she likely had been with him when we were married. That guy could move to Japan for all I cared.

"Ron," she said, again. "I'm going with him. I'm moving to New York."

"What about Caren?" I asked.

She was curt, her voice had an edge. "Of course, she's coming with me. I'm her mother."

"Of course," I said.

Why hadn't I tried harder? Why hadn't I been there more often? Why wasn't I different? Better?

She waited, as if she expected me to say more.

"Bye Joyce," I said. "Have a good trip."

I handed the phone back to Gary.

"FUCK! FUCK! FUCK!" I screamed, pounding his kitchen table with both fists. "FUCK!" Anguish engulfed me. My elbows on the table, face in my hands, my fingers grabbing fistfuls of hair—I gulped for air.

"I'm never going to see my daughter again," I moaned. "I'm never going to see my daughter again! She's taking Caren away, Gary! She's taking her away! Some other man is going to raise my daughter. Steven is her father now!"

He pulled his chair close to mine, then put his arm around me.

"Ron, you're going to get through this. I can't imagine the pain you're in right now, but you are going to get through this. Nancy and I will help. You're going to be okay. Someday, you'll be looking back on all of this, and it will be just a blip, a memory, something you went through."

"Stop," I said. "Please stop. Don't lie to make me feel better. I know what's true. I'm a loser and an asshole, just like my father. No, I'm worse. At least my father was *there*. I'm not even going to be there for her. What kind of a father am I? Who lets another man raise his daughter without a fight?"

"Man, you're my fucking hero," said Gary. "I wish you could see yourself the way I see you. You're just going through a bad time. This, too, shall pass. You'll see."

We sat there in his kitchen for what seemed like hours. The sun set. The sky darkened. The moon rose. He refused to leave my side. Eventually, Gary hoisted me up, walked me to the garage, and tucked me into bed.

◆ ◆ ◆

With Caren soon to be out of my life, my zeal to get better grew impossible to ignore. I wasn't going to let depression destroy my life—or hers. I was going to beat this. I was willing to do whatever it took. I had to get better. I had to.

While volunteering at the Haight Ashbury Free Clinic, I'd heard people talking about a new mental health day treatment program at UCSF Medical Center. Part of the Langley Porter Neuropsychiatric Institute, it catered specifically to hippies like me.

The morning fog still engulfed the city as I shuffled my way to the clinic. It felt heavy, more like honey than air. What was wrong with me? The mere act of walking felt like too much these days. All I wanted to do was sleep.

"So, what brings you to the day treatment program?" asked Dr. Rosenbaum, staring piercingly through his thick glasses. His movements seemed abrupt, aggressive even. Did something about me bother him? Did he see me for what I was, a total loser? Or was I reading too much into it? I was always doing that. I never knew what anyone meant. And whenever I tried to clarify things, people would get upset with me. What a total clusterfuck!

"I don't want to be alive anymore," I said. "Life feels too hard. Everyone would be better off if I were gone."

"Can you tell me more about that?" he asked. "Why do you think people feel that way?"

"Because it's true!" What was wrong with this guy? Why was he questioning me in this way? Didn't he believe me?

"Why do you think it's true? Lay it out for me. What's the evidence in favor of this belief that folks would be better off if you were gone?"

"Because everyone hates me. They see me as a failure. My ex-wife is taking my daughter to New York to go live with some dude named Steven. Obviously, she thinks I'm an asshole like my father. If she didn't, she wouldn't be taking my daughter as far away from me as she could possibly get!"

He looked at me quizzically. "Has your ex-wife told you that? Where's the evidence?"

"No! I just know, okay?" I responded, feeling angry. I wanted to feel better, yet this fool was making me feel even worse. It was as if I couldn't even talk about how I felt without failing. "I can tell by what she says. I can tell by what she doesn't say. Jeez."

"No need to get testy about it," he said. "I'm just curious if anyone has said these things to you out loud. Because, from where I'm sitting, it sounds like you're doing a lot of ruminating and mindreading. Do you have any control over that? That is, can you question your tendency to read into what people are saying?"

"Not really. How will I know what they mean?"

"Look, do you want to get better? I'm giving you a real suggestion that will work. But you have to do the work. I can't help you if you refuse to take the medicine."

"I don't understand what you're talking about," I said. "It's true! Everyone hates me! It started with my father, and it just got worse from there. I can't do anything right. I'm not reading people's minds. It's a fucking fact!"

"Okay, okay, calm down," he said. "It sounds to me that you may be experiencing ideas of reference, thinking that remarks are about you when they may not be. We can talk more about what those are and what you can do about them during our next session. For now, I'd like to prescribe some medication that will help."

After about a week or so, my long shuffle up Parnassus Hill to Langley Porter felt even more unbearable. The antidepressant that Dr. Rosenbaum prescribed numbed me out, dulling my senses. It felt like my thoughts were stuffed with cotton. I wasn't dead, but I also didn't feel alive. Along with the numbness, the depression clung to me like burs from a forest.

Just be patient, I told myself. *The meds will work. They have to.*

During group therapy, we sat on chairs in a circle. Everyone pretty much looked the same: long hair, unruly beards, tie-dye shirts, bell bottoms, and sandals. Some, like me, were depressed. Others were seeking help for drug abuse. Still others had ailments that I couldn't begin to understand. One of them, Ricky, spoke with confidence, but none of his sentences made sense.

"Raspberry ice cream cones on top of the lawn," he interjected, with great conviction, as if he were pontificating on one of life's most important truths. What the heck was he talking about?

The man next to him, James, interpreted for him, "He's trying to say that we're missing an opportunity here," said James. "We need to grab those raspberry ice cream cones and eat them. Get his drift?"

Raspberry ice cream cones on a lawn meant *that*? Why didn't I understand that? Was I even more mentally ill than I thought?

Ricky turned toward James, an expression of gratitude on his face.

"Anytime, brother," James said, gently placing his hand on Ricky's shoulder. "That's what I'm here for."

The two men transfixed me. James doted on Ricky in such a loving way. They were both sick and struggling. Yet it was clear that Ricky was struggling a lot more. He was barely able to function. Even though James had his limitations, he still cared for Ricky. Their relationship was beautiful. Despite all the numbness and heaviness that pervaded my body, seeing them together stirred me, just enough to give me hope.

The two men happened to live near Gary so, after group therapy, we walked home together. All along the way, James watched over Ricky. I loved watching them, being with them. I wanted to care for someone like that someday.

For several days, I fought through the numbness and depression to get myself to the day treatment program. Sometimes I met one-on-one with Dr. Rosenbaum. Most times, however, I either went to group therapy or participated in group activities. Each day I walked home with James and Ricky, always feeling a glimmer of hope that my depression might lift.

One morning, during milieu therapy, I played ping pong with another patient as Dr. Rosenbaum made his way around the room, checking in with each patient one at a time.

Eventually he made his way over to us.

"Ron," he said.

"Yeah," I replied as I whacked the ball.

"Stop that," he ordered. "Put that paddle down. Just put it down for a second. Listen to me. This is important."

I rested the paddle on the table.

"Look," he said, "you're being discharged."

"I'm what?" The haze and numbness made me feel as if he were a whole city block away from me. His words didn't make sense. Clearly, I'd heard him wrong.

More loudly, as if I were hard of hearing, he repeated "You're being discharged."

"I'm being discharged? That makes no sense."

"I've got your paperwork right here," he said, waving the papers in the air directly in front of me.

"But I'm still depressed. I feel horrible. Why am I being discharged? I'm not ready. Why are you discharging me? I don't understand. This doesn't make sense."

"See? This is exactly why," he said. "You're always like this. Questioning me instead of listening and doing what I tell you to do."

He seemed annoyed, angry even.

"Ron," he said, an edge in his voice. "Look, I'd love to be able to help you get better, but I just can't."

"What do you mean you can't? Isn't that your job?"

"I know this might be difficult for you to hear, but you remind me of the parts of myself that I don't like. You're going to need to find someone else to help you. I just can't do it."

"I don't understand. You don't like me and that's why you can't help me?"

"No, it's about me and not liking myself. You remind me of that."

"I told you no one liked me, and you're proving it to me. You tried to get me to believe I was wrong. But I was right! No one likes me! Even my psychiatrist hates me!"

"Ron, Ron," he stammered. "It's not like that."

"Yes, it is! I'm a failure at everything. I can't even do therapy right!"

"Ron, look," he said. "You'll get better. Someone else will be able to help you. I'm not the only psychiatrist in town. You'll see. There's hope. Don't give up on yourself."

"Right," I said. "Easy for you to say. What good are you? What fucking good are you?"

With that, I walked out the door. I felt as if I was the lowest of the low, the scum of the earth. Who else gets rejected by their own psychiatrist? I shuffled my way back to Gary's. Then I called Louise.

"I don't know what to do," I told her, "I need help. They don't want to help me."

"Fuck him!" she said. "What else would you expect from the establishment?"

"But I really need help. I'm drowning."

"Ron, it'll be all right. You're just going through a rough patch. It'll get better. It always does."

"No, I don't think it will. I've felt this way for so long that I don't remember feeling anything else. I'm a worthless piece of shit."

"Oh sweetie, don't talk like that," she soothed, "You know that's not true."

"Do I? How do I know that? I can't even succeed at therapy!"

"Come on now. Chin up."

"Maybe I should check myself into the state mental health hospital."

"You want to go to the hospi-jail? What are you thinking? Why would you do something like that?"

"I told you," I said, becoming increasingly tense. "Because I need help."

"It's the wrong move," she said, "They'll just mess with your head, make you even worse."

"Yeah, maybe."

"Honey, I love you. You're going to be okay."

"Maybe," I said. "Bye."

I stared at the phone, now resting on its cradle. Then I picked it back up and called my mother. She sounded beleaguered, as if she were bracing herself against a future that she did not want.

"Mom," I said quietly into the phone. "I'm a mess. I need help and I don't know what to do."

"Oh, Ronnie." Her voice became muted. She sounded far away,

as if her mind were elsewhere. Had she heard me? Why didn't she sound more concerned? When did this happen? She had once been the only person whom I could go to for comfort and to feel safe. She was the person who believed in me, and the person who was there for me no matter what.

"Mom," I said. "I'm stuck. I've felt like this for so long. I'm scared."

"I wish I could help you," she said, as if refusing to believe me or to feel anything. Had she packed up her emotions and stored them in a lock box? Where was she? Why wasn't she coming alive with love?

"Mom? I really need help."

"Oh Ronnie," she said, now sounding exasperated. "Isn't there anything you can do?"

How had things come to this? Was my own mother giving up on me? Was I that much of a disappointment?

After I hung up, I climbed into my microbus and drove three hours to Mendocino State Hospital, a state psychiatric hospital. The check-in process was a blur. Someone asked me a lot of questions. I signed a lot of forms. I handed over my keys. Someone walked me to a dorm and pointed me to a bunk. That's about all I remember.

I spent the first day settling in and undergoing an extensive psychiatric and psychological evaluation. Late in the day, an orderly came to find me.

"You're needed at the front office."

I followed him around a corner, down a long hall, and then around a final corner. Two police officers and several other staff members stood. One of the staff members approached me.

"We discovered your contraband. You can no longer stay here. These officers will take it from here."

"My contra what?"

"Your contraband. Your drugs," he said.

"What drugs?" I asked.

"In your microbus. We searched your microbus and found your drugs."

"Okay," I said, still not understanding. I was here to get help. I was doing the right thing.

"Hands behind your back," one officer said. He was young, wiry, and looked very aggressive.

He and another officer put me in hand cuffs and led me to a cruiser, drove me to the station, and walked me to booking. When offered a phone call, I dialed my mother. She wasn't going to be happy to hear from me, but I didn't know what else to do and had no one else to call.

"Mom, I need your help. I'm going from bad to worse. I checked myself into the state psychiatric hospital and they arrested me. I need you to get a lawyer to get me out of here. I'm desperate. Please. Help me."

"Okay Ronnie," she said. "I'll find you a good Jewish lawyer. You just sit tight. I know this is hard for you, but I'll work on it."

"I love you," I told her.

"I love you too, Ronnie."

I could tell from the tone of her voice that she was worried about me, and that buoyed my spirits. She would come through for me after all.

I followed the officer to a small cell with a metal bed, toilet, and sink. After staring at the wall for several hours, it dawned on me that I had not yet taken my medications.

"Officer!" I yelled from the cell. "Officer!"

A beefy man waddled over.

"Look," I said, "I'm on psychiatric medications. I'm on Imipramine."

"So?" he asked.

Why wasn't he getting what I was saying?

"They're in my microbus. I need to take them. I can't just go cold turkey!"

"Look, you put yourself here. I didn't. What is it with your generation? It's like you can't accept the consequences of your actions," he said.

"You're not getting it. It's dangerous. I need to take those medicines. Who knows what will happen if I don't?"

"Whatever man," he said.

"You can't deny medical care. It's against the Bill of Rights!"

"Fine," he said.

He walked over to a desk, opened a drawer, and then returned.

"Here," he said, pressing his fat fist through the bars. "Take these."

There were several small red pills on his sweaty palm.

"Is that Imipramine? It doesn't look like Imipramine."

"Take 'em or leave 'em," he said. "Your microbus is in impound. If you want drugs, these are drugs."

"No thanks," I said, curling up on the bed as far away from the bars as I could get.

Two days later, Michael Levine, a well-dressed attorney, came to rescue me. He was very tall, appearing like he might have played basketball in college, and very soft spoken. Most importantly, he was good at his job. My mother had come through. The man had somehow gotten me off without a single charge. I was free.

I retrieved my microbus from the impound lot and drove back to San Francisco. In the days that followed, my mother called me once or twice to check on me. I never heard from my father.

Gary and Nancy had already done so much for me. I didn't want to continually come and go from their pad, bouncing forward and back like a rubber ball. Instead, for a while I slept in my microbus.

News, however, had spread among my old CIPA friends about my sad state of affairs. Marty Lebowitz and his wife, Fran, continually checked in on me and nudged me forward. A nursing student, Fran helped me sign up and get approved for public assistance under the Aid to the Needy Disabled program from the San Francisco Department of Social Services. This provided me with the meager income needed to afford a spot in a rooming house. Then she helped me to enroll in a publicly supported day care program for the mentally ill.

Soon I was back on the antidepressant, as well as the antipsychotic drug, Stelazine. The combo left me feeling even worse than before.

My group therapy program was run by Mr. Northam, a short, clean-shaven guy who had previously worked as a high school shop teacher. He was gruff and assertive—the kind of person who told you what to do and what to think.

"Could it get any worse than this?" I wondered. "A woodshop teacher? The guy isn't even trained to help people like me."

"I don't know what's going on," I mentioned to the group. "I never know what anyone means. People say one thing but mean something else."

"Ron," said Mr. Northam, as he rooted through his bag. "I'd like to show you something. Hold on a second."

His hand emerged from his bag with a stiff, rectangular piece of paper. He held it up for me to see. As my eyes focused through my depressed and medicated haze, I realized it wasn't paper. It was a paint swatch.

"What do you see?" he asked.

"What does this have to do with anything?"

"Just play along," he said, "What color is this card?"

"Red," I said, crossing my arms over my chest and sinking back into my chair. I was here to get better, not to get tested on paint colors.

"Michael," he asked another group member. "What color do *you* see?"

"Looks burgundy to me."

"All right, Susan," he said to another group member. "What color do you see?"

"Scarlet," she said through clenched teeth.

"Steve? How about you? What color do you see?"

"Blue with sparkles. Sparkly blue. Far-out, man. That's outasight!"

Poor Steve. He was even farther gone than I was.

"You see, Ron," the group leader said, "everyone sees something different."

"So?"

"If you ask four different people the same question, you'll get four different answers."

"So? I'm not following you."

"You're trying so hard to make sense of a world that doesn't make sense."

"I guess," I said, sinking back farther into my chair. I wasn't sure how any of this was going to help me, but I had no other options.

◆ ◆ ◆

After several months of group therapy with the shop teacher, I dropped out. I'd been medicated into numbness, admitted to a state mental institution, arrested, and asked to identify paint colors. Where had any of it gotten me? I still felt as depressed as ever, and these jokers didn't know how to help me. In fact, I wasn't sure whether they knew how to help anyone. Louise was right. Psychiatry was just another prison. They didn't cure people. They merely kept us off the streets for a little while, saving other people from having to deal with us.

I was done. Totally done. This had to end. I couldn't stand feeling like this anymore.

"Just pick something and fucking do it," I told myself. "Take charge of your fucking life."

I found my way to San Francisco State College's Experimental College. With no admission requirements, I slipped right in. The courses were cheap enough for me to cover the cost from my monthly disability payments.

From the list of course offerings, I zeroed in on Encounter Group Training. The groups were popular at the time, offering a nontraditional way of helping people. I'd heard that the famed psychologist Carl Rogers was a big proponent. In addition, from what I gathered, they often included a nude session. That certainly sounded interesting. I figured I'd get trained to lead these groups. Who knew? Maybe it would lead to something bigger. At least I'd have something to do—and a purpose. Plus, it couldn't be any worse than group therapy with a shop teacher.

The training program involved participating in a group for ten weeks. About a dozen of us sat on folding chairs, very close together in a circle. Ted, our group leader, offered us conversation starters, thought experiments, and experiential exercises to work through together. I estimated that he was in his midthirties, and he sounded quite professional even though we never were provided with his credentials. Within the first few meetings Ted said, "Now, I'd like to do a feedback exercise. We'll focus on one person in the group. I'd like you all to stay in the here and now with this. Don't overthink it. Just say out loud exactly what you are thinking and feeling. Don't hold back. It's especially important to say the very thing you think you shouldn't say. Remember: this is about expressing your truest selves. Speak your truth!"

Pointing to me, he said, "Let's start with Ron here."

Feeling the attention of the group on me, I squirmed in my seat.

After a long silence, Ted said, "All right, all right. I get it. This is hard. It is very hard to say out loud what we're really thinking. I want you to take off the mask you display to the world. Be yourselves! Come on, now. Allow yourselves to be vulnerable."

I wasn't sure what feedback these people were going to have for me, after having known me for such a short time. Still, I wasn't sure if I was ready for an entire room of people to peer into my soul so they could describe the steaming pile of shit they found.

"All right, fine," Ted said. "I'll start."

He turned to face me, his sparkling eyes taking me in and caressing me like a lover.

"I think you're kinda cute."

How in the hell was I supposed to respond to that?

Despite my adventurous spirit when it came to all things sexual, intimacy with men was a hard stop. It wasn't that gay relationships repulsed me. I wanted people to be free to love whomever they wanted. That's what the Age of Aquarius was all about, but the male body held no attraction or interest. The only nude male body I ever wanted to see was my own—and, on some days, I wasn't so sure I wanted to see that nude body either.

"What's your response to that feedback, Ron?"

I didn't want to hurt his feelings. Yet, he wanted me to be true to myself. How could I walk that thin line?

"Um, okay," I said, stammering, shifting in my seat, wiping my palms against my Levi's. "Um, well, um, I guess, um, thanks for telling me, um, that."

"Anything else?" Ted pressed. "Remember, this is about freeing yourself. Don't be polite. Say what's really on your mind."

I looked at the floor, the wall, the ceiling, the clock, everywhere except the group leader. How long was this going to last?

"No," I said, "That's it. That's all that's on my mind. There's nothing else."

He waited, as if he knew there was more. I sat, staring at my hands clasped in my lap.

"All right," Ted said. "Let's move on.

And so it went, exercise after excruciating exercise, week after week. To free ourselves from our inhibitions, we jumped, danced, sang, and howled. To unleash pent-up anger and rage, we pummeled and thrashed pillows with Bataka foam bats. To build trust, we fell backwards into each other's arms. To peel back the layers of artifice and inauthenticity, we took off our clothes, folded them up, and placed them on the floor. Then we sat naked for the rest of the session. There was nothing titillating about it. The nude bodies of everyone around me were a lot less interesting than I would ever have imagined.

Following several weeks of work on removing our artificial restraints, everyone in the group spoke more freely, perhaps too freely. There was none of the politeness and civility that usually guided social conversations. Instead, we said how we felt, not worrying about how someone might receive the news. We were in charge of *our* feelings and expressions. They were in charge of *theirs*.

The various interactions left me swirling with anxiety, awkwardness, confusion, frustration—and, occasionally, rage.

"Today," Ted said, "I'd like you all to identify someone with whom you feel a strong reaction."

He went around the room, pointing to various people while asking them to identify others whom they felt strongly about. Folks lobbed insults back and forth as if they were tossing a football in someone's backyard. Tempers flared. Feelings got hurt. People cried.

"Okay, Ron, your turn," said Ted.

There was no question to whom I was going to point.

"Chris," I said.

Chris had been getting on my nerves for weeks. The man was loud, dominating, and opinionated. He always had to get in the last word. I hated people like him. He reminded me of my father.

"So, what's your beef with Chris?" Ted asked.

My mind went blank. Why did this always happen to me? Whenever anyone turned toward me, I froze.

"Just say the first word that comes to mind," Ted asked. "Remember, hold nothing back. What do you find difficult about him?"

"Ingratiating!" I blurted out.

No! That wasn't right! It wasn't what I meant! It was just the first word that had popped into my head. What was I trying to say? Grating? I'd meant grating!

"Well, you're an asshole," Chris said with a smirk. "There. Was that less ingratiating?"

By the close of the ten-week course I felt no better, no different, and no more in touch with my true self. I felt just as depressed as ever. Like a fish in a tank, no matter where I went it was all the same water. It mattered not whether I was in an encounter group, in bed having sex, or meandering through the Haight district. It all sucked pretty much the same.

So, I figured I might as well just keep going. Now that I was duly qualified by the Experimental College, I started my own encounter group. I co-led the group with a man named Tom—a sandy-haired, clean-shaven man who had recently moved to San Francisco from the Midwest.

After a few weeks, Tom and I developed romantic interests with two women in our group—Phyllis and Susan—with whom we soon hooked up. I was with Phyllis, a statuesque brunette, and Tom was with Susan, a petite blond. Within weeks the four of us moved into a cheap apartment in the Mission District.

We eventually became friendly with Dennis, a friend of Tom's, and Dennis's friend, Keith, who was into theatre arts and wanted to put on Aeschylus' play *Agamemnon* at a community theatre.

Phyllis loved the idea, and since I loved Phyllis, I figured that I had to love it, too. Further, at this point I was up for just about anything that would distract me from my depression.

We spent weeks learning the script and in rehearsals. As a member of the chorus, my part was relatively easy. Still, since acting was so far out of my wheelhouse, the experience was pretty stressful.

After opening night, Phyllis didn't come home from the celebratory party. I tossed and turned, the anger building. Clearly, she'd hooked up with someone else. I'd done this whole stupid play for *her*. I'd gritted my teeth through the entire humiliating experience. I'd hated it. I'd done it for *her*. This was how she repaid me?

The following morning I gathered my belongings, got into my microbus, and drove to Berkeley. I wanted nothing further to do with any of them again.

It was time to start over. Again.

TAKEAWAYS

All those chickens from my traumatic childhood had finally come home to roost. Diagnosing myself using current criteria, I suffered from major depressive disorder with mood congruent psychotic features, the latter part being the paranoia and ideas of reference that I experienced.

This chapter illustrates several important points:

Depression often brings with it suicidal ideation and even suicidal behaviors, such as my Stanyan Street attempt.

Good mental health care is a rarity, a problem which is even more pronounced in our postpandemic world.

Psychiatric medications (at that time) sometimes posed more side effects than benefits.

But there is also something else noteworthy about this period of my life: resilience. According to the American Psychological Association: "Resilience is the process and outcome of successfully adapting to difficult or challenging life experiences, especially through mental, emotional, and behavioral flexibility and adjustment to external and internal demands." Related to grit, and likely owing to the everlasting love from my mother, I was highly adaptive. I was willing to try anything—absolutely anything—to get better. And now I had additional motivation: I wanted to get healthy so that I could find a way to resume my relationship with my daughter. Readers, if you are going through a difficult period in your life, is there something that keeps you trying to solve the situation that you are in? That is, can you find your own resilience?

CHAPTER 9

Psychology and Psychedelics

(Late 1968–1970)

Before leaving the apartment, I phoned Lowell. He lived with another poet, Ken Irby, and I prayed Ken would be okay with me suddenly showing up.

"I'm kinda in a crisis state," I explained. "I need to get out of San Francisco. Can you put me up for a while until I figure it out?"

"Sure," he said, in his typical soft, soothing tone. "You can crash on our couch. I'm sure Ken won't mind."

Forty-five minutes later, I was at his front door.

"I see you've got your freak flag on, brother," Lowell said, looking me up and down. "The long hair and beard look good on you."

"Yes," I said, mechanically, struggling to seem normal.

"Oh, Ron," he said, sensing my numbness. He reached his thin arms around me, gently embracing me.

"Well, I suppose you might as well come in," he said, leading me into the small, two-bedroom apartment.

On the kitchen table sat a giant glass jar filled with pills of every shape and color.

He noticed me staring.

"You're arriving at a perfect time," Lowell said, clapping his hands together in excitement. "Ken, Fred, I, and some others are planning an Indian feast!"

"That's interesting," I said flatly. I tried my best to sound intrigued, but my voice box refused to cooperate.

"It's going to be at a cabin in the woods," Lowell went on, a soft lilt in his voice.

He seemed so animated. Full of energy. Happy.

When was the last time I'd felt anything like that?

"You know, Fred's got a relative who owns the cabin," Lowell continued. "It's a sweet pad, just lovely. It'll be the perfect place for you to drop acid for the first time."

"Right, right," I said. "Acid."

"You'll see, Ron," he said, resting his hand on my shoulder. "It's life changing. It's going to blow your mind."

Over the next couple of days, Lowell dipped into his glass jar repeatedly. Was he ever *not* tripping? Sometimes he seemed lucid. Other times, he rambled away, each sentence dramatically changing topic. There were no transitions. One non sequitur morphed into another and yet another. It was like listening to a radio while constantly changing the dial.

Is this what acid did to people?

Would it do that to me?

Did it even matter?

If I turned out like Lowell, wouldn't that be better than how I was? At least Lowell seemed enchanted with life.

I'd like to know what *that* felt like.

◆ ◆ ◆

Two days later, we piled into Fred's sedan, heading south. An hour and a half later, we arrived at a rustic A-shaped cabin in Santa Cruz, surrounded by towering redwoods and oaks.

Ken and Fred grabbed bags of food from the trunk, got set up in the kitchen, and proceeded to chop, stir, sauté, and bake.

Soon, the scent of cumin, butter, and fennel wafted through the great room.

They arranged dish after dish on a long table: Biyani, several curries, korma, saag, butter chicken, dal, palak paneer, momos, naan, and more.

It all looked so delicious.

Or, at least, would have looked delicious had I not been so depressed. Would I be able to enjoy any of this?

Lowell sauntered over, offered a side hug, and said, "Before you dig in, you may wish to partake in the main dish of our festivities."

He placed a white barrel-shaped pill on my palm. Given the unusual shape, it was certainly not an aspirin.

"It's a double-barreled Owsley," he said, with pride. "You've heard of Owsley Stanley, right?"

"I think so," I said, "Maybe?"

"Well, he's a chemist—the *best* kind of chemist," Lowell explained with excitement. "He made the gem in your hand. It's the purest LSD available. Get ready to leave behind all your problems, brother. You're about to have a truly special experience. I'm honored to be here with you."

He handed me a glass of water.

"It's time to get lysergisized," he said with a flourish. "Bottoms up!"

"Bottoms up," I said in my typical monotone.

I grabbed a plate, then sat on a chair. Fred placed the Dead's *Anthem of the Sun* on the turntable.

"Seems fitting," he said, winking in my direction.

He handed me the album cover.

"Just wait," he said. "In a few minutes, this is going to blow your mind. Stare at it. You'll see."

"All right then," I said. Could I sound any less enthralled?

The folksy, distinct sound of "That's It for the Other One" permeated the room. I rested my head against the back of the chair, my eyes fixed on the cover.

"Wait, what?"

Had I said that out loud? Or only in my head? I wasn't sure.

The colors pulsed and swirled to the beat of the music.

I couldn't look away.

Euphoria coursed through me.

Every cell felt alive, tingling with sensation. My senses blended. Sound was taste and taste was touch and touch was smell.

"I can taste the Dead!" I exclaimed.

"Groovy," Fred said. "It's a good trip then?"

"Far-out," I said, as I swayed and bobbed. "In-fucking-credible."

I scooped up some butter chicken with my naan, then popped it in my mouth.

My tastebuds soaked up the flavors like a sponge soaked up water.

"Wow! This is out of this world! Fred! Ken! This is amazing!"

"I had a little help," Ken said, winking. "Glad you like it, man. I'm happy to oblige."

Was it me? Or were the colors on the album even brighter than before?

Did the colors love me? Were they caressing my soul?

My entire body felt warm, relaxed, like that first moment just after an orgasm.

There was an urge to hug everyone in the room, all at once, and never let go. They were beautiful, wonderful, majestic, good people.

"I love you," I told Lowell.

"I love you too, brother."

"Fred, Ken," I said, "I love you, too. Gosh, I think I love everyone. I love the whole fucking world right now."

I turned to Lowell. "No wonder you're always tripping."

"Hey brother," he said, "I'm so happy I could be here for your first. It's an honor."

The shimmering, sparkling, psychedelic experience stretched on, one splendid hour after another.

The following morning, when I woke, it was as if I'd been

transported into a different world. No, a different body. Different fucking everything.

I walked outside, onto the wraparound deck.

The crisp winter air was saturated with the scent of evergreen and earth. Birds fluttered and chirped. Squirrels scurried up and down trees. A butterfly perched just below me. Its wings slowly unfurled, revealing two semicircles of bright red spots against a black backdrop.

Wind washed over my skin.

I closed my eyes, listening, feeling, and inhaling the world's beauty.

That's when it hit me.

For so many months, I'd been stuck in an emotional prison, a solitary confinement of my own misery.

Overnight, however, the dark walls of negativity had melted away.

What had once been opaque was now transparent. I could finally see what all along had been there: beauty, love, and goodness.

I was free.

I was finally free!

The depression was gone.

As the day unfolded, so did old feelings and sensations. I hadn't felt them in so long that I'd forgotten they existed. Yet, there they were, like a lost dog returning home after a long absence.

There was hope—so much hope.

Suddenly, everything felt possible, enticing, titillating. A searing sense of urgency coursed through my veins. I'd been stuck on pause for far too fucking long.

It was time to start living.

It was time to get my shit together!

During the drive home, as I gazed though the car window at the evergreens, I realized that I knew with conviction—without a single shred of a doubt—what I wanted to do with my life.

All this time, I'd thought I was a foot soldier in the

counter-cultural revolution. It was a noble concept. Yet, dropping out had done nothing for me. The experience had brought me no spiritual realizations. Nor had it transformed my life, the lives of people around me, or the world in general. If anything, it had only led to heartbreak and pain.

Dropping back in? That's where *my* revolution was going to be fought.

I was going to become a psychologist.

Yes, I would help poor souls like me—really and truly help them.

Fucking-A, someone needed to do it.

Why were there so many incapable losers in this profession? Paint swatches? Seriously?

Unlike the parade of incompetents who'd treated me, I understood what it was like to be depressed. I'd lived it. That had to count for something.

I was going to start something, change something, be something.

After I became a psychologist, people like Louise would no longer refer to psychiatric hospitals as "hospi-jails." I would make a difference. Unlike the jokers in San Francisco who herded sick people away from society, I would help folks get well. I would help them thrive. I would help them feel what I was feeling right now. That way they could drop back in, find their own individual paths, and start their own minirevolutions.

Once back in Berkeley, I hiked to the student union and perused the ads pinned to the bulletin boards.

Three graduate students were looking for someone to rent a bedroom in a single-family house in North Berkeley. I hopped in my microbus, drove over, and knocked on the door.

All of them were studying physics, which meant they were superbright, because this was Berkeley. They were also Delta Kappa Epsilon brothers, known as the Dekes. There was Greg, a tall lanky redhead who played lacrosse. Something told me we were going to get along.

Hans was a stocky blond rock climber.

Peter was polished and clean cut, the kind of guy who could have been class president.

They apparently liked what they saw, and I made plans to move in.

After that, I headed for Mandrake's Bar, which had advertised for a bartender. Located near the intersection of University and San Pablo Avenues, a good distance from my soon-to-be home, the joint offered entertainment on the weekends. The New Riders of the Purple Sage were regulars, as was the playwright Michael McClure, who staged complex productions, like *Spider Rabbit*.

It seemed like a fun place. More important, they only sold wine and beer. That was fortunate because I didn't know how to mix drinks.

They hired me on the spot.

◆ ◆ ◆

Getting into a doctoral program in clinical psychology in the late '60s was considered to be a lot harder than getting into medical school. To enhance my chances, I re-enrolled at Berkeley so I could earn a second bachelor's degree, this time in psychology. I had already completed all the other requirements so all I needed was to complete the major.

Within days, I found myself sitting in class, entranced by what my professors were telling me. I learned how Albert Bandura and a team of researchers at Stanford University had lugged an inflatable plastic doll, called a Bobo doll, into a room full of preschool aged children. The doll had been painted to resemble a clown. Because it was bottom-weighted, it rocked back and forth.

As the children quietly colored and attached stickers to paper, an adult kicked, punched, and threw objects at the doll, shouting things like "he keeps coming back for more" and "sock him in the nose!" This went on for about ten minutes. Then the adult left.

Later in the day, researchers observed the same group of children as they played.

The children who'd witnessed the doll being attacked played much more aggressively than another group of children who had not. Follow up experiments yielded similar results. Startlingly, a full eight months later, the children who'd witnessed the attack on the doll were *still* more aggressive than children who hadn't. Boys seemed most affected.

A chill went up my spine.

Was that what had happened to me?

Was that why I couldn't seem to escape the Curse of Wolf?

Had the trauma inflicted by my father and the neighborhood bullies socialized rage into my soul? Was that why I kept going off the rails—punching out the storefront windows in Long Beach and hitting Joyce?

If so, could the damage be reversed?

◆ ◆ ◆

Toward the end of January, Joyce returned to the Bay area to visit family and friends, which allowed me to spend the good part of a day with Caren.

I hadn't seen her in two years, and I'd worried she wouldn't remember me.

Yet, when Joyce dropped her off at the house, Caren raced toward me as if we'd never been apart.

I wrapped my arms around her and lifted her high into the air.

"Hi, Daddy," she said, giggling.

"Hi, sweetie."

"Why are you crying, Daddy?" she asked, her small hand pressed against my wet cheek.

"Oh, honey, that's nothing. I'm just so happy to see you. Some tears are tears of joy."

With my back groaning from strain, I put her down.

"Honey, you've gotten so big!" I said, "So big that I think you're ready to learn to ski."

"I am?"

"Yes, you are!"

"You know those Sierra Nevada mountains? Someday we'll go there together to ski. For now, though, you're going to practice inside skiing!"

"Inside skiing?" she asked, her face scrunched up in confusion. "What's that?"

"Let me show you," I said, with excitement. It was all coming so easily. I couldn't believe how effortless it all was now that the depression was gone.

I grabbed a pair of skis from the closet and strapped them to her feet, then pushed her around the living and dining rooms.

She squealed with laughter. "Wheeeeeeee!"

"You're doing it! You're so good at this!" I told her. "Someday, I'm going to be watching you ski in the Olympics."

Several hours later when Joyce returned, Caren and I were still at it, laughing and playing.

"It looks like you've really gotten yourself together."

It was night and day. The last time she'd seen me, I couldn't relate to the world. I didn't make eye contact. I probably didn't make sense.

Now I was engaged in my life, happy.

"Thanks," I said. "I'm feeling much better."

"It looks like it."

"You know," I said, "I'm thinking. It's going to take me about a year to finish up my second bachelor's. Along the way, I thought I'd apply to graduate schools on the East Coast. That way, I can be in Caren's life again."

"Ron, I'd like that," she said. "That'd be really good for Caren."

As I watched Joyce and Caren drive off, urgency engulfed my heart. I was going to do everything it took to get accepted to

Harvard or Columbia or another heavy hitter in the East.

Never again would I get arrested.

Never again would I blow off a class.

Never again would I show up for a test without studying.

This new version of Ron was no longer a drop *out*.

I was now dropping *in*.

◆ ◆ ◆

Seemingly in conflict with my sense of urgency and purpose, I felt drawn to psychedelics like a moth to a flame. A part of me worried what might happen if, like Lowell, I dropped acid too often.

Yet, another part of me worried about what might happen if I didn't drop them often enough.

LSD had cured my depression, at least for now.

Who was to say the depression wouldn't come back if I didn't keep dosing myself?

Psychedelics were my medicine. They were *how* I would drop back in—and stay in.

So, roughly twice a month, I scored pills from someone on campus, experimenting with every psychedelic that someone had to sell. Each trip left me feeling more grounded, more alive, and more filled with purpose. I figured I had to be doing something right.

When my roommate Greg indicated an interest in trying psychedelics, I felt compelled to help. It was a high honor to introduce someone else to the transformative experience. One didn't merely hand someone a free acid pill. No, one made that first trip very *special*, as Lowell had done for me.

"Spring break's coming up," I said. "What do you think about hitchhiking to the Grand Canyon? We can hike down to the Colorado River and then drop mescaline while we're surrounded by beauty."

"Far-out," he said. "Why mescaline, though? Why not LSD?"

"LSD gets all the attention, but I've been reading a lot about peyote cactus buttons," I said. "That's where they get mescaline from, you know? It's used in ceremonies among Native Americans. I've heard that Allen Ginsberg has described it as electricity. From what I've read, it sounds super mind-blowing."

"I'm all in. Let's do it."

We could have driven. We both had cars. It would have taken fifteen hours or so.

Yet, I wanted this to be the trip of a lifetime.

I figured hitchhiking would be way more fun—and memorable.

So, we loaded up our internal frame backpacks with sleeping bags, cooking gear, and many packs of dehydrated food.

Then we set off.

The trip went as smoothly as a multistate hitchhiking trip could have possibly gone. We met a lot of interesting people—folks we never would have met under other circumstances.

Two days later, at the South Rim entrance to the Grand Canyon National Park, we descended the seventeen-mile Bright Angel Trail until we reached the Colorado River.

It was late in the day when we arrived, so we found a spot to camp and made supper.

The next morning, we got up, had breakfast, and got ready for the trip. We each sat on a rock on the edge of the river. Then we dropped mescaline.

An hour later, the world transformed into a dreamy oasis, filled with brilliant colors, sparkling objects, and stunning beauty.

"Look at the pebbles," I told Greg. "In the river. Aren't they the most beautiful things you've ever seen?"

"Far-out, man," Greg replied, looking around. "Everything's so fucking beautiful. The sky. The river. The grass. The canyon. The fucking dirt. Everything."

"I told you this was going to be cool."

There we sat, for hours, staring, marveling, and basking in the beauty all around us.

Eventually another hippie ambled over.

"Your hands," I said.

"Oh, yeah, I scraped them up pretty good while rock climbing," he said, holding them outward.

"They're extraordinary," I said, gently grabbing his fingers. I bent forward to get a closer look. The sores, scrapes, and cuts formed angular patterns, full of bright colors.

"Greg," I said, "aren't his hands the most beautiful things you've ever seen?"

"Far-fucking-out!"

The guy hung out with us for a while. Then he left the same way he'd come.

We camped at the bottom of the canyon for a few more days, surviving on the freeze-dried vittles left behind by other hikers seeking to lighten their packs before they trekked upward. Then we reversed our trip, arriving back in Berkeley just a few hours before our classes began.

Greg became my regular tripping buddy after that. We often sipped sweet Bali Hai wine as we waited for the acid to kick in. Then we chatted about anything and everything, sometimes stumbling upon poignant ideas and realizations that we immediately jotted down in a notebook. In the morning our entries resembled nothing other than pure gibberish.

One weekend, while relaxing at a lake with a bunch of other hippies, we dropped purple LSD pills that turned everything—the water, the air, the people—purple.

We dropped psilocybin, along with a couple other hippies, as we maneuvered a small sailboat on a lake. We named that episode "Psilly Sailing."

One afternoon, alone, I dropped what I thought was LSD. As expected, it transformed everything around me into beauty.

The following morning, I woke and groggily shuffled to the bathroom.

I pulled my toothbrush from its holder, added toothpaste, and started brushing.

Then I looked in the mirror.

That's when I realized something wasn't right.

On the mirror, the old, splattered bits of toothpaste should have been white, maybe gray. Instead, they were bright red, bright green, bright purple.

Some of them sprouted arms, then legs. They formed an inner circle, then an outer, and another circle after that. They joined hands and spun. The mirror now looked like a kaleidoscope.

Were the toothbrush flecks performing a Busby Berkeley kaleidoscopic dance routine?

They were!

Clearly, I was still tripping.

But I shouldn't have been.

LSD trips never lasted *that* long.

The hallucinations went on for the rest of the day, throughout the night, and into the next morning, when they finally came to an end.

As I asked around, I learned that I likely hadn't taken LSD at all, but rather the amphetamine STP, which stands for "serenity, tranquility, and peace," and is known for being very long-lasting.

With each trip, I could feel a change. Compared to who I was a year before, I was exceedingly happy, enthusiastic about my studies, approached everything with gusto. Clearly, psychedelics were good for me.

◆ ◆ ◆

As spring unfolded, the Berkeley campus grew increasingly restless.

On any given day, Sproul Plaza was packed with students who'd gathered to rally against the Vietnam war. I was vaguely aware of a hubbub between students and the university, something to do with a muddy plot of land that the University wanted to transform into athletic fields.

The students, on the other hand, wanted to turn it into a public park. When the university turned down their requests, the students, along with some community members, forged on, planting trees, flowers, and shrubs.

The University, however, refused to bow to student pressure. By mid-May, they erected a fence around the property, sparking even more protests.

Though I supported the students, I rarely participated. My studies required too much attention. I no longer had time to save the world.

As I walked to class one morning, I could feel the excitement. The students seemed alive with purpose, streaming to the south side of campus and the park.

I headed to Tolman Hall, roughly a mile and a half from Sproul Plaza, the likely location of the rally. Then I entered the classroom for Professor Hugh Coffey's group dynamics class, looking forward to learning more about the phenomenon of "groupthink."

We were about forty-five minutes into class when loud sounds erupted from the hallway. People running and yelling?

Then my eyes were on fire. Everything looked blurry. My nose ran. My throat burned and swelled.

What was happening?

Everyone around me seemed to be afflicted with the same ailment.

Students coughed. Their eyes teared.

"I can't breathe," someone said.

"There's something wrong," Professor Coffey said, gasping, coughing. "Class is dismissed. Everyone—let's get out of here."

Chairs scraped against the floor.

I gathered my things.

Were we being poisoned? What was wrong? It was all so confusing.

The hallways were filled with smoke.

Bodies pressed up against me as I struggled to move forward, covering my nose and mouth with my shirt.

It was so dark.

People coughing. So much coughing.

Keep moving.

Just keep moving.

Tears streaming down my face. My eyes on fire.

Keep moving. You're still alive. Keep moving.

Finally, I got to the main entrance.

I emerged with hundreds of other students.

Papers fluttered in the breeze.

Cops and national guardsmen were everywhere, many in formation, three rows deep.

A large olive-green helicopter flew overhead.

There was smoke coming from the copter.

People screamed, racing in all sorts of directions.

Other students remained put, shouting in unison. "Killers off campus. Killers off campus!"

I noticed someone pick up a canister and hurl it toward the cops.

Fucking cops.

A canister whizzed through the air, landing with a thud near me.

I grabbed it, hurling it back.

Fucking cops.

What the hell was wrong with these pigs? Why had they gassed us out of class?

"I can't fucking believe this shit," I said to the guy next to me.

"Did you know they have tanks on the Marina," he replied.

"Tanks?"

"See that copter up there?" He pointed to the sky. "It's spraying us with tear gas."

"What the hell? Have they lost their minds?"

"They're patrolling Telegraph Avenue in jeeps with machine guns mounted in the back," he said.

I watched for a while, struggling to take in the constantly changing scene.

Then I walked to my microbus and drove to the Marina. I had to see the tanks.

I later learned that Governor Ronald Reagan had called in the National Guard to reinforce the California Highway Patrol and Berkeley Police, who were forcing students out of the park area. That had ignited a huge protest, with thousands of students packing Sproul Plaza.

The pigs had shot and killed James Rector, a student who'd been watching the unrest from a rooftop. Another person had been blinded by birdshot. More than a hundred students were hospitalized with serious injuries. When Reagan was pressed on why the police used such force, he answered, "It's very naive to assume that you should send anyone into that kind of conflict with a flyswatter."

The whole mess lasted for weeks.

◆ ◆ ◆

Yet another letter arrived from the government.

My heart dropped into my stomach.

While at Berkeley the first time, I'd gotten a draft deferment for "activity in study." Then, when the next induction letter had arrived, I'd applied for and was granted a different deferment, available to men who were married with children, as military service was considered a hardship. Then, while in medical school, I managed to postpone my service again with a deferment for medical study.

I'd been hoping and praying that the war would end before the Selective Service figured out that I was no longer married and no longer in medical school.

I slid my finger along the top of envelope, revealing the neatly folded piece of paper inside. Slowly I pulled the paper from the envelope.

There were hundreds of thousands of young people my age being forced to fight for a cause they likely either didn't understand nor believe in. By the end, more than 58,000 of them had died or were missing in action. So many lives cut short. So many grieving families.

So many hopes and dreams ruined.

So many young people who never had a chance.

I unfolded the paper. Across the top, in all caps, it said, ORDER TO REPORT FOR ARMED FORCES PHYSICAL EXAM.

Fuck! Fuck! Fuck!

I knew this day would come. Yet, somehow, I'd also hoped that the government would forget I existed, lose track of me, or decide they didn't want me.

I'd just started to get my life together!

My brother Lowell had already gotten his notice. He'd applied for and had received consciousness objector status. For the past several months, he'd been performing his alternate service as a participant in a study designed to test astronaut food and understand its metabolic effects. Every day he ate freeze dried morsels, with researchers monitoring his health, weight, even his pee and poop. He wasn't allowed to leave. He was confined to the premises.

I didn't want to go to war. I also, however, didn't want to put my studies on hold to be stared at like a lab rat on behalf of the US government.

As the date grew closer, I learned of several men who'd beaten the draft by showing up to their inductions drugged out of their minds. "Get yourself so fucked up that you can't even add," one of them told me, "then go to your physical and let them find out that you're unfit."

I stayed up all night before my induction physical, smoking hash, dropping LSD, guzzling cheap wine, and I even took a few pain pills for good measure.

With colors shimmering and the entire world vibrating, I walked into a huge room, where various tables were set up as induction stations.

I reported to the correct area, where a young man with a shaved head asked me a series of questions. I could barely figure out what the heck the guy was saying, or even what I was saying. The words floated into the sky.

"Why are you doing this?" I asked.

"Doing what?" the man asked.

"This! Do you know you are killing innocent civilians. You've killed a whole generation of young men. It's disgusting."

"I'm just doing my job."

"Isn't that what the Nazis all said? That they were just following orders?"

"Sir, let's just get through this, okay?"

Someone took my blood pressure, then listened to my heart.

On the desk was an object, shimmering, mesmerizing.

I had to have it.

I reached, grabbed, then shoved it down the front of my pants.

"What are you doing? Why did you do that?"

"Do what?"

"Give that back to me! I order you to return my stapler!"

"What stapler?"

"The one you just took off my desk!"

"I don't know what you're talking about!"

"Yes, you do! Give it back!"

Feeling a hard bulge against my crotch, I reached down.

"Why was this in there? That's weird," I said, pulling the stapler from my pubic area.

The man used a tissue to grab it.

"Stand up," he said.

"Okay," I said, getting out of my chair, bending my knees, sitting down on the floor, and then lying down.

"What are you doing?"

"I'm doing what you told me to do."

"That's not what I told you to do!"

"Yes, it is. You told me to stand and I'm standing."

"You're not standing!"

"I'm not?"

Similar routines were repeated at several other stations, taking up most of the afternoon.

Afterward, as I walked out, I realized I had no idea where I'd parked my microbus. I walked the surrounding streets, one street at a time, searching. It took several hours to find it.

Several weeks later, another letter arrived.

I'd pulled it off. I was unfit for active duty. I was classified as 1-Y, defined as "Registrant qualified for military service only in time of war or national emergency."

◆ ◆ ◆

By the end of that first quarter, I'd earned all As, two-thirds of which were A-pluses, which gained me acceptance into the honors program. That summer I was invited to participate in a small honors seminar that included only twelve students. Here I learned of the exciting work being done by Gregory Bateson, who—along with Jay Haley, Paul Watzlawick, and John Weakland—had been studying families with a member diagnosed with schizophrenia. They put forth the audacious theory that the schizophrenia symptoms were a response to faulty communication patterns in the family, which they called the "double bind."

It was in this class that I noticed a striking redhead named Anita.

After class I walked her to her car, and then suggested, "Why don't we get together some time?" She invited me over. Like me, she was very serious about her studies. Like some women I'd met, she was ready to hop into bed.

A month later, I brought her to the house to hang out.

As we all chatted, I couldn't help but notice: Greg wouldn't stop paying attention to her.

Was he *flirting* with her? Right in front of me?

I tried to put it out of my mind. Maybe he was just being polite.

Surely, he wouldn't try to steal her?

Two weeks later, as I parked near Anita's apartment, I noticed Greg's black Ford sedan. What was that doing here?

Wait. Was he with Anita?

It wasn't that I was especially heartbroken. That wasn't it at all. Relationships were so fluid. They were like clouds on a spring day. They formed. Then they drifted apart, changing shape, changing location, just changing with the breeze.

It was more the principle of the matter. He'd horned in on me. What kind of a friend does that?

I didn't want to disrupt the vibe of the house, so I drove away without confronting either of them.

Peter moved out. Jerry moved in. He was young, fun, and interested in LSD. He was also a photographer. Soon he and I were hanging out and dropping acid, as Greg and I once had done. We would take drives through rural areas and take pictures—one that I remember well was of two Model-A Fords rusting in a field.

◆ ◆ ◆

By the date of the Great Be-In, held at Mt. Tamalpais State Park, Anita was a distant memory. I'd since moved on to Heidi, at least sometimes.

A small blond, Heidi hung out at the house quite a bit. She'd slept with all of us, at one time or another, depending on her preferences that day and who was around. We affectionately referred to her among ourselves as "Heidi butt," because of her adorable rear end.

That morning, Heidi and I climbed into my microbus and drove across the San Raphael Bridge into Marin County, and on to Mount Tamalpais.

We weaved our way around the throngs of people already present, many of them walking around naked, found an empty patch of grass, and set up a blanket. Soon we were surrounded by other hippies, forming our own little community. I took off my shoes, then my shirt. It was such a beautiful day, and I loved the sensation of grass and dirt against the bottoms of my feet.

"I'm going to go walk around for a while," I told Heidi. "See you in a bit."

I sipped from a cup of acid-laced wine as I listened to the local New Age guru orate from the amphitheater. He meandered all over the place, not making much sense at all. Why did so many people love this guy?

Then the acid kicked in.

Suddenly, the guru was making sense! Thoughts that had seemed disjointed now congealed into a strong, powerful message.

"I get it now," I said, "Right on! Brilliant!"

The entire scene resembled the painting by Hieronymus Bosch, titled the *Garden of Earthly Delights*.

A young woman stood nearby. She was in a T-shirt, with no bottoms, her pubic hair on display. We locked eyes.

She approached me. I approached her.

I wrapped my palm around her small waist, pulling her toward me. As we kissed, she unbuttoned my jeans, grabbed the waistband, and pushed them and my underpants down. I lifted one foot, then the other. The warm air wafted against my behind.

She lay on the dirt. I crawled on top of her.

When it was over, we stood next to one another for a while, listening to the guru.

Then she drifted away. I never caught her name.

The line from the Doors song wafted through my head: "Hello, I love you, won't you tell me your name?"

Still naked, I walked back to our blanket, folded my pants, and left them there with Heidi and the other hippies we'd met earlier in the day, and continued wandering and tripping.

Hours later, I drove home. I have no idea how I got home safely. Nor did I know where Heidi ended up.

◆ ◆ ◆

Later in the year, Hans, one of the original occupants of our house, moved out. A beautiful hippie named Joannie Shalant answered our ad for a roommate. The ends of her long dark hair almost reached her butt. Sporting gold wire-rimmed glasses and a granny dress, she personified hippieness. I couldn't stop staring at her, nor she at me. It was soon decided. She'd move in with me, and we'd advertise for someone else to move into the spare bedroom.

Joannie blended with me in a way few women did.

She wasn't a passing cloud. I could tell, even during those first few days together, that she was going to become more of a permanent fixture.

The two of us learned how to make large cylindrical incandescent candles. We sold them on consignment at local craft and gift shops, calling our enterprise "Horatio Alger's Bargain Basement." It didn't pay the rent, but it helped.

Toward the end of 1969, Joannie, Jerry, his girlfriend Alana, and I attended the Altamont Speedway Free Festival. Billed as the West Coast equivalent to Woodstock, the counterculture rock concert was held at the Altamont Speedway outside of Livermore, California.

Along with hundreds of thousands of hippies, we sat on blankets as we listened to Jefferson Airplane.

The Stones would come on next. The anticipation was palpable.

"Look at that dude," someone said.

There was a huge man, completely naked, weaving his way

among the narrow areas of free space around the blankets.

As he neared the stage, Hell's Angels crowded him, whacking him with pool cues.

"Holy shit," I said.

The band stopped.

"Get out of here. Stop!" someone yelled from the stage.

It had no effect.

"What the hell?" Joannie screamed.

It was horrible, watching a crowd of men bludgeon another man.

"They're going to kill him," Joannie said.

"I think they are," I said.

People stood and ran. Thousands of people, running in various directions.

"Let's go," I said.

We raced back to Jerry's car.

The following day, in the paper, I learned that the Hell's Angels had stabbed a different man to death. I was horrified.

◆ ◆ ◆

Somehow, despite all the psychedelics, Be-Ins, concerts, uprisings, and sex, I did incredibly well in school. By December I'd earned all A's, half were A-pluses, and was awarded the Citation for Outstanding Undergraduate Accomplishment, designating me as the single best psychology student for that year.

Before the award ceremony, I took something that I thought was acid, but turned out to be speed.

During my acceptance speech, I could hear and feel myself talking too quickly. I tried to slow down. Yet, I couldn't seem to stop myself. The words kept pouring out.

Why wasn't I making any sense?

Finally, to end the embarrassment, I said, "Well thank you. That's all." Then I sat down.

TAKEAWAYS

Once again, I had a front row seat at the making of history, witnessing the massive amount of military force that Governor Ronald Reagan deployed against unarmed students during the People's Park protests—gassing us out of our classrooms and killing and injuring some of us.

I also caught the psychedelic wave, which fortuitously resolved my depression. In this respect, I was way ahead of my time, as psychedelics are only now being tested for the treatment of cases of mental illnesses (such as PTSD and depression) that have proven to be treatment resistant. Readers, if you are suffering from unremitting psychological symptoms, please do investigate if there are any clinical trials using psychedelics at your local medical centers. It might help you as it helped me.

The twenty trips that I took seem to have had lasting effects, in that I learned to see the beauty and grace of ordinary things.

During these years I also discovered my true and inherent passion—finding my calling as a psychologist—and I never looked back. It took a circuitous path from engineering to physics to history to medicine, and finally to psychology. But once I found it, I realized how well it fit me.

Readers, have you found your calling? What did it take for you to do that?

CHAPTER 10

An Imposter Earns a Doctorate

(1970–1973)

Joannie and I packed our clothes, candle supplies, my books, and our other belongings into a second, newer VW microbus. The boxes filled the back, leaving no space for us to sleep. Occasionally during the five-day, cross-country trek, we pulled into parking lots, parks, or to the side of the road, unrolled our sleeping bags, and slept under the stars. Once midway we checked into a cheap motel to shower and sleep.

Everything still felt unreal.

I'd run away from home, been arrested three times, gotten expelled from high school, and become so severely depressed that I'd attempted suicide and checked myself into a state psychiatric facility.

Yet, somehow, despite all of this, I'd earned acceptance into one of the top five universities in the world. Here I was, with all that I had been through, enrolled in a doctoral psychology program along with the brightest students in the country.

Psychologists were supposed to have their shit together.
Who would seek help from someone like me?
What would other students think if they knew my past?
No, they couldn't know.
No one could.
Absolutely no one.

◆ ◆ ◆

We had so few belongings that it didn't take long to carry everything into a cheap roach-infested apartment in Cambridge's Central Square Neighborhood. Within days, Joannie was busy exploring the city, searching for shops willing to sell our candles on consignment.

Before making the trek to Manhattan to reunite with Caren, I wanted to get settled with my classes. Everyone referred to Harvard's clinical-community psychology program in writing as CP^3, pronounced "cee pee three," which stood for "Clinical Psychology and Public Practice." Housed in a restored antique home in the Graduate School of Education, the program had been formed just a year before I arrived.

It was unique, to say the least.

I learned the trade from talented faculty. There was Chester Middlebrook Pierce, a psychiatrist and Naval commander who served as a senior consultant for Sesame Street and coined the term "microaggression."

(He would go on to become the first Black full professor at Harvard Medical School-Massachusetts General Hospital.)

Ira Goldenberg, another professor, had trained at Yale under Seymour Sarason, the founder of community psychology. David McClelland was considered one of the world's leading experts on human motivation. John Shlien had been Carl Rogers' protégé at the University of Chicago. They were just a few of the many highly credentialed and revered faculty—and they tore up all the traditional rules.

They often stated that they didn't want to churn out graduates who "counseled the wealthy elite in fancy offices on Park Avenue." Rather, their goals centered on using psychology to lift marginalized communities out of poverty.

To achieve these lofty goals, Professors Pierce, Goldenberg, McClelland, Shlien, and others preferred to admit students like me who had prior experience as campus activists. They even gave me credit for my work in CORE and CIPA.

Rather than organize the program around a clear, sequential, graded curriculum that followed American Psychological Association accreditation guidelines, the professors asked us to demonstrate competencies. They expected us to work on social action projects with them, based on the philosophical premise that, faced with challenging projects, we would learn what we needed to know to complete them.

New first year students were required to be present during the summer before classes formally began in the fall. I was assigned to Professor Shlien, a medium-sized man who played tennis and drove an older convertible sports car. Because of his white hair, students referred to him as "White Owl."

During our first meeting, Dr. Shlien asked me to participate in a group conducting a needs assessment of the people in the so-called catchment area served by the new Erich Lindemann Mental Health Center. The Center was located in a part of Boston that had been catastrophically impacted by urban renewal. The area that housed the Lindemann Center and Boston City Hall, called Government Center, had been a working class Italian American neighborhood known as the West End, whose vitality had been beautifully captured by Herbert Gans in his book *The Urban Villagers*. To add insult to injury, both the Lindemann Center and City Hall were constructed in the architecture style known as "neo brutalism." Designed by Yale Architect Paul Rudolf, the Lindemann Center building was made of poured concrete that had been systematically chipped, yielding a very rough and dangerous appearance, not what any reasonable person would recommend for a mental health center.

Erich Lindeman Mental Health Center. Photo Credit: Ari Bowman

As soon as I heard the words "needs assessment," painful memories surfaced. Images from the Mission District Project crowded my mind. I'd already failed at this work before, and it had ignited my downfall.

It was because of the Mission District Project that I'd lost the CIPA election.

It likely had helped to bring my marriage to an end.

The Mission District Project had contributed to my depression, my stay at the state psychiatric institution, and my third arrest.

It had ruined everything.

With uneasiness coursing through me, I struggled to pay attention.

This would be different. I would make it so!

Along with a half a dozen other students, I attended a few classes, read required materials, and quickly learned how to strike up conversations with strangers.

Within days, I found myself in East Boston—referred to as "Easta Bosta" by the Italian American residents—with a pen and clipboard in hand.

I stood in the doorway of a business, talking to a shopkeeper, asking him about his experiences.

The building rattled.

What was happening?

The man pointed up.

There was a giant plane, coming toward us, flying so low it seemed as if I could reach up and touch it. The man gestured wildly, but the roar of the engines made it impossible to hear what he was saying.

By his facial expression, it was clear. He was enraged.

Eventually the roar subsided enough for me to hear him.

"See?" he said, thrusting his hand upward. "This is what we're forced to deal with. It goes on all day long—and even late into the night!"

I made my way down the street, talking to one person after another. Without fail, the topic always led back to Logan Airport. Located on an island in Boston Harbor, the airport was initially used only by the military. To expand it to include commercial jets, the government dumped piles of debris into Boston Harbor to artificially expand the island. In the early 1960s, the airport took more land, including the forty-six-acre Wood Island Park. This expansion not only took the pride of the East Boston neighborhood—their beautiful park—but also pushed many residents out of their homes by eminent domain.

Outrage over those decisions was still fresh, as if it had all just happened.

By day's end, I'd completed nearly a dozen interviews—twelve more than I'd managed to do for CIPA's failed Mission District project. As it turned out, a needs assessment wasn't difficult. CIPA could have handled it had we had just a smidge of guidance. Had we succeeded, maybe I would have remained in charge of CIPA. Had I remained in charge of CIPA, maybe my marriage wouldn't have failed.

Maybe I would have never become so depressed.

Maybe.

Just maybe.

If only I could go back. If only I could do it over.

◆ ◆ ◆

It was dark when I woke.

What was that sound? Was it scratching?

I poked Joannie.

"Did you hear that?"

"The scratching sound?"

"Yes," I said.

We sat and listened.

"I don't know. Maybe it was a tree branch scraping against the side of the building," I said.

We went back to sleep.

The following morning, when I opened the door, I noticed the wood around the latch had been gouged away, as if someone had chipped away at the door with a screwdriver.

"Look at this! Remember that sound last night?" I asked. "I think it was someone trying to break in!"

"Shit!" she said. "Thank goodness they didn't!"

"What if they had?"

"I don't want to think about it!"

"What if they had a weapon?"

Joannie didn't want to be alone after that, and I didn't blame her. Neither did I.

I clearly couldn't leave her alone in that apartment for a whole weekend while I went to New York to see Caren.

Yet I couldn't exactly bring Joannie with me.

How would Joyce react?

How would Caren?

"I'll figure it out," I told myself. "I'll figure it out."

Before I knew it, summer was over, the East Boston surveys were complete, and I was being assigned to complete a much more demanding assignment—my first clinical practicum.

I had yet to get to New York.

◆ ◆ ◆

In other clinical psychology doctoral programs around the country, graduate students started small. Before they ever saw a client, for example, they spent a semester role playing and learning interviewing skills. Then they might counsel one client. Over time, they might increase their client load to four, then seven.

Harvard did the opposite.

They thrust us into the most challenging of clinical situations and expected us learn on our feet.

So, on day one of the first semester I was placed in a practicum two days a week in the men's unit at Boston State Hospital. It was the same kind of state hospital that I'd admitted myself into a few years earlier, except for one difference: this unit was locked.

I imagined bedlam—patients screaming, throwing things, taking off their clothes, upending tables, talking in gibberish, drooling. What if they attacked me? Each other?

I wondered if the CP[3] professors knew what they were getting us into. They had expressed a great deal of respect for us students, as if we were the "chosen" few. I wondered if they expected that we had already mastered the basics on our own?

After a fitful night—with vivid dreams of mentally ill patients chasing me through a blood-soaked asylum—I dropped by my supervisor's office in the administration building on the grounds of Boston State Hospital.

"What's on your mind?" Dr. John Arsenian asked in his thick Armenian accent.

"Dr. Arsenian," I asked. "Are you sure I'm ready for this—to be in a locked unit? This is my first day of graduate school. I have no formal training."

"I see," he said. "How old are you?"

How was that relevant?

"Twenty-eight," I answered.

"Not so young then," he said.

"I suppose not," I said, still not sure where this was going.

"I know you are a student in this new cockamamie clinical program at Harvard that puts its students into placements before any preparatory course work," he said.

What did he mean by cockamamie? "Yes, but—"

"At age twenty-eight you probably know how to make friends, right?"

"Sure," I answered.

"Okay," he continued, "it's almost 10 a.m. now. This is what I'd like to do. I'd like for us both to go to the unit together. I'll let you in, and I want you to make friends with as many of the men as you can. Then at noon I'll come for you, and we can go to the cafeteria and have lunch and discuss your experiences."

"Make friends?"

"Yes," he said. "Just relate to them the same as you'd relate to anyone else."

I wasn't sure how that was going to be possible, but I nervously agreed to give it a try.

Once inside the four-story red brick building called the May Building (named after Dr. James V. May, a former superintendent of Boston State Hospital), we were greeted by the powerful stench of chemical cleansers, smoke, and urine. Our feet clopped against the vinyl flooring as we made our way down a series of drab halls.

Then we came to a huge metal door.

Dr. Arsenian inserted his key, turned the deadbolt, and lugged open the door.

"Ron," he said, "you're going to be okay. You really are."

As I swallowed the tension in my throat, I tried to appear confident, forcing a smile.

"Thanks," I said, my face feeling tight.

The door closed behind me. Then there was the sound of Dr. Arsenian's key turning the lock.

The Lucy Show blared from a television set.

A man was lying on a couch.

Others were pacing, smoking one cigarette after another.

One man sat on the edge of a chair, his hands neatly folded in his lap, his back as straight as a ruler. He stared into the distance, expressionless, as if he were concentrating on a point on the wall.

I approached a middle-aged man. Bald and skinny, he didn't look as scary as the others.

"Think of him as a friend," I reminded myself. "He's just a guy sitting next to you in a bar. You're just getting to know him."

"Hi," I said, "My name is Ron Levant. I'm a graduate student in psychology. I've been placed here by my program. I'd like to speak with you about your experiences here. Are you open to having a conversation?"

"Shuah," he said, his thick Boston accent already coming through. "Whaddaya wanna know?"

"Well," I said, buying myself some time. What *did* I want to know? "What was your life like before you, um, came, um, here?"

"You see," he said, "I was a weldah. I was damn good at it too."

"I see," I said. "Why did you stop?"

"I had a psychotic break, you see. Then I got help and I was okay for a while. Then I had anothah one. And anothah one. My job they uh, well. They didn't trust me with the tauch after that, ya know? No one wanted to work anywheah neaah me so they uh. Well, they canned me."

"I'm sorry to hear that," I said. "So how did you end up here?"

"My wife, you know, she didn't want me around the kids anymore. She thought I might lose it again. She didn't want them to see any of that again. Neithah did I if I'm being honest. I miss them. I love them. But it was foah the best."

"What was for the best?"

"She had me committed."

"I'm so sorry to hear that." My heart ached for this man. "How long have you been here?"

"Eh, I dunno. Um, Rahn, you say your name is?"

"Yes," I said.

"It's nice to talk to you, Rahn. Thanks for visiting us. We don't get many visitahs around heah."

He seemed just like any other person I might meet. It didn't make sense, him being here. It was heartbreaking.

I thanked him and moved on to the man who in the chair who seemed fixated on the wall.

"Hi," I said, "My name is Ron Levant."

He didn't respond.

"I'm a graduate student in psychology," I continued. "I've been placed here by my program. . ."

Still, no reaction.

"I'd like to speak with you about your experiences here. Are you open to having a conversation?"

He didn't move—not his mouth, not his head, not his pupils, not any part of him. His eyes remained fixed. I'd heard of catatonia, but I'd never seen someone with it.

"Yaw new heah."

I turned away from the catatonic man. Standing to my side was a huge man with a white towel around his neck. Another one was wrapped around his left hand.

"Jim," he said, reaching out to shake my hand.

"Ron," I replied.

He was friendly, gregarious, talkative.

I launched into my spiel about the program. All the while, he grinned, as if he were overjoyed to be in my company.

"Are you open to having a conversation?"

"Shuah," he said, "But fuhst, I've got a tip foah ya."

"Okay," I said, shifting my weight to the other leg. A tip? About this place?

"Weah one of these," he said, reaching forward to wrap a white towel around my neck.

"Thanks," I said. Why would I need to wear a towel around my neck?

"Did you used to—"

"You heah that?" he asked, interrupting me.

"Hear what?"

"The messages," he said.

"What messages?"

"What's wrong with yoah hearin'? You really can't heah them? The messages coming from the boob tube over theah?"

"From *The Lucy Show*?"

He leaned in close, as if he were sharing a secret.

"Theyah watching us," he said. "Through the boob tube. You be caheful because theyah watching. Don't tell the othahs. They won't believe you."

Not knowing what to say or how to respond, I moved on to the next patient.

On this went—me sitting with one man after another. Some were receptive. Others weren't. Still others shared many details about their lives, their fears, their regrets, their hopes, their dreams.

Later, when Dr. Arsenian came to retrieve me, I felt as if something inside of me had changed.

"So?" he asked. "How was it? As scary as you thought?"

"Not at all," I said as our steps echoed against the floor. "You were right. Don't get me wrong. Some of the men had some seriously deluded ideas, but those delusions were not all-encompassing. They also had distinct personalities and lives. They had families, and they had vocations. They're human beings, like you or me, but they happen to have an illness. They aren't their diagnosis. They're so much more than that."

At that point I recognized how ingenious our faculty were. A typical program would have had me taking courses on psychopathology and diagnostic assessment before I ever saw a client, to the point that I would have been fixated on the illness, rather than the person. Days into my program I knew that the person was not their illness, a profoundly humanistic learning that stood me in good stead early in my career.

◆ ◆ ◆

In addition to the two days a week at the State Hospital, I attended classes and meetings, guarding my every word.

I worried: If I talk, they'll know. They'll figure it out.

I was ashamed of my history—all of it. The childhood fights, my father's abuse, running away, the expulsion, the arrests, the depression, the psychosis, the stay in a state institution, the addiction to cigarettes. I worried that, if I didn't carefully monitor everything I said, something would slip out.

At the end of each week, I briefly thought about driving to New York to see Caren. Yet I was so exhausted, and there was always a string of activities that needed my attention: Helping Joannie with the candle business, studying for a class, reading up on mental illness so I could better communicate with the men at the hospital, searching for a new apartment in a safer neighborhood.

It was all so time-consuming.

"Next weekend," I'd tell myself. "I'll go next weekend."

It wasn't until early winter, when Joannie and I moved to Somerville and a safer neighborhood, that I finally climbed into my microbus and set off for New York.

Guilt trailed me like my shadow. It had been so long. Why had I waited? Had I really been too busy? I imagined her jumping into my arms, excited to see me. I couldn't wait to hug her, throw her in the air, and play. I promised myself. I'd come more often. Nothing else would get in my way.

Nothing.

I drove around their block multiple times as I searched for a parking space. Groups of men congregated on the street corners, playing cards, checkers, and dominoes. Small children frolicked on the sidewalk. Teens sat together on curbs. Trash filled the gutter. The apartment buildings seemed shabby, long past their prime. Graffiti cautioned folks that "the streets belong to the people" and to "stop the bullshit."

Caren answered the door.

"Caren!" I exclaimed, excitedly, reaching my arms forward, bending my knees, and bracing for one of her wild running hugs.

"Hi," she said shyly, not making eye contact. "Would you like to come in?"

She was quite a bit taller.

Her round cheeks had narrowed. Her once babyish arms were now skinny. At age seven, she was no longer a child. She was blossoming into a preteen.

"Honey, you've grown so much! Wow! You've gotten so big!"

She stood quietly, politely, so reserved. So standoffish.

"Would you like me to show you the apartment?" she asked.

It was all so formal.

"Well, sure!" I said, perhaps a little too passionately.

I wanted to put her at ease, but how?

She walked backward a few feet and pointed to a small, decorated tree.

"Well, this is our Hanukkah bush," she said.

"And this is where we have our kitchen," she said, pointing to the small kitchenette.

On it went, her walking me from the kitchen to the bathroom to a small bedroom and back to the living area.

"That's where you'll be sleeping," she said, pointing to the small couch.

There was no warmth.

The sickening realization pressed in from all sides. It had been far too long. I'd blown it. She'd forgotten me. I might technically still be her father but, to her, I was no more than a stranger.

"Thanks for the tour, Caren. I need to get some smokes from the store," I told her. "I'll be right back."

Caren quietly walked me to the door, politely opened it, and ushered me through. Then she closed it behind me, locking it.

In the drab hallway, I stood motionless, my thoughts racing loops in my mind, tangling me in regret.

If I'd come sooner, everything would have been different.

Why hadn't I come sooner?

Barely aware of my surroundings, I shuffled down the hallway, down the stairs, and out into the street. I needed a smoke. I wasn't going to get through this without one.

Without a whole pack.

Maybe two.

As I emerged from the bodega, I noticed two men positioned oddly on the street, as if they were searching for prey. Were they walking toward me? Were they going to jump me?

I took off running.

Down the street.

Into their building.

Up the stairs.

Down the hall.

My heart pounding, I banged on their door.

"Everything okay?" Joyce asked.

"Yeah," I said, lowering my voice, quickly shutting and locking the door.

I glanced Caren's way. "Let's talk in the kitchen."

Joyce handed me a glass of water.

"Look, Joyce," I said. "I think these two guys just tried to jump me. I raced all the way back here."

"That's terrible!" she said. "Are you sure?"

"Why wouldn't I be sure?"

"Well, you know, you tend to suspect the worst in people. Remember when you thought the CIA was spying on you?"

"That's different. That's from before," I stammered, "before I got better. I'm sure of this."

"Why are you so sure?"

"It's how they were looking at me. They were both approaching me from different directions. You know the crime rate in Manhattan. All you see on the news are stories of people getting shot or bludgeoned to death. It's just not safe. This neighborhood isn't safe."

"What do you expect me to do?" she asked. "I'm a social worker, Ron. I'm a single mother. Do you think I can afford a penthouse on Park Avenue?"

"Of course not. I'm just saying that—"

She cut me off. "Look, it hasn't been the easiest for me since Steven died."

"I know Joyce. I was so sorry to hear about that. Cancer? It must have been hell for you."

"And Caren," she said. "It was hell for both of us. She'd grown quite fond of him."

"I see."

"I never intended to be here, in New York, single, trying to make rent on just my income. But that's how it is. That's where I am. I'm doing the best I can."

"I understand, but—"

She interrupted me again.

"You have no say, Ron," she said. "Where I live is my decision. Not yours. End of story."

Every couple of months after that, I drove to New York to see Caren, taking her to museums, the zoo, playgrounds, whatever I could come up with. Sometimes she was slightly warmer, but never like she'd been when I'd last seen her in California. No matter how hard I tried, I couldn't seem to break through. She remained distant, always on her best behavior, never relaxed or carefree.

"Just keep trying," Joannie told me.

"That's all I can do I guess," I said. "I just wish I'd been there. I wish I'd done more."

"You can't change the past," she said.

Joannie was right of course, but that didn't make things any easier to accept.

That January Joannie enrolled in Northeastern University's master's degree program in counseling. Like so many times before in my life, the relationship withered, with both of us focusing on our own things. A year later, after Joannie earned her degree, there was little left to keep her in Boston. We were cordial, but not in love. She returned to California.

◆ ◆ ◆

Jerome Miller, Massachusetts's commissioner of youth services, was in the process of closing the Institute for Juvenile Guidance. The effort was the culmination of several years of investigations that had led the Massachusetts Senate to declare the twenty-seven juvenile facilities that were spread throughout the state "a continuing nightmare."

Some of the children had done nothing wrong—other than having been born into unfortunate circumstances. Their parents had been deemed unfit, for example. Some of the children had been addicted to drugs. Others had intellectual or physical disabilities. Of the thousands who languished in these youth prisons, fewer than twenty had committed murder or manslaughter.

Yet the children had been treated like hardened criminals. Each evening before bed, the boys had to strip to nothing and allow a staff member to inspect their naked bodies. There were no toilets in their cells. Mattresses were soaked in urine and smeared with feces.

When the children misbehaved, they were locked in rooms in only their underpants. Or they were put in isolation cells. Or mechanically restrained. Over the years, staff have been accused of raping, even impregnating some of the children.

Miller faced a challenge. For one, what he was attempting to do had never been done before. At the time, every other state in the nation relied upon juvenile jails. On top of that, after serving time in these facilities, the children couldn't exactly be released back onto the streets. They needed to go somewhere where they could learn skills.

But where?

Harvard's CP³ program wanted to be a part of what would later be known as The Massachusetts Experiment. My advisor John Shlien founded the Robert W. White School, a private therapeutic day school for disturbed and delinquent adolescents, housed in the Lindemann Center.

I was tapped to serve as the assistant director.

We soon took in thirty formerly institutionalized students.

I sat with each student for an intake and assessment, asking question after question. Many were so childlike, with skinny arms, round cheeks, and high-pitched voices. Their appearance offered a shocking contrast to their past. One, Steven, fifteen, diagnosed with minimal brain disorder and severe personality disorder, mentioned that his father was in prison for murder. The authorities considered Steven very dangerous.

Another student, Dennis, thirteen, had been in and out of nineteen foster homes. His artificial eardrum and kneecap hinted at past violent encounters.

Alice, fourteen, always wore a wig covered by a hat—I knew not why—and long pants to conceal a sharpened screwdriver that she used to defend herself as needed.

Michael, age eleven, had wavy blond hair and blue eyes that made him seem angelic, yet a lit cigarette bobbed from the corner of his mouth as he spoke. He'd landed in reform school for stealing taxi cabs to collect the fares.

Tony, age sixteen, was considered to be an accomplished thief.

These children had all been through so much—too much. I couldn't believe someone had locked them away. I felt driven to help them.

After the intake, some of the students went to woodworking. Others went to learn how to play guitar. Still others went to try photography. None of them were forced to sit in typical classrooms with a teacher at the front, lecturing them. In fact, we didn't even force them to stay. They were able to come and go as they pleased.

We wanted to provide a destination that they wanted to go to—not one that they felt they had to go to. It was also a place where they felt empowered to make their own decisions—and not disempowered. Frankly, it was the opposite of everything they were used to.

The idea stemmed from Robert W. White's concept of competence motivation. If attaining competence was its own reward, students, we thought, would feel motivated not only to show up, but also to learn. With ten teacher-counselors for thirty students, class size was small enough to manage.

At least, that was the hope.

Within an hour, one kid called another kid a "mutha fuckah" and a fight erupted. Kids were screaming, punching, pushing, shoving, kicking, and tackling one another.

I didn't want to tackle or restrain any of them. They'd already been through enough of that. Instead, we gently pulled kids off one another, led them to our offices, and talked to them about what had transpired. Yet, an hour later, another fight erupted. It went on like this throughout the week.

During one of these encounters, someone messed with Alice's wig. She backed away from the student, then whipped out her screwdriver. A staff member talked her down.

Again, and again and again the fights erupted. I wondered if we could ever make an impact.

Near the end of the day, I stepped outside for a smoke. Some of the kids milled around in the parking lot, which doubled as the school's de facto playground.

I noticed Michael eyeing up a Dodge Challenger. At first, I thought nothing of it. He was into cars. Plus, I figured, he knew I was watching. What could he possibly try to do?

He looked back in my direction, smiled, and waved.

Then he stepped closer to the car.

His little body shimmied.

Before I could react, he was inside the car.

I strode over.

"Wanna see me hot wiah the caah?" he asked.

"No, I want to see you get out of the car," I said.

By the end of that week, several cars had gone missing. We couldn't prove what had happened, but the implications were clear. The center added a security guard to patrol the lot.

We organized a meeting.

"We'd like to set up some rules," I said.

Their bodies tensed.

"Here's the thing: These aren't going to be our rules, Dr. Shlien's or mine. They'll be your rules," I said.

"Whaddaya fucking mean by that? What the fuck ah 'owa' rules," asked Debbie. She had a mouth on her like I couldn't believe.

"Well," I said, "you all get to decide what the rules are going to be."

There were whispers and gasps.

"What's the catch?" asked Tony.

"There's no catch," I said. "We want to create a school that you want to come to. To want to come here, to enjoy yourself here, to feel safe here, what do you need?" I asked.

"Fewah fuckin' fights," said Alice. "And no one touchin' my wig!"

"I know," said Dennis. His bangs partially covered his eyes like a lowland sheepdog. As he talked, he slumped forward with a concave chest and rounded shoulders.

"We have too much muthah insulting around heah and it's causing a lot of fights," he continued with an eloquence that stunned me. "No one likes it when theah muthah is insulted. So why don't we all agree to not do it?"

The kids were quiet for a minute as they mulled over the suggestion.

"Okay, everyone, how about we put Dennis's suggestion to a vote? Everyone in favor of the No Mother Insulting Rule, raise your hand."

To my shock, every single hand went up.

◆ ◆ ◆

A state senator came to tour the building.

As he walked through a common area, I noticed Debbie milling about in the room.

I cringed, knowing what was coming.

"What's that muthah fuckah doin' heah?" she asked.

I could feel the staff members tense up, but the senator didn't react.

Had he not heard what she'd said?

The next day, we got our answer. John Shlien, Gerald Klerman, the superintendent of the Erich Lindemann Mental Health Center, and Milton Greenblatt, the commissioner of the Massachusetts Department of Mental Health, were called before a Senate hearing to answer heated questions.

The senator asked, "What are these kids doing in this nice new facility?"

It was as if he thought they were too poor and too wrong for his nice new government complex.

"These are disturbed children that your commissioner of youth services released to the community to an alternative placement," Dr. Shlien calmly explained. "We are duly certified by the commonwealth. We are providing therapeutic education to help them learn how to live constructive lives. What's wrong with that, Senator?"

He had no answer.

That was the last we heard from him.

◆ ◆ ◆

As the year unfolded, it became increasingly clear that the White School was making an impact.

For example, when Tony heard that the school was undergoing a temporary financial crisis, he came in with some medical equipment that he had stolen from a community clinic. We accepted his desire to help but told him that we could not accept stolen property. He returned the equipment to the clinic with an apology. This was his first experience of returning something that he had stolen.

The other kids had also transformed. It was truly amazing to see it.

The kids wanted to come to school, wanted to go to class, and wanted to learn. This was even true of foul-mouthed Debbie—whose school records had given her the notorious title of "the worst school phobic in East Boston." She turned up every morning, on time, sometimes even early. Alice's screwdriver remained out of view.

Steven was coming out of his shell. The kids were learning, growing, and thriving. It was wonderful to see.

On top of that, we weren't only welcoming the kids, but we'd also opened the doors to their parents. In this way, we hoped to uplift an entire community, teaching these folks skills that allowed them to break free from poverty. It was clear: people had the tools to solve their own problems. Once psychologists like me believed in them, they found the confidence to believe in themselves.

The school was no longer a social experiment.

We'd proven our approach.

My dissertation evaluated the effects of the school on its students, focusing on their *re-engagement in the process of learning*. Remember, these children had been out of school for quite some time. We measured three stages in this process:

1. Coming to school
2. Going to classes
3. Engaging in productive work in class

The rate of improvement was high for the first step (87.5 percent), and moderate for the second (62.5 percent) and third (58.3 percent) steps.

We also weren't an anomaly. The positive changes were taking place in community-based therapeutic educational settings all over Massachusetts. Juvenile recidivism dropped by half, falling far below the rate in other states that still relied on so-called reform schools. As a result, other states began adopting the Massachusetts approach.

As I thought about it all, I couldn't help but wonder how my childhood could have been different. My mother had always believed in me. That was true, and I was thankful for that. Yet, what might have happened if my dad hadn't been abusive? If I hadn't lived in an antisemitic neighborhood? Would I have engaged in so many delinquent acts? Had so many problems with alcohol? Gotten expelled from high school? Gotten arrested? Would I have messed up my marriage? Become so incredibly depressed? Lost touch with my daughter?

I would never know.

One thing was clear. My past allowed me to connect with the kids. I understood their pain, their rage, their desire to lash out. I saw myself in them.

I'd grown especially close to Billy, a tall sixteen-year-old with a wave of blond hair that partially covered his right eye. Several times a week, he and I had chatted in therapy about his upbringing and life experiences. He'd been through so much—way too much.

I felt like I was breaking through, truly helping him.

I yearned to have the same relationship quality with Caren.

◆ ◆ ◆

That summer Caren traveled up on the train and stayed with me for several months.

Given the White School was closed for the summer, I had a lot of time to focus on her.

In the evenings, she'd go to bed around eight or nine. I'd then start writing my dissertation about what we'd learned at the White school, often staying up until four in the morning.

Before going to bed, I'd leave her a kid-friendly set of instructions and fun activities. She'd wake to word searches and hangman games, along with a to-do list of how to get her breakfast. That allowed me to sleep until ten. Once I woke, we'd spend the day together, which often involved me taking her to arts and crafts activities.

As each day progressed, she seemed to relax. The coldness seemed to be melting. We were finally growing closer, like we had once been, years before.

Maybe, just maybe, she and I would resemble a typical father and daughter.

◆ ◆ ◆

Early that fall, someone knocked on my office door.

It was time for my appointment with Billy.

Without asking, I opened the door.

Billy shoved me several feet backward. We tumbled into my desk. Pens and books thudded against the walls and floor.

"I'm going to kill you!"

I raised my forearms to block his punches. I didn't want to fight back. I didn't want to touch him.

He climbed on top of me.

He was bigger than I was.

He was trying to kill me.

The desk screeched as it slid sideways.

My body flew into the wall.

I didn't want to hurt him.

"What's going on?" Counselors poured into the room. Someone pulled him off me. Someone else led Billy away.

Papers littered the floor. Books were everywhere. A framed photo of myself and Caren was on the floor, the glass shattered.

Later, I called his psychiatrist, who surmised that Billy had attacked me because of what he called "homosexual panic." This is an older diagnostic formulation, based on the idea of rigid gender roles. Boys were expected to avoid feminine emotions, and they certainly should not feel close to another male. Billy had been starting to feel close to me, a man, and he couldn't tolerate it. In his world, men weren't supposed to feel emotionally close to other men. He'd grown up in a society that had taught him: real men were straight. They were masculine, and they didn't feel.

I had to stop counseling him, and it saddened me.

Soon after, I was promoted to director.

◆ ◆ ◆

Meanwhile I was still in grad school, taking courses. One of the courses that I took was Psychological Assessment. As part of that course, we were paired off and required to administer various psychological tests to each other, including two I.Q. tests: The Stanford Binet and the Wechsler Adult Intelligence Scale (WAIS). I scored 147+ on the Stanford Binet, and 140 on the Wechsler, both in the gifted range. I always knew I was smart, and my LACC instructors could see it as well, but here was definitive proof. It is said that with an IQ score of 120 one can navigate any obstacle that society throws up for advancement.

During my years at Harvard, I attended Grand Rounds after Grand Rounds, soaking up as much of Boston's psychiatric life as I could. In one of them, psychologist Joseph Cautela explained how someone could use the power of their imagination to overcome a range of mental health issues, including addictions. He called it "covert sensitization." In his original article from 1967, Cautela described the technique as useful for the "treatment of alcoholism, obesity, homosexuality, and delinquent behavior." Of course, that was seven years before the American Psychiatric Association removed homosexuality from its *Diagnostic and Statistical Manual for Mental Disorders*. We would now say that this technique works on things that can be changed (addictions) and not on things that are innate (sexual orientation, gender identity).

In therapy, Cautela asked alcoholics to imagine themselves with a drink in their hands. As soon as the drink touched their lips, however, they visualized themselves feeling sick and then violently vomiting. They were told to imagine it so vividly that they felt nauseated. Then, they imagined themselves turning away from the alcohol and gradually feeling better. When practiced consistently, the technique led to impressive results. Only two out of every seven people who tried it resumed drinking over six months, compared to three out of every four alcoholics who weren't taught the technique.

As I listened, I grew excited. I felt ashamed of myself for smoking. Clinical psychologists weren't supposed to be addicts! But now I had a possible solution. I could use covert sensitization to quit smoking!

I got started that weekend. Whenever I got the urge to smoke, I logged in the time. Then I visualized a series of increasingly distressing images: the smell and look of a full ashtray, coughing up brown phlegm in the morning, an X ray of a diseased lung, a movie I'd seen of cancer patients smoking though their tracheostomy tubes, and my own funeral. Once the urge passed, I rewarded myself by visualizing pleasant scenes: listening to music, having a steak dinner, having great sex, enjoying a vacation, and growing old surrounded by family.

That first day, the urge to smoke struck roughly every five minutes.

By the end of the weekend, it was every seven.

Within about two weeks, I had no urges at all.

That was great, and I was absolutely delighted! I had overcome my addiction to nicotine. But there was an interesting twist. At that time there were great debates between psychoanalysts—like most of my supervisors—and behaviorists like Cautela. The behaviorists argued that psychoanalysis failed at symptom relief. The psychoanalysts retorted that behavioral techniques might remove symptoms, but they did nothing to change the unconscious mind. In my case, the psychoanalysts were right. Although I had completely lost the urge to smoke tobacco (for which I remain eternally grateful), in my dreams I was a smoker—for at least a decade.

Finally, at the risk of getting too far ahead of my story, I will note that after I quit smoking, I resumed my participation in athletics and outdoor activities, which had been on hold since high school. I resumed running in 1972. At first, I could only make it for one city block, but I gradually extended that. At my peak I ran sixty or more miles a week. Following an interval training protocol, I systematically varied the length of my runs as follows: five, ten, five, ten, five, ten and then a long run on Sunday, from fifteen up to twenty miles. I ran in several half marathons and attempted one full marathon (the 1978 NYC Marathon) but made it only twenty-three miles. As I continued running, I began to experience knee problems and was advised to pick another sport. The orthopedist pointed to the x-ray, and said "You have two choices, run now or walk later." So, I took up cycling and eventually completed five centuries (one-hundred-mile rides), two of which were back-to-back (the Pan Mass Challenge of 1992, two hundred miles over two days.).

I also skied cross-country locally and backpacked in the White and Green Mountains of NH and VT. The most memorable backpacking trip though was a five-day hike starting in the Hermit Creek wilderness section of the Grand Canyon. This trip was led by a psychologist, Larry Morris, who had also written a book on hiking in the Grand Canyon. Our plan was to descend to the Colorado River and hike along the Tonto Trail (a flat trail that runs about 1000 feet above the Colorado River) to the Bright Angel trial and then ascend to the South Rim on our last day. As we were making camp the night before the ascension, a hiker approached our camp, who had only trekking poles and a water pack. He was a trail runner and he stopped to chat. He had started that morning at the place where we had started five days earlier! He asked if were from here, and Larry, whose hair was completely white, said no but that he had relocated there some time before, to which the trekker asked, "What for, retirement?" We all groaned. He had to rub it in.

◆ ◆ ◆

Things felt off as soon as Caren, now nine years old, emerged from the train at South Station.

I reached my arms out to hug her, but she retreated. She didn't seem to want to be touched.

"How was the trip?"

"Okay," she said.

"Just okay?"

"Yes."

"I'm so happy to see you!"

"Yeah, okay," she replied.

"We're going to have such a fun weekend together!"

"Whatever."

It was as if she'd been forced to come, as if she didn't want to be here.

Why couldn't I break out of this cycle?

Why couldn't we move on?

The kids at the White School had bloomed under our direction and guidance. Yet my relationship with my own daughter seemed eternally fraught.

Why couldn't she accept me? I knew I'd screwed up in the past. I got that. But how long would it take before I'd made up for it?

A simmering anger bubbled in my cells, tensing my muscles.

During the ride back to the apartment, I continually tried to start a conversation, yet her answers never expanded beyond one word.

Good.

Okay.

Uh-huh.

Fine.

Yes.

No.

As we walked into my apartment, I asked if I could get her something to drink or eat. That's what my mother always did to warm me over. Maybe it would work with Caren?

We sat at the table as Caren sipped her orange juice.

Her hand held the glass so casually, as if it were a wadded-up piece of paper that she was about to drop into a trash can.

"Honey," I said, "You need to hold onto the glass. You're going to drop it and spill it."

"No, I won't!" she replied. "Jeez."

She was pouty, irritated.

I needed to back off. The White School kids had taught me that. She needed to find her own way. She needed autonomy.

Still, why did she have to be so difficult? Why couldn't this be easier? Why did things have to be so hard?

Dejected, I looked away. Maybe I'd never break through. Maybe it was hopeless. Maybe it would always be like this.

There was a crash.

Orange juice poured over the table and dripped onto the floor. Shards of glass were everywhere.

The rage felt like a storm-churned ocean powering its way through a floodwall.

"I told you!" I screamed. "I fucking told you!"

Her reaction seemed delayed, almost in slow motion, as if she'd been expecting this.

As if she no longer cared.

As if she'd grown numb to it all.

My face burned.

The urge to destroy surged through my chest and down my arms.

"You're cleaning this mess up! I told you and you refused to fucking listen. I can't believe this!"

"Sorry," she whispered, refusing to make eye contact.

She was quiet, sullen, resigned to her fate.

I hurled a roll of paper towels at her.

"Clean it up!"

I had to get away from her; I didn't trust myself.

My hands on my head, I strode from the room, in a circle, and then back to the kitchen.

"You're going to have to go home! I'm calling your mother."

The rage clung to me as I checked the train schedule. It was there as I called Joyce. It was there as I returned to the kitchen and told Caren to pack up her things. It followed us into the car, to the train station, and onto the platform. It wasn't until the train pulled away from the station that I realized what I'd done and who I'd become.

I was him.

I was my father.

I'd thrown paper towels; He'd thrown a radio.

I deserved to have a daughter who hated me.

TAKEAWAYS

The first lesson is: when life gives you lemons, make lemonade. In other words, use what you have, even if you do not immediately recognize its value, or much worse, even if you feel ashamed of it. I was able to draw on my experiences as a juvenile delinquent to establish empathic and compassionate relationships with the students at the Robert White School, who were in fact adjudicated delinquents. Readers, have you had this experience of making something good and valuable out of something that you had felt not so good about? What helped you to do that?

The second lesson is: trauma leaves a deep well of rage. A qualitative study found that unresolved trauma from childhood was closely linked to current levels of adult rage[5]. Here I was again, unleashing my rage, this time at my daughter. Admittedly she was uncommunicative, or more truthfully, she was highly communicative—letting me know that she did not want to be with me. And I was my father. Just like him, who felt neglected when my mother paid attention to me, I felt rejected when Caren was so transparently cold. And just like him, I reacted with rage.

---

5 McKay MT, Cannon M, Chambers D, Conroy RM, Coughlan H, Dodd P, Healy C, O'Donnell L, Clarke MC. Childhood trauma and adult mental disorder: A systematic review and meta-analysis of longitudinal cohort studies. Acta Psychiatr Scand. 2021 Mar;143(3):189-205. doi: 10.1111/acps.13268. Epub 2021 Jan 18. PMID: 33315268.

CHAPTER 11

My First Professorship

(1974–1983)

After I earned my doctorate at the end of November in 1973, I needed a postdoctoral year of supervised clinical experience to qualify for licensure as a psychologist. I took a position as a treatment team leader at the Human Resources Institute (HRI) in Brookline, MA, a private psychiatric hospital.

I managed a team of five therapists who cared for ten to fifteen patients. To make extra money, I moonlighted in the outpatient department (OPD), providing psychotherapy to former inpatients. That's where I met Evan Longin, a large man with long hair and a full beard. Also serving as a treatment team leader, Evan had recently graduated from Boston University's doctoral program in counseling psychology. In the OPD, I also became friendly with Carol Beaudoin, who had moved from Florida to Massachusetts for her doctoral work. She was completing her dissertation on suicide in Boston University's counseling psych program using data from HRI patient records.

She was blond and slender, and I felt drawn to her. I asked her to dinner, then a movie. The sex came soon after, and it was amazing. We began dating, which quickly slipped into the serious relationship phase. I fell head over heels in love with her. I couldn't stop thinking about her. I couldn't wait to see her. I was obsessed.

There was one problem: Carol was still involved—no, entangled is a better word—with a former boyfriend, Jay, who was a psychiatrist. It had been a complicated—kind of "sticky"—breakup. She would end the relationship. Then he'd show up, they'd have a fling, and he'd be gone again. I wished he would drop off the face of the earth.

It felt as if I kept repeating the same pattern. Carrie, my high school sweetheart, had maintained a relationship with an old boyfriend. I believed that Joyce, my first wife, had been cheating on me. Phyllis, my girlfriend from my hippie days, also stepped out on me.

I felt stuck in a cycle that I couldn't seem to break.

◆ ◆ ◆

The year flew by, during which I was also looking for academic jobs.

John Silber had been president of Boston University for several years, and he had a vision. He wanted to transform BU from a sleepy commuter school into a renowned research institution that rivaled Harvard and MIT. To turn this into a reality, he needed more faculty, especially in the physical sciences and medicine.

Thanks to my time at HRI, I knew several BU students and grads, including Carol and Evan. Those connections, coupled with my experiences in family therapy at the White School helped me secure a tenure-track position in the Counseling Program. When BU offered me the job, I felt blessed and privileged. The position allowed me to remain on the East Coast and close to Caren.

That first semester, however, was a baptism by fire.

Family therapy had gained tremendous popularity, and there was enormous pent-up demand for training opportunities. As a result, ninety students enrolled in my family therapy course, making it nine times larger than the typical doctoral-level course. Furthermore, many counseling students had returned to school after working in the field for years with a master's degree. As a result, they were older and potentially more experienced than I was. At times, I wondered whether they were the ones who should be teaching the course. Over time, I gradually got better at it. Still, the weekly three-hour sessions left me drained.

Soon after the semester started, President Silber asked all of BU's psychology professors to meet with him in a large conference room. There were a lot of us, from colleges of arts and sciences, education, medicine, social work, and divinity.

"Do you know why we're here? It looks like every psychologist at BU is here," asked the psychologist next to me.

About fifty of us sat at desks, awaiting Silber's arrival.

"Not a clue," I said.

"I've heard folks either love him or hate him," the professor whispered.

When Silber walked in, I couldn't help but notice his right arm. It was stub-like, a congenital disability that stemmed from his mother's use of the drug thalidomide during her pregnancy.

"You're probably all wondering why I asked you here," Silber said, pointing with his congenitally shortened arm. "Well, I'll tell you. You've all made a terrible mistake."

What was he talking about? He seemed so sure of himself, belligerent, as if he couldn't wait for someone to debate his reasoning. I glanced around the room. Everyone looked as puzzled as I was.

"YouknowwhatImean," he said, his words jumbled so closely together that I had to slow them down in my mind and spread them out to get his meaning. "I am talking about when you split from philosophy in the nineteenth century. You say you are evidence-based, but the vast majority of papers I see coming out of psychology are pure rubbish. I tell you, they're barely worth the paper they're written on. And you liberals . . . Your skin is so thin. You should welcome criticism. Stop falling in love with your views! Welcome pushback and deep thought—or else stop calling yourself intellectuals!"

He pontificated on like this for nearly a half hour. It seemed he was still miffed from something that had happened in the late

19th century when a German psychologist had agitated to break psychology free from the discipline of philosophy.

It was now 1975. What did he expect us to do about it? We weren't even alive in the late 19th century. Why was he telling us this?

"I am going to address the problem you caused," he said, his brow furrowed. "I hired Sigmund Koch as a university professor, and he is going to write books that expose psychology as epistemopathy, with the aim of performing an epistectomy."

Translation: he thought of us as illegitimate and wanted to prove it to us. His furor over it all didn't make sense. It wasn't as if philosophers ever walked into a state mental hospital and offered to help the patients heal. Clearly, the two disciplines were distinct.

What was wrong with this guy?

As I walked back to my office, I didn't know what to do with what had transpired. I'd accepted the job. I was here. I didn't want to leave. So, I did my best to put it all out of my mind.

◆ ◆ ◆

To eventually earn tenure, I needed to do more than teach. I had to publish, so I concentrated on setting up my lab to conduct research while also writing a graduate-level family therapy textbook. I read every paper I could find, explored every theory, and traveled to workshops every chance I could get. Of all the family therapy approaches, one made more sense to me than the others. Developed by the psychiatrist Murray Bowen, Bowenian Family Therapy looked at patterns that persist in families, sometimes over many generations.

When I learned that two of Bowen's disciples were running an institute, The Center for Family Learning, in New Rochelle, NY, just a few hours away, I was on it. I listened intently as Phil Guerin and Tom Fogarty interviewed a family, on stage, in front of a large audience of therapists of all stripes, showing us how to use Bowen techniques in a live therapy session.

"You see, the less differentiated a person's self, the more they try to control the people around them," Guerin said.

I leaned back in my seat. Was that why my father had controlled every aspect of his home life?

"Your experiences during childhood and adolescence determine your level of differentiation of self," he continued. "When someone has a well-differentiated self, they recognize their dependence on others, yet they can stay calm and clear-headed, even in the face of conflict, criticism, and rejection."

If I didn't work on differentiating myself—on becoming a mature adult—was I destined to become just like him?

Toward the end of the session, the trainers encouraged us to apply the Bowen Theory to our own lives.

Several months later, when I flew home for a family visit, I decided to try it. During the flight, I imagined how my father would likely needle me. He'd tell me I was doing something incorrectly. That was a given. He'd micromanage everything I did—also a given.

My job wasn't to change my father.

It was to change my reaction to him.

When I walked in, I hugged my mother and kissed her. My father shook my hand.

As I entered the dining room, he sneered, "Hey, get those bags you left in the foyer. Go put them in the bedroom right now."

He sure hadn't changed. It was as if he still saw me as a boy. Would he talk to another grownup like that?

"Sure thing, Dad," I said, forcing myself to sound chipper.

On it went, him correcting and belittling me at every turn. It didn't matter what I did. In his eyes, it was wrong.

Later that evening, around 10 p.m., they both went to bed, as they always did.

I pulled out some work, looking forward to many hours that didn't include him.

"Turn off that goddamned light!"

Really? Try shutting your fucking door, asshole! Why did he

have to be such a fucking bully?

Rage seeping from my pores, I flipped off the light but refused to sleep. There was no way I'd give him that.

For the rest of the visit, I refused to give him the satisfaction of an easy conversation. No matter what he asked or said, I responded with monosyllable words. Yes. No. Right.

By the end of the visit, I felt that I had regressed back to my old teenage self.

On the plane ride home, I dissected everything, trying to understand better where I'd gone wrong. In the evenings, I could have been more proactive. Instead of simmering in monosyllabic rage, I could have said, "Dad, I'm not going to go to bed right away. I've got some work to do. I will not make any noise, and I'll shut my door, but the light will be on." Next time, I promised myself—next time.

◆ ◆ ◆

Gary was rambling.

"Wait, who's listening in on our call?" I asked.

"I told you," he whispered, so softly I could barely hear, "Skeeter."

"I'm sorry. I think I should know this. Who is Skeeter?"

"Ron, keep your voice down. She's listening."

Why would keeping my voice down even matter? We were on the phone. Even if Skeeter was listening, talking quietly would mean Gary couldn't hear me either.

"Okay," I said more softly. "Who is Skeeter?"

"My girlfriend. My ex-girlfriend. She's been following me, spying on me."

"How so?"

"It's like she can hear my thoughts."

I leaned into my forearm against the kitchen wall. I'd heard rumblings. Now a pediatrician, Gary canceled patient appointments at the last minute. Sometimes, he didn't show up for work for hours.

Nancy had divorced him several years before because he often didn't come home. At the time, their daughter was only three. Nancy still loved Gary, but his behavior bewildered her. She didn't know what else to do.

"How do you know that?" I whispered.

"She just can," he said.

I couldn't argue with his paranoia. If I pushed too hard, telling him that no one was listening, he'd see me as one of the enemies.

"Okay, I said, let's say she can. Let's say she's listening right now. Is that bad? She loves you, right?"

"Well," he said, "she used to."

He'd always been there for me.

Yet I was in Massachusetts. He was in California. As an assistant professor, I still barely made enough money to fly home once or twice a year to visit my parents. Gosh, why hadn't I looked Gary up during my last visit?

"What do you think changed?" I asked.

"She doesn't understand me. No one does."

"What makes you think that?" I asked.

"Do you hear that?" he asked.

"Hear what?"

"That click?"

"Um, I don't think so."

"You didn't hear it? How could you not have heard it?"

"I just—"

"Ron, come on, man. Are you lying to me? You must have heard it?"

"I . . ."

"Forget it. I gotta go."

"Gary, I care about you, man. Come on. Let's talk."

"No, man. I gotta go. Bye."

The next sound was the dial tone.

◆ ◆ ◆

Yet again, I found myself disembarking from a plane at LAX, renting a car, and driving north to Oxnard, praying that I'd be able to manage the visit without blowing up.

In addition to trying to remain mature, I planned to use another strategy straight out of Bowen Theory: detriangulation.

Bowen theorized that families with low differentiation formed triangles in which two people (often parents) deal with conflicts in their relationship through their disparate treatment of a third party, usually a child. For example, one parent might be very strict with the child, meeting out punishments for minor infractions, whereas the other parent might be permissive and indulgent.

Looking back on it all, I could see the dynamic clearly. My mother doted. My father was ultrastrict. It had been present since I'd come into the picture. My father had been on a ship at sea during the war. When he arrived home for shore leave, he was no longer the main attraction in my mother's life. She now had an infant to care for—and he didn't like that. She'd loved him. Of course, she had. If only he could have seen that. If only he would have talked to her about it. That might have cleared things up.

Instead, he resented me. To be fair, it is not uncommon for expectant fathers to resent their unborn child in cases where their wives are too uncomfortable due to the pregnancy to have sex. Even more to the point, it is not uncommon for new fathers to be jealous of their newborn infant, because their wives' attention is focused on them. But this seemed different, not only in degree, but also in kind.

But it all made sense in a weird sort of way. He zeroed in on my faults because he wanted to prove to her and himself that he was better, more worthy of her attention.

Of course, that wasn't all that was wrong with him. He had other issues. His skin was extraordinarily thin. He had obsessive-compulsive traits. And he definitely met the diagnostic criteria for intermittent explosive disorder. It took so little for his resentment to ignite into full-blown rage. But I wasn't here to diagnose and treat him. I merely wanted to find a way to visit without losing my mind.

Figuring out how to interrupt this dynamic wasn't difficult. As soon as my mother doted on me—and she always did—I would redirect her attention to my father.

That was the intention, anyway.

As I pulled into the driveway, I felt a strange mixture of anxiety and anticipation. I wanted this to work. Yet I braced myself, nonetheless. I was used to things not working out with him.

As usual, we exchanged pleasantries in the foyer. To avoid triggering him, I brought my bags straight to my room. Then I headed to the kitchen. I was hungry.

I stood, fridge open, examining the contents when I heard my mother.

"Honey, what do you want? Can I make you something to eat?"

"No, Mom," I said, "I've got this. I can make something for myself."

"Don't be silly, Ronnie," she said, gently pushing me away from the fridge. "There's left-over meatloaf. Or I could make you a sandwich?"

My father's impatience filled the room. If this went on for much longer, the complaints would start. He'd tell her to leave me alone or that I could take care of myself. Or he'd zero in on something I was doing wrong, perhaps getting a crumb on the table.

Yet my mother wouldn't stop fussing, so I changed tactics.

"Mom," I said, "You know, I'm not hungry. Maybe Dad is. Why don't you see if he'd like a sandwich?"

It was a lie. I was hungry. Yet, it was a small price to pay. I'd live.

She turned toward my father. "Would you like something, honey? How about a salami sandwich? That's your favorite, I know."

The irritation evaporated. His body relaxed. Was that a smile?

He sat at the table with me.

"So, Ronnie," he said, "How's Boston?"

◆ ◆ ◆

According to my old medical school buddies, Gary was doing poorly.

"Someone caught him injecting drugs," Marty said.

"Where? What?"

I wanted to believe that it was no big deal—that it was the cops overreacting. Gary had been the stable one—the person who'd helped me.

"In his car," Marty said. "He was in the driver's seat of his car, a needle in his arm, and a cop saw him."

"Fuck!" I said. "Still, I don't understand. He wasn't doing heroin, was he?"

"No, apparently, it was a synthetic pain killer. Talwin. Ever heard of that?"

"Talwin? Are you sure?"

"Yes," Marty went on. "It sounds like they're going to take his medical license away."

"Fuck! Fuck!"

"I know."

The silence was uncomfortable. Neither of us could find a way to fill it.

Finally, I said, "What can we do?"

"I don't know what we can do," said Marty. "He's an addict, you know?"

"I do, but he was always there for me. He probably saved my life. You both did. I owe him."

"He needs to reach out. You can't help him if he doesn't want to be helped. You were different. You knew you needed help. He's not at the point where he thinks he has a problem."

"I see," I said.

What else was there to say? I'd likely been with Gary the first time he'd shot up. Hell, we'd done it together. Why had he gotten addicted, and I hadn't? It seemed like such a nothing drug. All it had done was create some pleasant tickling sensations in my throat.

It was all so sad.

◆ ◆ ◆

By the time Caren and I pulled into the parking lot at the Stowe ski resort, we were worn out from arguing.

How had the fight started? I kept rewinding and watching the conversation in my mind.

I'd picked her up at the airport. I'd hugged her, but she'd remained limp, her arms at her sides.

She hadn't hugged back.

I'd tried to ignore it. She was a teenager—thirteen now. Teenagers were tricky. Plus, she'd just gotten off a plane. She'd warm up. She usually did.

We'd walked to the car, and I'd started driving north.

Along the way, I continually tried to start a conversation, to make her smile, to cheer her up.

Yet she fought me at every turn, emitting snide comebacks rather than engaging.

Finally, I asked, "You sound like you're angry with me. Would you like to tell me about it?"

That question had lit a match.

She'd told me I reminded her of Archie Bunker.

I'd asked, "The bigot from *All in the Family*?"

She'd said, "Yes."

I pushed back. If anything, I was like Michael, the son-in-law who Archie repeatedly referred to as "Meathead." Archie? He was my father—not me.

I'd said all of this—and she'd disagreed.

We'd debated the topic until we'd become too tired to argue.

All I could gather: she didn't like Archie Bunker, and she also didn't like me.

We headed to the slopes. I'd never skied downhill, only cross-country, so I signed up for a lesson. Caren had been skiing for years, so I suggested she go on without me for a while.

By the end of the lesson, another man challenged me to try the Black Diamond trail. Never one to back down from a chance to prove myself, I agreed.

Soon I was on the lift, not completely understanding what I'd just gotten myself into. The man and I set off down the slope, with Caren just behind us.

Within seconds, I knew I was in trouble. I couldn't slow down. Nor could I steer. I kept picking up speed, and I was headed straight for a cliff.

Frantically, I tried to do the snowplow maneuver they'd taught me, but it wasn't working.

This is the end, I thought. *I wish Caren didn't have to see this.*

I felt a whoosh, almost like wind.

Then I saw a flash of purple—Caren's snowsuit.

She was inches from me, so close that the fabric from her coat made a zipping sound against mine.

Then she was slightly ahead, pressing the sides of her skis into mine, nudging me away from the cliff and back toward the slope.

As the bottom of the hill came into view, I felt enormous relief.

When I finally came to a stop, I hugged her. I didn't care if she hugged back. I was so proud of her. She was so skillful, a true ski pro.

She likely saved my life.

♦ ♦ ♦

By 1978, I was three years into my time at BU. One day, Norine Johnson, a pediatric neuropsychologist, gave me a call.

"Hi Ron," she said. "You don't know me, but I'm familiar with your work. I'm the chair of the Board of Professional Affairs for the Massachusetts Psychological Association and I'm looking for another psychologist to serve on our board. Do you have any interest in serving in a leadership role?"

Did I have any interest? Of course, I did! I'd soon be up for tenure. Serving in a leadership role could only help my cause. Plus, it would allow me to connect with other psychologists, helping me to keep my research in the spotlight.

"Absolutely," I said.

Soon she introduced me to Lane Conn, another psychologist, and the three of us started working together to develop a white paper on the two-class system of psychology in the Commonwealth of Massachusetts. To be called a psychologist in the private sector you needed to be licensed, for which you had to have a doctoral degree, whereas in the public sector, all you needed was a master's degree. This was a common problem in many states at the time, which we tried to address with our white paper.

The experience hooked me on organized psychology, helping me to see that a group of psychologists working together could influence policy and legislation to enhance the practice of psychology and services to the public. As time went on, I became more and more involved.

◆ ◆ ◆

Carol and I were still dating, and I was still drawn to her. I couldn't get enough of her. I thought about her all the time.

Still, I couldn't muster the courage to pop the question. Things hadn't worked out with Joyce. Heck, they hadn't worked out with most of the women in my life. Plus, there was Carol's messy breakup with Jay. It had left me feeling insecure, as if I was crazier about her than she was about me.

I didn't want to get married again, only for it to fail.

Instead, I bought a 1294-square-foot three-bedroom home in Cambridge near Fresh Pond for $48,000.

This was big step for me, solidifying my status as an established adult, something that had been a long time coming.

Soon after, Carol moved in. Soon after that, Carol mentioned that her period was late. I hovered steps away as she used a home pregnancy test. Sure enough, human chorionic gonadotropin was detected. The test strip turned pink. She was pregnant.

Neither one of us welcomed the news. Carol didn't feel emotionally ready to become a mother. I was still proving myself at BU and had a way to go before applying for tenure. BU's President Silber had already denied tenure to several senior psychologists, making me wonder if it was possible for someone like me to earn tenure at BU. Were I not to earn tenure, I might have to find a job somewhere else—perhaps several states away. Would Carol drop her thriving practice to join me? That wasn't a given. I had missed several critical years of Caren's upbringing, and my absence seemed to have affected her deeply and perhaps permanently. I didn't want to do that to another child.

Thankfully, Carol and I were able to discuss this calmly and thoroughly. We agreed to have an abortion. It was an in-clinic procedure, and not a very big deal from a medical point of view. However, Carol did have some regrets afterwards, but we worked our way through those, with me providing emotional support.

◆ ◆ ◆

Three years later, as 1981 dawned, dating was starting to seem silly. We'd been together for seven years. Surely marriage was justified. Surely, we were right for each other.

Still, something nagged at me. I couldn't begin to describe it. Deep in my gut, I felt I was making the wrong decision. I told myself that it was just jitters. My previous divorce had left me insecure. It wasn't that Joyce and I had parted badly. As far as divorces go, it had mostly been amicable. The divorce had irrevocably changed my relationship with Caren. Had Joyce and I somehow found a way to stay together, she and Caren likely wouldn't have moved to the other side of the country. Caren and I would still have been close. Things wouldn't have been so tense between us.

That's, at least, what I wanted to believe.

I loved Carol, but I worried about repeating the same pattern. What if she and I had a child together? What if things didn't work out? Would I have brought another child into the world only to become partially estranged? I couldn't face that possibility. I couldn't go through it again.

Partially to help myself get past this sticking point and partially because I'd wanted to do it since grad school, I signed up for intensive psychoanalysis. The three 50-minute weekly sessions cost $100 a piece, and insurance only covered ten sessions total per year. During each session, my therapist asked me to free associate, helping me to glean insights from my unconscious mind and helping me to understand my more perplexing behavior.

Ivan Boszormenyi-Nagy, an important family therapist, had theorized that trauma may leave the survivor with a sense of "destructive entitlement," which roughly translates as "the world has to pay me back for what I have suffered." As one session blended into another, I began to see how I embodied this tendency. I was seriously pissed off—at my father, at antisemitism, at so many goddamned things. Parents are supposed to champion their children, to love them, to mentor them. My father had done none of that. He'd constantly made me feel like I wasn't good enough.

Now this hurt traveled with me. When it congealed into rage, I lashed out— as I had at Joyce. Destructive entitlement animated my behavior when I'd become enraged at Caren for spilling her orange juice.

After several months of analysis, I finally asked Carol to marry me.

The nagging feeling, however, refused to abate, despite the therapy.

I figured that, eventually, I'd get past it.

Yet it dogged me as we planned the wedding.

It was there as we drove to Belmont for the ceremony.

It remained with me as I looked around, seeing Carol, the rabbi, and Carol's parents.

Everyone seemed so happy.

The uncomfortable feeling swirled and grew, making itself impossible to contain.

Just before the vows, the rabbi noticed my watery eyes.

"Oh, look at those tears of joy," he said.

I forced a smile.

The tears, however, were anything but joyful.

I couldn't explain it. Yet, deep in my bones, I knew the truth.

This was a decision that I would live to regret.

◆ ◆ ◆

That fall, Caren enrolled in Boston University as a first-year student.

I couldn't believe how quickly she'd grown up. Caren had blossomed in high school, graduating in three years instead of the typical four. She was also an athlete, making the girls' swim team. I was so proud of her and happy that I could play an important role in her next phase of life.

I'd worked some connections to help her get her into one of the nicer dorms. It was more of a semiapartment than the typical dormitory with bathrooms in the hall.

Several times a week, she stopped by my office. Each time, the conversation followed a familiar pattern. I'd ask how she was, how her classes were going, and how things were going with her roommates. The answers were always the same: "good" or "okay." Eventually, I'd run out of questions, the space between us would become heavy with awkwardness, and she'd say, "Well, I should be going."

I yearned for an easy relationship in which the conversation flowed easily, where everything felt warm and comfortable. Yet I had no idea how to foster it.

◆ ◆ ◆

By now, Carol was thirty-five, and her biological clock was ticking.

She now felt ready to become a parent. I didn't, but I loved her. It seemed so important to her. I went along with it, though without much enthusiasm. "It will work out," I repeatedly told myself.

Month after month, when her period came, I pretended to feel as deflated as she did. I tried to support her, to be there for me. Inside, however, the process wore on me.

The sex? It had once been the highlight of our relationship. Now that we were timing intercourse to her body temperature, everything felt forced and mechanical. Rather than turning to her with sexual hunger, I felt an overpowering pressure to perform—to give her the swimmers she needed to make the baby she wanted.

Month after month after month, her period came, and she became increasingly despondent.

By late fall, Carol and I had moved on from sex during ovulation to what most people refer to as the "turkey baster method." Intracervical insemination involved me masturbating and capturing the semen. Then I placed it into a large syringe, inserted it deep into her vagina, and pressed the plunger to deliver the semen as close to her cervix as possible.

Each time, she remained on her back, with a pillow under her hips, for as long as a half hour, giving the semen more opportunity to swim upward.

As Carol grew more despondent, things started to fall apart.

At first, we picked at one another, voicing small irritations over where items belonged in the bathroom or whose turn it was to take out the trash.

As time wore on, however, the fights grew more passionate.

Around this time, Caren showed up at my office in tears.

It was unlike her. Usually, she was so reserved, her every emotion hidden from view.

"I can't do it," she sputtered between sobs.

"What can't you do, honey?" I asked, as I put my arm around her, my heart breaking for her.

"Anything. I can't do anything. I can't handle it. My life feels all messed up."

"Did something happen? I'm confused. Just a couple of days ago, you told me you were good. What's this about?"

"You don't understand!"

"I'm trying to. I really am. I just . . . could you tell me a little more about what's going on?"

Her face was swollen, her eyes red. I handed her a box of tissues.

"I'm drowning. I don't know what I'm doing."

"Okay, tell me more about that. What don't you know?"

She couldn't get the words out. It was as if part of her wanted to tell me, and another didn't.

She blew her nose.

She said nothing for a while.

"I'm failing," she finally said.

"What class?"

"All of them," she said. "I'm failing all of them."

That couldn't possibly be true, could it? She'd been at the top of her class in high school. Maybe she was struggling. I didn't doubt that. But failing every single class?

"There's more," she said.

"Okay," I said. "I'm here. I'm listening."

"I've been doing some . . . I've been . . . I . . . I'm on drugs," she said.

"All right, honey," I said. "That happens."

"That's not all."

Not all? What else could there be?

She couldn't get the words out.

"Okay," I said. "There's nothing—absolutely nothing—that you could say that would stop me from loving you. You know that, right?"

"Dad," she said, "I had sex."

"Okay," I said. "That's normal and age appropriate. Did you use—"

"No, Dad. Stop. Let me finish."

"Sure, honey. I'm here. Go on. I'm sorry I interrupted you."

"I had sex with another girl."

"I see," I said.

I knew I needed to choose my words carefully. I didn't want to say the wrong thing. She was clearly in crisis, and I didn't want to make it worse.

I gently touched her chin, drawing her gaze upward so she could see my facial expression.

"Honey, there's nothing bad or wrong about that, okay? Absolutely nothing."

Her tears gushed forward as I held her. She gasped for air.

"I don't know," she said. "I don't know who I am."

"Okay, honey," I said. "It's going to be okay. We'll get through this, okay?"

Soon after, she disenrolled from BU, moved back home, and went into therapy. I used my network connections to hook her up with a good psychologist in her area.

◆ ◆ ◆

As I boarded the plane for California, all I could think about was when Gary and I had sat in his kitchen, him comforting me after I'd learned Joyce was taking Caren to New York.

He'd been so understanding, so warm, so steady—the proverbial rock.

No matter how erratic I became, his support never wavered.

If I'd found a way to repay that kindness—if I'd called more often, visited, written more often—would he still be here?

His ending. I couldn't stop thinking about it.

He'd lost everything. His marriage. His career. His home.

In the end, he sat in a chair in his trailer, wedged the stock of a shotgun between his feet, wrapped his mouth around the muzzle, and pulled the trigger.

I couldn't fathom how he'd managed to do it.

It's not easy to shoot yourself with a shotgun.

Yet, he'd found a way.

The darkness he must have felt—the despair.

Why hadn't I been there?

Why hadn't I reached out more often?

He could have gotten help.

He could have beat the addiction.

The same process that had helped me quit smoking would have likely helped him.

Maybe? I would never know now. Why hadn't I suggested it? Why hadn't I done more?

The guilt followed me from one side of the country to the other.

When I pulled up to his mother's home in Calabasas, it was still there, heavy, gripping, and painful.

Fuck, Gary had saved my life. Could I have saved his?

I walked up the driveway, knocked on the door, and waited.

"Oh, Ron," his mother said. "It's so nice to see you. Come in. Come in."

She had a towel wrapped around her. Her hair was wet.

She'd always been the cool mom we all wanted to be around. There were the usual boring and annoying parents, and there was Gary's mother. She seemed to understand us in ways our parents didn't.

"We're in the pool. Did you bring swim trunks?"

I followed her through the house and out into the backyard.

"This is George," she said, introducing me to her current boyfriend. We shook hands.

The two jumped in the pool.

They seemed so carefree, normal, almost unfazed by everything that had happened.

"I'm sorry," I said.

"Oh, Ron," she said. "Don't feel sorry."

"What do you mean?"

"Look, honey. There was nothing you or anyone else could have done, okay?"

"Yeah, sure," I said. "I just. I don't know. Why didn't he reach out? He didn't have to do this."

"Honey," she said. "What would he do? He'd lost his ability to make a living."

A rift opened between us.

Why was she so callous? Why didn't she care? How could she move on so quickly?

It angered me. Gary deserved to be remembered. He deserved to be mourned.

He deserved more than this.

He deserved to still be here.

"Come on," she said. "Get in the pool. It's so refreshing. You'll feel better."

I obliged, but I didn't feel any better.

◆ ◆ ◆

I sold my small home near Fresh Pond, and purchased a big old Victorian house in Cambridge, off Massachusetts Avenue near Porter Square, one mile north of Harvard Law School. Built in 1894, it was a huge triple-decker with ornate gingerbread trim and a wraparound porch. The peeling, nicked-up plaster walls hinted that the old home needed work. Still, we figured the two first-floor rental units would help to offset the mortgage and any required repairs.

The home quickly turned into a money pit. We'd hired a contractor to mend the nicked-up walls. Rather than giving us a firm bid for the job, he provided an estimate, which seemed like an amount we could afford.

Yet, week after week, the work dragged on. He continually told us about complications and problems he hadn't foreseen, all adding to the growing price tag.

Each week I received a bill totaling thousands of dollars we didn't have.

To make up for the difference, I began working ridiculous hours, teaching classes at BU during the day, and seeing patients in the evenings. I usually arrived home around 10:30, ate dinner, went to bed, and woke early the next morning to do it all over again.

In the past, when I'd poured my time and energy into work, my relationships had withered. That's what had ended my relationship with Joannie. It's likely what had become between me and Joyce as well, with my involvement with CIPA.

I should have known.

I should have seen it coming.

Soon after buying the home, the nitpicking turned into huge arguments that seemed to erupt over the most minor issues. We were either fighting or not talking to one another. There was no in-between. I couldn't remember the last time we made love.

How had things gotten so bad?

I didn't know how to turn it around. I also didn't have the energy to try.

I was up for tenure, which required much of my focus.

After reviewing my extensive dossier, which included my textbook and many journal articles, book chapters, and conference presentations, as well as evaluations of my teaching performance—the retention, tenure, and promotion (RTP) committees in my program, department, and school, as well as the University Faculty

RTP Committee (with members coming from many different schools at BU), had all recommended me for tenure and promotion to associate professor. Now it was up to the provost, the next-to-final step in the long process. It was clear that I'd satisfied the university's tenure standard.

"You've got this," Evan reassured me.

"I don't know," I said. "Lots of other psychologists before me were turned down."

"They weren't you," he said.

"They were quite accomplished."

"You've already gotten so far. There's no way they'll turn you down."

"They all got this far too! It's as if Boston University has a policy against granting tenure to psychologists."

"Come on, Ron," he said. "That's crazy talk. Think positive."

"I'll try."

I thought back to the day soon after I'd arrived when President Silber had told us we'd made a terrible mistake. Maybe he was talking about more than something that had happened in the late 1800s.

But maybe he meant we'd made a terrible mistake by coming to Boston University—because psychologists weren't welcome there.

I wanted to be wrong, but the idea gnawed at me as I awaited the decision.

Finally, the letter arrived.

I slid my finger under the flap and opened the envelope.

"We regret to inform you..."

Oh, no.

No.

No!

Why? How?

What would I do?

This couldn't be happening! There had to be another explanation.

A mistake? This had to be a mistake!

I reread the letter.

It was clear.

I'd never become a tenured professor at BU.

Never.

I opened a beer. Then I canceled my appointments for the rest of the day.

I lit a joint.

I opened another beer.

I inserted ZZ Top's *Afterburner* into a tape player and cranked up the volume.

The phone rang.

It was Evan.

"So, any news?" He sounded so hopeful. Why did he have to sound so fucking hopeful?

"Yeah, I didn't get it. Fucking Silber. He hates psychologists! I knew this was going to happen. I fucking knew it!"

"I'm so sorry, Ron," he said. "This sucks."

"It does. Yes. It does. I guess he got his revenge on the ghosts of William James and G. Stanley Hall. Fucking bastard."

"So, what are you doing?" he asked.

"I'm drinking and drugging, listening to ZZ Top, trying to turn myself into Texas roadkill."

I'd meant it as a joke, kind of.

Yet my words sounded more ominous than intended.

"Are you going to hurt yourself?"

"I don't know."

It was the truth.

"Look," he said. "I'm going to clear my schedule. I'll be over in a bit, okay? You don't have to face this alone."

"Yeah, sure, okay."

After hanging up, I took another drag off the joint and opened another beer.

The album ended. I rewound the tape and played it again, cranking the volume.

Someone was knocking at the door.

At first, I assumed it was Evan.

But he couldn't have gotten to me that quickly. It would have defied the laws of physics.

The knocking grew louder.

What were they saying?

The police?

Were the police at my door?

What the hell?

There was a joint in the ashtray and more cannabis here and there all over the house. There was no way I would let them in. They'd arrest me. That was the last fucking thing I needed right now.

The last fucking thing.

The knocking continued.

I ignored them.

They'd go away.

Wouldn't they?

More knocking.

"We can hear the music. We know you're in there."

Fuck. Why had I turned up the volume?

I sat on the floor with my knees pulled into my chest.

Go away. Go away. Go away.

"Sir? We're just here to check on you. Open up, okay?"

Evan must have done this! Evan must have called them!

Fucking Evan!

There was a cracking sound.

The door opened.

They'd popped the lock.

Two officers were now inside.

I glanced at the ashtray.

I was fucking toast.

Why had Evan done this?

"Sir," one of them said. "We're just here to check on you. We got a report that you were going through a hard time. Could you tell us how you are?"

"Look," I said, "this is all a big misunderstanding. I see that now."

"Okay, sir. Can you tell us how it's a misunderstanding?"

I glanced at the ashtray.

How would I recover from this?

BU would probably fire me as soon as they learned of the arrest.

"I had a bad day," I said. "I got some bad news—terrible news. And I was talking to a friend and made a joke that he thought was serious. I'm okay. I really am."

"Do you have plans to hurt yourself?"

"No! No! Not at all! I was just blowing off some steam—listening to music and having a couple of beers. Yes, I admit, I also smoked some cannabis. I'm not proud of that. It was a mistake."

"We don't care about that, sir," one said.

"You don't?"

"No, we're just here to check on you. So, you're feeling okay?"

"Yes."

"You're not going to hurt yourself?"

"No, I'm not going to hurt myself."

"Hang in there, okay," one of them said.

"I will."

Then they left.

I stood in the doorway, staring at the busted lock.

That's when Evan showed up.

He tried to hug me.

"Get away from me!"

"Ron, what?"

"You fucking called the police?"

"I knew it would be a while before I could get here. I wouldn't be able to live with myself if you'd done something and I was too late."

"You fucking called the cops?"

"Yes, I did. And I would hope you'd do the same for me."

"Look at my fucking door! They broke it down! As if this day wasn't fucking hard enough!"

"I needed to know you were okay."

"I didn't need the fucking police at my house. What would have happened if they'd arrested me? Had you thought of that?"

"Look, Ron," he said.

Something unleashed itself. The urge to destroy surged down my arm and into my fist.

Evan stumbled backward. He swayed from one side to the other. His hand cradled his jaw.

"I think you broke it," he said.

"Fuck you."

"Ron." He sounded wounded, startled, yet still loving.

I turned my back and walked away.

Yet again, I'd become my father.

Yet fucking again.

TAKEAWAYS

Readers, what is your relationship like with your parents? Are you satisfied with it? If not, do you find, as I did, that you lose your adult self when visiting them, and wind up behaving in immature ways, ways that you are not proud of? If so, you might benefit from applying some elements of the Bowen approach to your family.

Bowen recommended frequent short visits, during which one tries to hold on to one's adult self as long as one can. By that I mean operating from a clear sense of who you are and what you value. If you find yourself getting emotional—that is, angry, sad, fearful, etc.—then you have likely regressed from your adult self. If that is the case do whatever works for you to calm down—count to ten, take a walk, focus on your breath—in order to regain your composure. Then re-engage as the adult that you are.

Also, can you identify repetitive patterns of interaction with your parents? Is one of them more indulgent toward you while the other is very strict? If so, you may be caught in a triangle, as I was, which you can analyze and figure a way out of, as I did.

But, however good this work had been, I was not yet out of the woods. I still had an explosive temper and was prone to violence.

CHAPTER 12

Fathers: The Forgotten Parent

(1983–1988)

I'd spent years preparing for a moment that was never going to arrive. How had I been so naïve? Why had I deluded myself into believing my future would be any different than the other psychology professors who'd also been turned down for tenure? Why hadn't I seen it six years earlier, when President Silber had told us we'd all made a mistake?

Silber was right about one thing that day.

I'd certainly made a mistake, but it had nothing to do with choosing psychology as a profession.

Had I taken a position somewhere else, literally anywhere else, I'd have had tenure by now.

I'd have a job for life.

Was my career always going to be in this state of stagnation?

Thus was my state of mind when I learned that Paul Warren, dean of BU's School of Education, wanted to see me.

He stood, pensively gazing out of his large bay window, looking out onto Commonwealth Avenue as the Green Line train pulled up for a stop, his hands gently clasped behind his back.

"Please sit," he said, motioning to the armchair near his desk.

"I suppose you're wondering why I asked you to come here," he said.

"Well, I assumed it had something to do with me being turned down for tenure."

"That's right. I'm so sorry about that," he said. "I thought you had a strong case."

"I thought I did as well."

"Yes," he said, "I expect you did."

He took a few steps forward, then slowly turned, almost in a circle, as if something was on his mind.

It was clear he was choosing his words carefully.

"You know how much I value your contributions," he said. Despite whatever Dean Warren might have felt about President Silber, the man knew the chain of command. He wasn't going to question Silber's decision, not openly, not publicly. Still, he didn't need to say more. I knew he disagreed with the decision. If it had been up to Dean Warren, I'd be a tenured associate professor. There wasn't a doubt in my mind.

"Yes," I replied, "I do. Thank you for recommending me for tenure. Obviously, I wish everyone felt the same way."

"I expect you do. So, Ron, as it turns out, I have a proposition for you."

"Okay," I said, curious. "I'm all ears."

"How do you feel about taking on a five-year contract position with us? It wouldn't come with tenure, of course. I can promote you to associate professor, but it would be on a clinical line—that is, as clinical associate professor. The position I have in mind would come with releases from some of your course load."

"Okay," I said, not sure where this was going. What would I have to do to make up for the course reduction?

"You're probably aware that BU has been expanding into Allston and Brighton. The residents there aren't the happiest with us," he said with a wry smile. Was that a dig at President Silber? I wasn't sure.

"So, I was thinking. We need to do something to improve our relationship with those communities. I'd love to start a community-facing program, something that gives back to the community, something that helps the community see the value of the university. What do you think of the idea?"

"It sounds like a great idea to me," I said.

"Now, this also involves your colleague Eileen Nickerson, the chair of the counseling psychology program. She's running a counseling program for women in the surrounding community with one of her recent graduates, Mary Ann Gawelek. I was thinking, given the dissertation research your student Greg Doyle did, that you might want to run something for men or possibly fathers?"

Under my mentorship, Doyle had done an interesting study. He'd taught parenting skills to a group of fathers (the "experimental group"), using a curriculum that he and I had developed together during our long training runs. He compared them to another group of fathers, a "control group." Before and after the eight-week class, Doyle asked the men and their families to fill out several psychological scales. The results: after taking the fatherhood class, the experimental group men (as compared to those in the control group) improved their communication skills, were more sensitive to their children, and were less likely to engage in undesirable behaviors (e.g., blow up or do something else that they would later regret). In addition, significantly more experimental than control group children perceived positive changes in their relationships with their fathers, and the experimental group fathers changed their view of the ideal family.

"I can offer you a conference room and start you off with some funding. A lot of funding to be precise."

"That sounds intriguing," I said. "I'd like to think it over for a few days, talk it over with my wife. Could I get back to you later in the week?"

"Of course," he said. "I understand that this is a big decision."

That evening Carol and I weighed the various pros and cons. On the downside this wasn't a job for life. After five years, I'd need to find a new position somewhere else.

On the plus side, however, it would provide gainful employment for at least five years. That was a long runway, long enough for me to figure out my next move.

It also kept me in Boston.

Despite the friction between us, I still loved Carol, and she still loved me. However, she was clear: she had a thriving practice, and she had no intention of starting all over again somewhere else. If I left Boston, I'd be leaving without her.

Boston was also relatively close to Caren, which was important to me. She had recovered from her unfortunate experience at BU and was a young adult now, attending classes in the School of Visual Arts in New York City. I wanted to work somewhere that was close enough to visit regularly.

The following day, I accepted Dean Warren's offer.

I used the funding to extravagantly equip the conference room with state-of-the-art video equipment. In the early 1980s video was all the rage. We had three cameras on tripods which were each adjacent to a microphone coming down from the ceiling, and there were several AV carts with decks, monitors, and special effects generators, which allowed me and Greg to split the screen to capture two different people in an interaction.

We used the Parent Education for Fathers curriculum that Greg and I had already developed for his dissertation. It included a leader's guide for the eight-session program, and a father's workbook with homework exercises. It wasn't lost on me that I would soon be teaching men to do something that I couldn't seem to do for myself.

"I might suck as a father, but I'm a pretty good psychologist," I told myself. "I'm teaching these men basic psychological stuff: active listening skills, self-expressive skills, emotional self-awareness skills. This is like what I teach master's degree students."

We placed public service announcements in the Boston Globe and on the NPR-affiliate radio station in Boston, WBUR, announcing seats in a nonacademic credit fatherhood education course for two hundred dollars. Ten men signed up. They were from many social class levels—plumbers and electricians, small businessmen, and lawyers. What united them? They wanted to be better dads.

On that first day, the men sat in a circle, uncomfortably glancing around, seeming as if they regretted what they'd gotten themselves into.

"Hi, I'm Ron Levant, a clinical associate professor of counseling psychology at Boston University and this is Greg Doyle, a recent graduate of the program. We're happy you're here. I guess you're wondering: what's all this video equipment doing here?"

"I figured you guys have got it going on!" one of the men joked.

"We think we do! We're going to use this equipment to teach you how to become better fathers in the same way you might have learned how to perfect your golf swing or your tennis serve. You'll role-play problems you might be facing at home, and then we'll watch the footage for insights. Before we get to any of that, however, let's get to know one another. How about we go around the room and introduce ourselves. Say your name along with what brings you here."

"Great," I heard one of the men say sarcastically, "circle time."

The men shifted in their seats—their faces stony. No one offered to go first.

I turned to the man next to me. Dressed in jeans and a flannel shirt, he ran a plumbing business in Allston. "Why don't you get us started?"

He sighed. Then he wiped his hands on his pants.

"Hi," he said. "My name's Steve. You know, my wife, she uh, she gave me the class as an, uh, birthday gift."

He paused, then asked, "You think she was trying to send me a message?" The man laughed.

The next few men used the same line. They'd gotten the course as a gift.

Was that all true? Or were they unwilling to admit that they might need some help with parenting? There should be no shame in that. After all, parenting is one of life's most difficult jobs, and the one for which we tend to receive the least preparation.

About halfway around the circle, a well-dressed man sat, his arm's crossed, his eyebrows knitted, his lips pressed into a scowl.

"Clyde, right?"

"Yeah. That's my name."

"So, what's going on? You appear tense. Would you like to say anything?"

"You want to know why I'm here?" he blurted. "I'll tell you why I'm here. I'm here so that my son doesn't feel as bad about me as I do about my dad. There. I said it."

Clyde's words hit the room like a hurricane. The other men sat up. Their eyes came alive. The uncomfortable silences gave way to a spirited discussion, with the men interrupting one another and sometimes talking over one another.

"You know it. My old man? I could never do anything right in his eyes! I do not want my son to feel like that, ya know?"

"My dad was not the happy-go-lucky, take-you-out-to-the-ballgame type of guy. In fact, he was the opposite. He was morose most of the time. I just tried to stay out of his way.

"Mine was extremely strict. I got the strap for nothing—these stinking minor infractions. If I left a ball out on the lawn, he tanned my ass. I don't want to do that to my kid. But you know? I think I am doing it. It kills me."

"I never knew how my dad felt about anything. He never talked about how he felt! It's strange to say, but I don't feel like I know him."

"When I was a kid, everything I did always had to be corrected. It was as if he hated everything about me. Damn! I hope I'm not doing that to my kids."

"Mine was there, but not there, you know? His body was in the house after work, but he didn't interreact much with us, other than short one-word answers."

"Mine was there but not there as well, but that was because he was almost always drunk."

I was shocked. Like many men, I rarely talked about my personal life, particularly not about my childhood, and thus assumed that I alone had this terrible excuse for a father. While it was a relief to see that I wasn't alone, it also made me very sad to know that many men shared the same upbringing.

Although some facilitators might choose to act differently, I did not feel that this was the time or place for me to share. Still, I related with these men. As children, we'd promised ourselves. We'd sworn. We would never be like our fathers. Yet here we were, wondering if we were stuck in the same destructive cycle.

The mood in the room was very dark. The feelings seemed to go very deep for many of the men. We continued to process this difficult topic for a while and then did a couple of role-play exercises. As they filed out after that first session, I silently made a promise: I would teach them—and myself—to be better men. I wanted to do my part to break this vicious father-to-son cycle.

A couple of weeks into the course, we taught the men how to see things from their child's perspective. The content was based on a psychological concept called "theory of mind." Humans often assume they know someone else's thoughts and motives. However, we can't read each other's minds. We can only infer what someone might be thinking based on their behavior, statements, and body language. That inference is a theory. Sometimes the theory proves correct. Other times, however, it's wrong.

When the theory is correct, one can see things through the other person's eyes, "walk a mile in their moccasins," as the Native American expression goes. From that vantage point, one can vicariously experience the other person's feelings—that is, empathize with that person. As you might imagine, when the theory is wrong, it generally leads to misunderstandings, arguments, and hurt feelings.

Hank was a small guy, wiry, who ran a dry-cleaning store. He'd told me about an insightful conversation he'd had with his eight-year-old son recently, so I asked him and another man to role play to illustrate the concept.

Hank pretended to watch from a window while Steven, the other father, crouched on the ground, watching an imaginary worm on the pavement. Steven whipped out his pocketknife and sliced the worm in half.

"What the?" Hank said, acting enraged, as he'd been when the incident had first unfolded. "Who does that? What the hell? What's wrong with him?"

He then confronted the other man who was pretending to be his son.

"Why did you do that? Why would you do such a thing?"

"Dad," Steven said, play acting. "I thought the worm was lonely, so I gave him a friend."

The session dramatically revealed that the eight-year-old not only had a mind of his own, but also a mind that saw the world quite differently than the mind of his father.

The father had seen a cruel boy. But the boy cut the worm as an act of kindness.

"Wow," said Hank. "That's amazing. It never occurred to me that my son had a mind of his own." This was quite a revelation from a guy who had been very quiet in the class up to this point.

It did not surprise me that he'd never realized his son had his own mind. In my experience, many parents think of their children simply as extensions of themselves.

In a later class, Tim, a somewhat overweight middle-aged dad who worked in construction, seemed out of sorts.

I asked him about it, and he said that his son had stood him up for a father-son hockey game.

"How did that make you feel?"

Tim pointed his finger and angrily exclaimed, "He shouldn't have done it!"

"All right," I said. "I agree, but that's not how you felt. How did you feel?"

Tim stared at me, blankly.

"I don't know."

It was perplexing. As an observer, I thought I knew how Tim must have felt.

Why was he struggling to put that emotion into words? Was it really that difficult?

Pulling a couple of chairs over to a video camera, I asked Tim to role-play himself and another father to role-play his ex-wife as she delivered the news that his son had forgotten all about the date.

Then I played the recording back, showing Tim's face falling into a frown and his shoulders slumping. I stopped the tape and asked, "Tim, what were you feeling right then?"

With his hand on his chin, concentrating intently, Tim said "I guess I must have felt disappointed."

He "guessed"? He "must have felt"? Why was he so uncertain?

To gain some perspective on the situation, I reflected on how a mother in a similar circumstance might react, let's say to her daughter standing her up for a shopping date. I imagined her saying, "Well, I was surprised because it's not like her to forget a shopping date. Then I felt angry at being stood up. I was also hurt that she acted with so little regard for my feelings. And I was also worried that that she was perhaps upset with me, and this was her way of letting me know. In the end I was disappointed and annoyed. I had planned my whole day around it and now the day was ruined."

The contrast was striking.

As a grad student at Harvard, I had studied developmental psychology, so I returned to this literature in search of answers to my questions. What I learned from the research on "emotion socialization" was revelatory. Boys start out life as neonates more emotionally expressive than girls. Over time, however, they become less verbally expressive, and a bit later lose their facial expressiveness.

All that suggests a suppression of emotional expression, which I theorized had occurred as a result of socializing boys to restrict the expression of emotions because that was considered feminine.

This man, however, seemed completely out of touch. He didn't seem to know what he felt.

How many other men were like him?

Over the weeks, we taught the men a toolbox full of skills, and we watched them transform. The uncomfortable silences gave way to animated conversations, with the men supporting and comforting one another. The men told us that family life improved. They grew closer to their spouses as well as to their children.

For example, Jerry, a fifty-six-year-old attorney, set up a weekly "guys get-together" with his two sons, age eight and ten, every Wednesday evening. During it, they ordered pizza, watched TV, and talked.

"I am so glad I did this," he told me. "I have gotten to know my boys so much better, and now they are opening up to me with their worries and questions. It is truly marvelous at how much closer we are!"

It was a beautiful transformation, and I felt proud to have been part of it.

◆ ◆ ◆

BU's public affairs office pitched stories to the media about the Fatherhood Project. A local newspaper did a story, quoting a father saying, "I think every parent should take the course. I found it also has application for adult communication."

The *Christian Science Monitor* also responded right away, with an article titled, "My Dad spends time with me now," by Diane Casselbery Manual. It spanned the entire Lifestyles section and was syndicated to 310 newspapers.

BU's President Silber sent a copy of it to Dean Warren, along with a handwritten note, asking, "What is this Levant doing? Is he trying to turn fathers into mothers?"

Dean Warren forwarded the clipping and note to me in interuniversity mail with a note, "I thought you might be interested in this."

What a dumb shit, I thought.

Silber was a traditionalist. I got that. He thought fathers should be tough and dominant. Yet, I was starting to see that these very social constructions were likely what held men back from living full emotional lives. Whether Silber liked it or not, fathers *were* involved in parenthood these days. It was becoming very visible. In Harvard Square, fathers were glimpsed pushing strollers and carrying infants in Snugli chest packs. Fathers got kids up and dressed in the mornings, and they fed them breakfast. They picked kids up from school, settled them into their evening routines, and helped them with their homework.

This was the '80s, not the '50s.

The times, they had a-changed, as Bob Dylan foresaw.

Fathers were no longer the sole breadwinners who came home to dinner on the table and a wife with a cocktail in hand.

Women worked, too. They had incomes. They were no longer financially dependent on men.

No, I wasn't turning fathers into mothers. Au contraire, I saw that parenting was just that—parenting. It was quotidian. There was no gender attached to it. The only parental things men could not do by virtue of their gender was gestation and lactation.

I was helping men create their full, complete lives. I was saving marriages, and I was interrupting a harmful cycle.

Over the next few years, I got more publicity than any other faculty member at BU, with appearances on *The Oprah Winfrey Show*, *20/20* with Barbara Walters, and a huge spread in *People* magazine.

My graduate students were publishing study after study too.

Since the Fatherhood Course was based on the original

program that I had created for foster parents, I spun off several other parenting courses. These were for parents who both worked (so called "dual-earner parents"), single parents, and stepparents. One project, headed by graduate student Wendy Nelson, offered a deeper dive into child development, and was called "What children teach their fathers about growing up."

Every single win offered a satisfying "fuck-you" to President Silber. I doubt he regretted turning me down for tenure, but he should have.

On top of that, my relationship with Caren was improving. Now several years into my intensive psychoanalysis, I was learning how to connect with her in new ways. I was less angry, frustrated, and prone to blowing up. Thanks to everything I taught the men in the fatherhood class, I was also more attentive.

I was a better man.

At the School of Visual Arts in New York, Caren met a young man named Adam Shanker. He was the son of Al Shanker, the labor and civil rights leader who founded the United Federation of Teachers. One year Al led so many teachers' strikes that Woody Allen gave him a shout out in the film *Sleeper*, in which he said that Al Shanker was trying to start World War III.

Together Caren and Adam started their own business, called Best Shot Video. Adam was the videographer and Caren handled postproduction. By the time 1986 dawned, the two were planning their wedding.

I was thrilled for her, and—truth be told—a bit anxious, given my history of failed pairings. I hoped my romantic afflictions weren't heritable.

The wedding was held in New York City and was attended by my immediate family, Joyce and her family, and Adam's family.

The rehearsal dinner was held at a fine Manhattan restaurant. As we dug into our salads, my father admonished Lowell, "What's wrong with you? You're using the wrong fork."

"Whatever," Lowell said quietly, not used to my father's critical side.

Usually, Dad reserved the venom for me. For our entire lives, Lowell had gotten a pass.

"The one I'm using works just fine," Lowell said, clearly annoyed.

"No, you're supposed to use the small one for the salad and the big one for your meal."

"Dad," Lowell said, "I've got it."

"No, clearly you don't."

His voice was rising. People were staring.

This. Again. Like usual. My father was making a scene. At Caren's rehearsal dinner.

I shot Lowell a compassionate glance as I lifted my small fork to my mouth. With my eyes, I tried my best to communicate, "Yes, he's an asshole, but let's not ruin this for Caren."

"You're right Dad," Lowell said in his gentle way, picking up his small fork.

Now that I had an adult daughter who was getting married, my father seemed to see me more as another adult—and not as someone who needed to be nitpicked over every tiny detail. In Bowen Family Therapy, this was known as "terminating the intergenerational hierarchical boundary," in which parents became "former parents," disburdening themselves and forming "I-Thou" relationships with their former children. The termination takes place earlier in many families, often when a child leaves home, gets married, or has their first child. For me, all those milestones came and went without my father acknowledging my adulthood. Now, with my daughter's wedding, it had finally happened.

Lowell was two years younger than I was and he'd escaped Dad's wrath for so many years. But because he was neither married nor a parent, I feared that, without any such milestone markers of maturity, our father may very well treat him like a child until the day one of them died.

A year later, Caren gave birth to her first child, Adrian.

I was delighted to have a grandson, figuring I might be able do better with a boy than with a girl. And of course, there is that old joke that grandparents and grandchildren get along so well because they have a common enemy. But in this case Caren wanted me in Adrian's life and worked hard to create opportunities to visit. I jumped at every offer, spending as much time with her family as I could. Things between us finally started to feel settled, warm, something resembling what I imagined the father-daughter relationship should feel like. I felt blessed.

On the other hand, my marriage to Carol was withering away, and no amount of psychoanalysis was going to save it.

One evening, as we quietly talked it over, Carol and I agreed: things weren't working out. We were like two people in a canoe, rowing in opposite directions. She decided to move out.

Over the next few months, I nursed my emotional wounds, wondering if I'd ever be able to maintain a long-term relationship with a woman. I wanted a life partner. Yet, I seemed caught up in a never-ending nightmare. One relationship would end. Another would start, and it would follow the same story line as the one before it.

Nothing ever changed.

Then, one evening, several months after the divorce was finalized, I attended a singles dance held in a ballroom in the Hyatt Hotel on the banks of the Charles River in Cambridge. I looked across the room and noticed a woman with long dark hair and the sweetest of smiles. Our eyes met. Soon we were chatting. Her name was Carol, the same as my ex. Like me she was recently divorced. The music was getting louder, so we decided to go outside so that it would be easier to talk. There was something about her. Despite my long history of failed relationships, something told me that this time, things would be different.

We exchanged numbers, began dating, and fell in love.

TAKEAWAYS

Readers: Is there some unfinished father-child business that continues to weigh on you, or that casts a shadow on your life? Do you have questions for your father? If so consider an exercise in which you write down the questions you'd like to ask your father. There are a lot of ways this can be done, but I suggest spending several days on it, for no more than fifteen minutes each day. After you have done this, reflect on how it feels to have put all this down on paper. If your father is alive, consider asking these questions in person. If your father has passed away, consider going to the gravesite to ask your questions there. This activity may cause you to experience acute feelings of grief, so it might be a good idea to bring along a significant other who can offer encouragement and support. It will likely be difficult, but it can help you achieve closure.

CHAPTER 13

From Research to Practice in the Psychology of Men

(1988–1994)

As my five-year contract at BU came to an end, my relationship with Carol grew more serious. We weren't living together—she had her house in Reading, a suburb north of Boston, and I still had mine in Cambridge—but we spent nearly every weekend together. There was something about her that felt like a perfect fit.

So, as I feverishly applied for tenured positions at academic institutions, I mainly focused on the Northeast Coast. It was a risky decision. Academic positions were like winning raffle tickets. I was competing with dozens of psychologists for a single post. What if no one made me an offer? I'd still be with Carol in Boston but have no job.

Finally, Rutgers, the State University of New Jersey, made me an offer.

I was relieved—and proud.

Years before, when I was a boy, an older cousin, Sheldon Baker, had attended Rutgers. At the time, everyone in the family was impressed. At several family gatherings, I'd overhear grownups talking about it, saying how proud they were of him.

My father would never tell me that he was proud of me. I knew that. If anything, he'd be jealous, taking it as a slight.

Still, I imagined extended family members on my mother's side—because Uncle Joe, Sheldon's dad, was my Grandma Edith's younger brother—sitting around and talking about how Ronnie had gone far, earning a role as a tenured professor at Rutgers, the same great school that Sheldon had attended decades earlier.

The current chair of the counseling psychology program was planning to retire. Thus, the position was cast as the "chair apparent." The dean of the School of Education promised that I could build the program from its current size, three professors, to at least five, allowing the program to apply for accreditation from the American Psychological Association.

Growing a program and putting it on the map? I was in.

I was getting a great opportunity here to build a first-rate doctoral program. Initially, everything seemed perfect.

Carol and I hadn't been together long enough for me to ask her to move. She had a great job at Houghton Mifflin. I couldn't ask her to give up her career. Plus, I doubted I could get a good price for my Cambridge home. The housing market was too depressed.

So rather than move to New Jersey, I commuted.

Each Sunday evening, I flew into Newark International Airport where I had arranged with a driver to take me to Rutgers. I stayed in a succession of different faculty apartments, one nice, the second one not so much, and then later in a hotel. I got around the area with a bicycle equipped with panniers, so that I could buy groceries. Then, every Thursday evening, I reversed the trip.

Health service psychology programs at Rutgers and beyond encouraged their faculty to keep their clinical skills sharp so that they could adequately supervise the students. So, each Friday, I counseled patients in the office of my former wife, Carol Beaudoin, having rented it from her for one day a week.

I spent the weekends with Carol Slatter.

During that first year, I mentored my doctoral students, teaching them the way I was taught at Harvard, by immersing them in projects in which they worked as apprentices. Rather than lecturing, I encouraged my students to work with me to complete a research project from start to finish, including publishing our work.

◆ ◆ ◆

The dominant theoretical perspective in psychology had viewed masculinity through what's known as a "gender essentialist" lens. It assumed masculinity was synonymous with being male, and that masculinity was largely due to biological factors. Gender essentialists held that children needed to adopt the personality traits that were (stereotypically) associated with their sex or be at risk for maladjustment and psychological problems. For example, in the 1950s, boys who did not conform to stereotypes of masculinity, but rather exhibited "effeminate" traits, were considered to be so much at risk of developing serious mental health issues that they were sent to a Child Guidance Clinic for mental health treatment.

This didn't make sense to me.

If masculinity were synonymous with maleness and resulted from biological factors, one would expect uniformity over historical time and across cultures. Yet, masculine norms were anything but uniform. One needed only to see any number of photographs of Franklin Delano Roosevelt as a child to know how quickly these norms could change. In many of them, he has long hair, and he's wearing what appears to be a frilly dress, which was the norm for children during the late 1800s. Similarly, a current masculine norm in the US is to restrict the expression of affectionate behavior between men. The norm was the exact opposite in the US by the middle of the twentieth century: men were expected to be physically and verbally affectionate with their close male friends, even going so far as to sleep in the same bed when visiting each other. Finally, the current masculine norm in some Latin countries (such as Italy) is for men who are relatives or close friends to kiss each other.

It seemed to me and a growing number of psychologists that someone's maleness or sex (their chromosomes, genitalia, and secondary sex characteristics) was different from their masculinity (the set of beliefs that governed how they should and should not think, feel, and behave.) The latter constituted a gender role, defined by a set of social norms.

More importantly, based on what I already knew from counseling men, these masculine norms likely *harmed* men and certainly didn't help them.

With my graduate students, I set out to investigate it.

The first step: create a scientifically reliable and valid scale that would allow us to measure people's beliefs about how boys and men should think, feel, and behave, and more importantly, should *not* think, feel, and behave. We included women in our study, because anyone can have such beliefs, irrespective of their biological sex and gender identity.

Taking an existing but imperfectly developed masculinity scale (the Brannon Masculinity Scale) as our starting point, my students got to work. Soon they had a revised scale that we called the Male Role Norms Inventory (MRNI). It measured seven traditional masculine norms: avoidance of femininity, negativity toward sexual minority men, self-reliance, toughness, dominance, importance of sex, and restrictive emotionality. In addition, one subscale measured nontraditional masculinity. Each norm was measured by several belief statements, such as "a man should prefer football to needlecraft" and "fathers should teach their sons to mask fear." Respondents indicated the extent to which they agreed or disagreed with each belief statement using a seven-point scale, ranging from strongly agree to strongly disagree.

To evaluate the scale, the students administered it to a sample of participants and did an exploratory factor analysis. That began the process that ultimately established the dimensional validity of the MRNI. That is, through this and subsequent studies we were able to show that the MRNI truly measured the seven norms that we had proposed, something the Brannon Scale lacked. This made me proud. Robert Brannon was a significant leader in the field. Yet he'd hit a wall when trying to devise a scale to measure masculinity. My students and I eventually solved a problem he'd thought of as unsolvable.

Our new scale could be used by mental health professionals to help assess male clients. For research, it would allow us to determine how their beliefs about masculinity correlated with depression, substance abuse, poor health habits, violence, and other harmful behaviors.

◆ ◆ ◆

Toward the end of my first year at Rutgers, I decided to run for a seat on the Committee for the Advancement of Professional Practice (CAPP), an important committee that controlled the budget and strategic priorities for the practice side of the American Psychological Association. My opponent: Rogers Wright, a powerful and influential practitioner.

The word about Rog was that he was an aggressive son of a bitch, but he was *our* son of a bitch. As one might expect from a person with such a reputation, Rog alienated many people and, perhaps as a result, I wound up winning. I was a nobody, and yet here I got elected to the very apex of APA boards and committees, defeating the Father of Professional Psychology.

As I climbed up the ladder at the APA, I found myself jogging in place at Rutgers. I put in my request to recruit a new professor; however, the dean demurred. We met in her commodious and tastefully decorated office.

"Ron," she said, "as you know, we're in the middle of a recession."

"Yes, I'm aware," I said, "but you'd promised me that I could hire a line a year when I came in. I'm only asking for one position at this point."

"And a year ago, when I hired you, I meant that," she said. "I had no reason to believe that I wouldn't be able to expand the program. In just one short year, so much has changed. Unemployment has risen from 3.8 to 5.5 percent. Real estate values have dropped.

Businesses are either laying off workers or freezing new hires. The state government is faced with a growing budget shortfall. They're cutting expenditures for public schools, hospitals, and, yes, higher education. No one is immune from this belt-tightening. I wish I had better news for you. I wish things were different. In this climate, there's just no way I will get approval to hire another line. Hell, I'll be lucky if I manage to keep all the hires we have."

"We only have three faculty in the counseling psychology program," I said. "Duncan's about to retire, which means we're about to only have two. Yet, staff of the APA Commission on Accreditation told Duncan that we would need a minimum of five full-time tenure track faculty even to consider applying."

"Yes," she said. "I'm sympathetic to your situation. I'd love to give you the needed lines to get your program accredited. My hands are tied here."

"Well, when do you foresee this situation changing? Do you think we can at least replace Duncan next year?"

"I don't know," she said. "I'm hesitant to make any promises."

"The year after?"

"I don't know."

"I see," I said, deflated.

Being stuck in an unaccredited program would not be a good look for my career.

But, as I thought about it further, the dean's stance might solve a lot of problems.

The housing market was still depressed, meaning selling my house in Cambridge would result in a financial loss. Yet, if I didn't sell that house, I couldn't afford to buy one in New Jersey. Plus, the commute was wearing on me. Really wearing on me. Not to mention, it was also very expensive.

In the Spring of 1990, I resigned from my job-for-life and returned to Boston.

◆ ◆ ◆

We were surrounded by family and friends who had gathered to celebrate my parents' fiftieth wedding anniversary.

People had traveled from around the country to be with us in Southern California.

Yet, here was my dad, asking people to keep the noise down.

Drink in hand, I leaned against the wall, wondering what held the two of them together.

Why had my mother stayed with him? Had she *loved* him? Just the idea of it seemed ridiculous. He was so crass, mean, gruff, and just plain uncomfortable to be around—and that described his *best* behavior.

When I was just a kid, I'd assumed she'd stuck around for me and Lowell. Yet, she'd remained by his side long after he and I had left home.

What could she possibly see in him?

I would never understand it.

As he loudly criticized my cousin, I rolled my eyes. It was embarrassing to be related to the man.

"He's a piece of work, isn't it?" Uncle Arwin, my dad's youngest brother, said quietly.

Unlike my father, Uncle Arwin was polite, soft-spoken, and encouraging.

"Yes, he is, Uncle Arwin. But I have a theory: I think he has PTSD," I said. "From when he was in the war. He was on a construction ship. Of course, it wasn't a battleship, but I'm guessing it was under attack, at least occasionally. Plus, it must have been terribly loud. Maybe that's why he hates noise? Maybe that's why he feels the need to control everyone and everything around him?"

"No, Ronnie," Uncle Arwin said, matter of factly. "Your father was always a bully. That's how he came out of the womb."

My Aunt Merle, Arwin's wife, added, "He's got the Curse of Wolf."

"The curse of what?"

"Wolf," she said. "Tomashinskii. Your great-great uncle. People say he was mean as hell. Once punched a horse in the head. Knocked the poor beast out. Grandma Sarah took after Wolf and passed that down to your uncle George and your father. It's a genetic mean streak. That's my take anyway."

I wanted so badly for my father to have an affliction. PTSD from war trauma? At least it allowed me to see him as a good person damaged by circumstances beyond his control. I could feel compassion over that situation. But him being born an asshole? It was too depressing to even contemplate.

◆ ◆ ◆

I thought back to the fatherhood courses I'd taught at BU. I'd encountered men who struggled to put their emotions into words. If I asked them how they felt, they usually responded with just one word, "Dunno." They also lacked theory of mind. It was as if they were oblivious to the thoughts and feelings of others around them. This inability to identify and describe their own emotions, and to sense the feelings of others seemed to hold these men back, ruin their relationships, and lead to all manner of unfortunate outcomes.

To find a way to help these men, I leased, furnished, and insured my own office and worked to expand my practice. I also accepted a part-time position in the Department of Psychiatry, Harvard Medical School at Cambridge Hospital, first as lecturer in Psychology, then as associate clinical professor of Psychology.

Then I dug into the research. Soon I formed a hypothesis and coined a new term: "normative male alexithymia." *Normative* referred to the influence of masculine norms, particularly the norm to restrict the expression of emotions. *Alexithymia* is the clinical term for an individual's difficulty identifying and describing their emotional experiences. It literally means "no words for emotions."

If my hypothesis was correct, men would meet criteria for this condition more frequently than women. Indeed, a narrative literature review and subsequent meta-analysis (in which the results of numerous studies are statistically aggregated) both revealed that men met the criteria for alexithymia significantly more often than did women. The effect was small, but that was also true for most sex differences in psychological attributes.

One of my students, Emily Karakis, later found that, among college men in heterosexual relationships, normative male alexithymia was negatively related to relationship satisfaction and communication quality, meaning that the greater the alexithymia, the lower the relationship satisfaction and communication quality. It was also positively related to fear of intimacy.

It was clear alexithymia was harming men.

Now it was time to figure out how to help men overcome it.

I asked my colleagues at Cambridge Hospital to refer to me the men whom their women clients complained about. I soon had a practice filled with men, some of whom were alexithymic, affording me a laboratory to experiment with techniques to treat alexithymia.

Over several years, I tried many approaches.

Eventually, as I worked with more and more men, I developed a step-by-step process that seemed to help.

Rick, one of my clients, had been married for fifteen years. When his wife informed him that she was pregnant, she became alarmed by his reaction—or more accurately, his lack of a response.

He'd shown no emotion. He wasn't freaked out. Nor was he overjoyed.

It was as if she'd told him that she'd purchased a new set of towels for the bathroom.

Concerned about what this might mean, she encouraged him to go into therapy.

Like so many of the men I worked with, Rick didn't want to be there, in my office, talking to me about his "feelings." He seemed closed off, a little like a trapped animal.

I had my work cut out for me.

During the intake interview, I asked, "When was the last time you cried?"

"I don't know. Maybe ten years ago? Yeah, that's when my dog was hit by a car and killed."

Ten years without crying? Crying is one of life's most effective means for relieving sadness. Tears flush stress hormones from the body, helping people to release negativity. As people cry, the brain releases oxytocin, a bonding hormone, and endorphins, which help to blunt pain.

By not crying for ten years, he was robbing himself of this ubiquitous means of catharsis.

"What are you feeling right now?"

"Nothing."

"What did you feel yesterday?"

"Nothing."

"How do you feel about your wife telling you to come here?"

"Nothing. I usually feel nothing."

When I asked about his family of origin, he described his parents in flat, one-dimensional terms. He mentioned their titles, their ages, what they did for a living, and their hobbies.

It was most striking when I asked him about his father, who'd died of a heart attack while Rick had been serving in the US Army.

"So, what was your father like?"

"He was a World War II vet, serving in the Air Force," Rick said. "He was a ball turret gunner—he sat in a bubble at the butt end of a bomber with a machine gun, fighting off enemy aircraft. He talked about this a lot, stating that he was 'one second from death.' He loved talking about the war and, of course, collected World War II memorabilia. And he also published the city's local newspaper."

Rick's tone was flat, his face expressionless. It was hard to tell how he felt. Angry? Sad?

"So those were things that he did. What was he like?"

"He was a good man, a family man, a hard-working man," Rick said, yet his tone of voice and facial expressions didn't match up. Something was off. I suspected there was more, hidden deep under the surface.

It was clear that Rick was alexithymic, so I used the evolving alexithymia reduction treatment program that I'd been developing.

We started with him naming words for emotions—because, if he didn't have words for emotions, he wouldn't be able to identify them.

"Before you come in for next week's session, I'd like you to do some homework," I said. "Would you be willing to write down as many words for emotions as you can on a piece of paper? Then bring your homework to your session next week."

"So, when I think of a word for an emotion, just write it down?"

"Yes, words that name an emotion is what we are looking for," I responded.

"Okay," he agreed, sounding a little confused.

I worried he might not complete the assignment at all. Or that, given the severity of his alexithymia, he might only list a few words. So, I threw a little more fuel on the fire.

"The guy I saw before you brought in thirty words," I said. I figured Rick's masculine competitiveness would encourage him to outdo that number.

The following week, Rick delivered, with thirty-one words. Like so many of the men I worked with, most of his words were descriptions of either anger (pissed off, furious, mad, frustrated, upset) or stress (zapped, burned out, overloaded.)

It was a start, but he still had a way to go. I encouraged him to keep this exercise up.

Next, I worked with him on reading emotions in other people, thinking that that would be easier than learning how to read his own emotions. I instructed him to read and understand nonverbal cues like tone of voice, facial expressions, body language, as well as paralinguistic qualities like sighs and gasps. During the session, we talked about what various nonverbal clues typically mean.

"Here's your homework for next week," I said. "When you're with a person or even watching TV, ask yourself, 'What are they feeling?' Go back to your vocabulary list from the last homework assignment and pick out the word or words that you think best describe what you are seeing in someone's nonverbal cues."

It took a couple of weeks before Rick became somewhat proficient at reading other people's emotions. For the third stage, I worked with him to identify his own emotions. I knew that some alexithymic men didn't experience emotions in the same way most people did. Most of them, however, did at least experience bodily sensations resulting from the physiological changes that accompany emotions: a lump in the throat, a hot face, weakness in the legs, tight shoulders, butterflies in the stomach, heaviness in the body. The problem: they didn't associate these sensations with emotions.

Rick and I talked this over for a while, with me explaining the psychophysiology of emotions.

Then I assigned more homework.

"I want you to pay attention to your bodily sensations for the next week. Whenever you notice one, write down what you're noticing in your body, along with some notes about what was happening around you just before you noticed the bodily sensations. In other words, who was doing what to whom, and how did that impact you?"

The following week, he arrived with several three-by-five cards, all of which contained handwritten notes about sensations and surrounding circumstances.

On one of them, he'd written, "My neck was kinda stiff."

He told me that, when he noticed that sensation, he had been waiting for a performance evaluation.

"So, what emotion do you think a stiff neck in that situation might represent?"

"Fear? Apprehension?" he asked.

"That sounds like an accurate assessment."

As one week slid into the next, I watched him transform.

Now that he had words to describe how he felt, Rick began to use them to talk about emotional wounds from his childhood that had been deeply buried.

"It was as if I had to bid for my father's attention," he said. "He never seemed interested in me. I even became the editor of my high school newspaper just so I would be able to talk to him about his work as a publisher. We could talk about the rights and responsibilities of the press. Even that didn't work. It was like he didn't fucking care about me at all. All he cared about was his stupid World War II experiences. I was fucking invisible to him."

"You seem furious."

"I am! It's not as if he couldn't socialize! He always had friends and colleagues at the house. He laughed and chatted with them for hours. He had no trouble spending time with them, talking about World War II. It was as if he just didn't care about me at all."

"Is this why you didn't go home when your dad had that first heart attack?"

"Yeah, probably," he said. "When I got the call, I was in the Army. I could have gotten leave. But I thought *fuck him*." Rick flipped the bird with both hands as he said it.

This likely explained why he "felt nothing" about his impending fatherhood. He had so many difficult unresolved feelings about his own father, he could not begin to imagine himself in that role.

"It must have been so difficult for you as a boy," I said. "To try so hard to make your father proud only to be ignored."

"It was," he said quietly. "It was. I just wanted. I just. . ."

His body tightened as if all the cells in his skin were preventing his inner contents from spilling out.

He leaned forward, cradling his face in his hands, and sobbed.

I nudged a box of tissues toward him. This was a huge step, him openly expressing the prohibited masculine emotions of sadness and grief.

"I'm sorry," he said, taking one and blowing his nose.

"Please don't apologize. That's how you're feeling. It's normal and healthy to cry. Crying is one of life's best methods for relieving sadness."

I sat with him for a while, giving him the time and space to process his grief.

Then I said, "Here's what I'd like to suggest. I imagine you have a lot of questions that you would like to ask your dad if he were alive. Could you write them down on those index cards that you have been using for your emotional response log? I'm not saying he could have answered them back then. He obviously can't answer them today. But it's important for you to know what you want from him."

The following week, Rick arrived with a stack of cards, each one listing a question, which we spent some time discussing. He remained flat and unemotional during this discussion.

So, I suggested a new task: visit his father's grave and ask the questions. This had to wait until he visited his mother at the family home in Minnesota. But he arranged his schedule to do it a couple of weeks later.

At the gravesite, he asked question after question. What did you think of me? Were you ever proud of me? Why didn't you spend more time with me?

Anger gave way to grief.

He sobbed for nearly twenty minutes.

Then he was done. He had been able to fully experience the grief he had long felt about his father's emotional absence in his life.

Having made significant progress in recapturing his ability to tune into and verbalize his emotional life, Rick began to experience some strong feelings about his expectant fatherhood, including fear, worry, and anxiety. He worried over whether the baby was going to be all right, given his wife's age. He investigated some obscure genetic diseases that ran in families of Scottish descent. I encouraged him to address his worries directly by attending one of his wife's visits to the obstetrician. He did so and was reassured about the baby's health. When he heard the baby's heartbeat, his fear turned to joy and excitement.

We terminated one month before the baby was due. Several weeks later, a postcard arrived in the mail. It was from Rick, informing me of the birth of his son:

"Ron, the baby was two weeks late. But he's a big guy, 8 lbs. 13 oz. And he definitely looks Scottish," Rick wrote with pride. That last sentence connected the dots from his son to him to his father and beyond.

As a postscript, I want to add that I made a teaching videotape of my work with Rick[6]. I showed parts of this tape during a workshop that I gave in Canada, and five minutes into the tape a member of the audience raised his hand and asked: "Were you trained by a first generation Rogerian?" Of course I was, but I had not realized that the training that I received from John Shlien was so indelible. The questioner himself had also been trained by another first generation Rogerian, William Kjell.

◆ ◆ ◆

As the years unfolded, I formed close friendships with other psychologists who were also doing work on men and masculinity. Eventually, we created a new APA division, Division 51, The Society for the Psychological Study of Men and Masculinity, along with a new journal, showcasing the research and clinical work of a growing number of psychologists working with boys and men.

The findings of my colleagues confirmed my initial hunches.

Gender role socialization caused boys to feel ashamed of their vulnerable and caring emotions.

---

6 https://www.psychotherapy.net/video/psychotherapy-men-ron-levant

Boys are expected to not show any vulnerability, nor any tenderness or need for another person because the most honored way to be a man is to never need another person for anything. They cannot be affectionate with another boy lest they be accused of being gay. They cannot express affection to a girl because children play in sex-segregated groups, and boys demonize girls (do you remember how boys would say that girls had "cooties"?). They cannot express affection to their mother lest they be denounced as a "mama's boy." Finally, fathers who subscribe to traditional masculine norms stop expressing physical affection to their sons around the time they enter school, out of fear that they will emasculate them.

As they grow up, boys learn that they must fit into the mold of a narrow set of stereotypical masculine traits. For example, aggression is a masculine expectation. We have scales that can measure aggression. If one were to administer one of these scales to one hundred boys, one would see a distribution of scores from very low to very high. If your boy scored very low on this scale, and you forced him to be aggressive, you would not only be straining his personality, but also you would put him at odds with the foremost tenet of Western Civilization—that of Individualism (as contrasted with the Collectivism of Eastern Civilization). From Aristotle to Shakespeare, we have been admonished, "To thine own self be true," "Be that self that one truly is." Or, as Oscar Wilde put it, tongue-in-cheek: "Be yourself. Everyone else is taken." Boys who are made to behave in a manner different from who they are cannot be true to themselves and thus are at odds with this overriding cultural imperative.

As boys confront these norms, they learn to stuff down their vulnerable emotions. Some boys also learn to transform these vulnerable emotions into anger, aggression, and even rage. Imagine a boy pushed down on the playground by another boy. At some level, he probably feels hurt, sad, and maybe also afraid. But he knows he must come back up with his fists flying, and certainly not with a face full of tears. That is, he must transform his vulnerable feelings into aggression and attack the other boy. Men who have had such experiences as boys have been known to fly into a rage, igniting much like a match struck to magnesium, when someone hurts their feelings.

The inability to identify emotions and put them into words blocks some men from utilizing life's most effective means known for dealing with all forms of stress. I am referring to identifying, thinking about, and discussing one's emotional response with other humans. Having an emotionally honest conversation about a stressful or hurtful situation with another person can provide empathy and emotional support, allowing the person to put the incident into perspective and figure out an emotionally satisfying way to handle it.

TAKEAWAYS

Readers, conduct an honest self-assessment. Do you struggle to know how you feel? Or how someone else feels? You can improve your emotional self-awareness (some call it emotional intelligence) with a little bit of work over a few weeks. Simply follow the exercises described in this chapter. There are four steps.

1. Build up your emotional vocabulary. Include words for vulnerable emotions—those that make you feel vulnerable—like sadness or fear.
2. Learn to read other people's emotions by focusing on *how* they say what they say. That is, what does their tone of voice or facial expression suggest about how they feel?
3. Learn to read your own emotions by keeping an emotional response log. If you have a feeling, or a bodily sensation that may be the physiological component of a feeling that you can't identify, write it down. Then ask yourself "who is doing what to whom and how does that affect me?" Then go through your vocabulary list to pick out the word or words that best describe what you are likely feeling.
4. Finally, practice, practice, practice. Emotional self-awareness is a skill that can be developed with practice.

CHAPTER 14

My Dad Dies

1994–1997

My father's car had veered into the shoulder. Adrenaline coursed through me. Had he fallen asleep? What had just happened? Why was his car, a well-maintained late-model Chrysler sedan, drifting to the right and onto the road's shoulder?

"Dad..."

Before I could say more, he jerked the wheel, yanking the car back into the lane.

"Dad," I said gently. "You seem to be misjudging where the shoulder is."

"Don't worry Ronnie," he spat. "It's nothing."

His words were full of sharp edges. He didn't want to talk about this.

Still, how could I let it go? This wasn't normal.

"Dad," I said as gently as I could. "Why don't you talk to your physician about it?"

"I'm healthy as a horse. I'm going to live to ninety," he said as if I were a grunt in the army and he was delivering my orders.

Healthy as a horse. How many times had he told me that? How could he possibly know?

How long would it be before I got the news that he and Mom were involved in a horrible car accident?

As he pulled into the driveway, I tried to put it out of my mind.

The man wouldn't listen—not to me, not to Mom, not to anyone. What could I do?

Several months later, my mother called.

Her voice was high-pitched, as if someone had put a tight vice around her voice box. She could barely get out a few words between sobs.

"Your father," she said.

"What is it, Mom?"

"Your father . . . Your father. He. . .He. . ."

"It's okay, Mom. Take your time. I'm here."

"He . . . he had a stroke."

I could hear her gulping down air. I yearned to hug her, to comfort her.

"Oh, Mom. I'm so sorry. How is he?"

"I don't know. He is in the hospital now, but he can still talk."

"I'm so sorry, Mom. I'm so sorry."

"We were just sitting down for lunch, and he complained of a headache that seemed to get worse, so I drove him to the ER."

I tried my best to comfort her, but she was inconsolable.

"It's okay, Mom," I told her. "I'm here."

Eventually, she told me she had to go. She wanted to get back to the hospital.

As I sat in my office, thinking over what she'd just told me, my thoughts traveled back to my teenage years. She'd threatened to leave him just after I'd run away. I'll never understand what stopped her.

Had she left him all those years ago, I doubt the man would still be in my life. As it was, he had become more of an obligation than a father. I visited because he was married to my mother, whom I loved, and not because I wanted to see him.

Last summer when he'd swerved off the highway, had he had a transient ischemic attack (TIA), a temporary period of symptoms like those of a stroke? Had that been what was wrong? Had we had a better relationship, I might have more aggressively pursued the matter and pushed him to get himself checked out. Had he mentioned it to a doctor, he could have gone on blood thinners. That might have prevented the big one.

But we didn't have a better relationship, and I didn't press the matter.

She hadn't asked, but I knew what Mom wanted. She wanted me to visit—to sit in his hospital room all day and night, to play the role of the doting son. Yet, it was the middle of the semester. I was teaching several classes. For me to visit, I would need to line up substitutes to teach my classes and supervise my students. I also would need to make arrangements for the clients in my practice.

Had a million things been different, maybe I would have thought nothing of dropping everything and arranging a flight.

But a million things weren't different, and I felt no urge to be there for him.

Winter break was coming up. It was just seven weeks away. I'd fly down then. It was the best I could do.

◆ ◆ ◆

He died several weeks later, long before winter break.

Regret swept through me.

Should I have canceled my psychotherapy sessions and lined up subs for my classes? Had I done so, would he and I have reconciled?

It was doubtful.

For one thing, the stroke had probably impaired his ability to communicate, making him incapable of deep conversation. More importantly, even if he hadn't been impaired, I didn't think he could ever have answered the questions that weighed down my heart. Why had he terrorized me? Was he proud of me? Was there anything about me that the man liked?

Had he lived for a decade longer—had I visited dozens more

times—I would likely be right where I was now, wishing things could have been different.

But here we were. The family gathered for the funeral. Most were in Southern California and simply drove to the VFW lodge in Oxnard. Caren flew in from LaGuardia, and Carol and I flew in from Boston.

After we boarded the flight to LAX, Carol sat beside me, quietly reading as I stared at the blank sheet of paper on my tray table. What could I possibly tell people during my eulogy?

At funerals, no one mentions the negative.

I was supposed to tell people about his service in the war, and his entrepreneurial spirit, how he'd scrimped and saved to buy a business and build it up, and how he'd provided for his family.

I was supposed to say that I missed him, that he'd given me great advice, that he'd been there for me, that he was a wonderful father.

I couldn't.

"This is difficult for me primarily because of all of the unfinished business I have with my father," I wrote. "And while a part of me continues to nurture the hope that, had he lived longer, I would have been able to finish my business, I have to acknowledge that this is not true."

I read over the words. Was this okay to say at a funeral? Who knows? I was going to go with it.

I thought back to the men taking my Fatherhood Course. It seemed as if we'd shared similar experiences. Maybe, instead of making this about myself and my father, I could make this about them.

My pen scurried across the page.

"In the Fatherhood Course that I teach, this issue of son-father business usually comes up in the first class. We might be talking about why the men decided to enroll in the course, and after a few guys give the standard reasons and others make some quips, the mood palpably shifts to serious as one father speaks, lower lip quivering." I then quoted what Clyde had said over a decade earlier:

'You want to know why I am here? I'll tell you why I am here. I am here so that my little son will not feel as bad about me when he's grown up as I do about my dad.' Clyde's words were bracing. Soon the theme of father-son business was on every man's lips. The fathers then become sons and talk about the grief, pain, and bitterness they feel toward their fathers."

I continued writing, listing what these men said about their fathers, talking about what I'd learned through my research—hinting that it applied to me but not explicitly saying it.

The pen came to a stop.

I'd have to talk about myself.

It would be weird not to do so.

I hated the fact that I found this so hard.

"So where am I in all of this? Obviously, I find it easier to talk about other people and things in general than to talk about myself as a son in relationship to my father. And, of course, this reflects the fact that I do have unfinished business with him."

I wrote about my yearning for a close relationship, how I wanted to know that he loved me, the questions I wished I'd asked him, and some of his good qualities. Yes, he had been a good provider. He was self-sufficient. He did have spectacular talents, like his ability to perform complex arithmetic in his head.

"He did the best he could with what he had."

It was a cliché. It would have to do. What else could I say?

I neatly folded the paper and slid it into my suit pocket.

◆ ◆ ◆

Before cremating my father, as he had wished, the funeral home invited us to view the body. Caren and I accepted the offer, but Carol demurred.

Without calcium ions flowing in and out of his cells, his facial muscles were flaccid. The characteristic furrow between his brows was gone. His jaw was relaxed, his mouth still open from his last inhale.

He no longer looked like someone a few seconds away from an explosion. Now, he seemed small, defenseless, and weak.

I leaned forward, gasping for air.

Caren wrapped her arm around me, slowly stroking my back.

Why was I sobbing?

I felt out of control, bewildered, wailing, and not knowing why. She never left my side.

◆ ◆ ◆

I looked out at the crowd of people gathered at the VFW to pay their respects. My mother appeared deep in grief. Lowell was expressionless, stoic, as usual. Caren was composed. She had always been afraid of my dad's anger. Carol's face wore an expression of deep sympathy. Other mourners seemed uncomfortable, perhaps a little bored.

"What was it like for him to be my dad, especially during the early years when he was stationed on a ship in the Pacific during WWII and saw me only rarely?" I asked. "What did he think about during those long absences? What did he feel when he learned that, as a two-year-old living with my mother and maternal grandparents, I would open the shirt of any man who came to the house to check and see if he had enough chest hair to be Dad? What was his reaction when I packed my pockets with snow upon leaving Minnesota to reunite with him in California because I thought he would really like snow? Why was he always so tense and unhappy in that house on Ledgewood Road? Why was he so disapproving and angry at me?"

I took a breath, looking at the faces in front of me.

His buddies from VFW, his home away from home, seemed puzzled, not understanding the meaning of my words. Had they known a different side of my father?

I continued.

"He fully lived up to his standards, which were the standards of his generation, a generation unlike my own whose worldview was shaped by the severe hardship of the Great Depression and the near calamity of WWII."

The crowd seemed unmoved.

I folded the paper, slid it into my suit pocket, and sat down. It was over.

◆ ◆ ◆

After the funeral, I stayed with my mother for a week, lining up support services for her, as a social worker might. Mom was suffering from macular degeneration and only had peripheral vision, so I consulted with the local chapter of the Braille Institute, enrolled her in some adaptive classes, and found out that prismatic glasses would help her see, so we got her a pair of those. The glasses were a godsend, allowing her to watch her favorite TV shows. I also lined up transportation resources so that she could go to the grocery store and attend her appointments with her doctors.

The day after the funeral, Mom asked Lowell and me to meet her in the dining room. On the table were family heirlooms and valuables, including her engagement ring and diamond earrings.

"There's no reason for me to hang onto all of this anymore," she said, dabbing away a few tears with a tissue. "I'd like you and Lowell to have these."

"Mom, are you sure?" I asked.

"Yes, Ronnie," she said. "They were once important to me. Your father is no longer with me, and I no longer get dressed up to go anywhere. I have no use for these things. Perhaps you boys could make use of them?"

Lowell picked up my father's wedding band.

"I'd like to have this, Mamala."

"Sure, honey," she said.

"Lowell, would it be okay if I take the engagement ring?"

"Sure, brother," Lowell said with a wink. "You have more use for that than I ever will."

I cradled the ring between my thumb and index finger. I'd never looked at it very closely before. Made from white gold, it had one large diamond in the middle surrounded by a ring of smaller ones.

"When your father first proposed to me, he didn't have enough money to buy a ring," Mom told us. "I didn't have one for many years. He surprised me one day with this ring after he purchased the printing company."

I turned to Carol and said, "As you just heard, this was my mother's," I said. "I would like you to have it. The past several years have been the best in my life. Would you do me the honor of being my wife?"

She took the ring from the box, slid it onto her ring finger, and hugged me.

TAKEAWAYS

Readers, are you in the situation of having lost a parent with whom you have unresolved issues? Grief is challenging under the best of circumstances but is made much more difficult if you have never achieved reconciliation. It is very hard to grieve when you are angry at the person that you lost. Furthermore, our understanding of grief is limited. Kübler Ross's stage theory attempts to make sense of grief, but research suggests that it does not capture the full picture. Most of us grieve in ways that do not fit any existing model.

What worked for me was to find a way to *exonerate* my dad—to forgive him for his flaws. I used the fact that he was said to have the "Curse of Wolf." I reasoned with myself that his cruelty was a family trait that he had inherited. Given this I could more easily accept the fact that he truly did the best with what he had. And then I could give him credit where credit was due. He did serve his (adopted) country during World War II. He did become a small businessman. He did provide for his family.

But given his extraordinary mathematical abilities, I have often wondered who he might have been if he'd had the advantages that I have had in my life.

CHAPTER 15

Hitting My Stride

1995–2005

As 1995 dawned, my life felt as if it was coming together on multiple levels. I was moving up the ladder at the American Psychological Association. After finishing my sixth year on CAPP, the last two as the chair, I ran for an at-large seat on the APA Board of Directors and won. There was talk, among some in APA, that I was now in line to become APA president.

My personal life had also taken on a predictable rhythm. Caren and Adam now had two children, Adrian and Jeremy. (They later divorced, and Caren eventually remarried). Carol and I visited them several times a year, always bringing an enormous quantity of gifts. I would always buy them clothes, and the boys liked the styles at Bugle Boys. Of course, there were also fun things, including entire boxes of Topps sports cards, baseball in the spring, football in the fall. Each box contained hundreds of cards and just as many sticks of gum. Adrian and Jeremy tore through their boxes, feverishly searching for rare gems like Mickey Mantle, Willie Mays, or Hank Aaron. As they discovered doubles, they pushed them aside, stacking up the dozens of sticks of gum. Once they'd organized their cards, they excitedly traded. I loved seeing them so animated and happy.

I poured everything into these visits, playing with the two of them for hours. After several days, I felt like I needed a vacation from my vacation.

That winter of 1995, Carol and I flew to Key West, booking a room at a resort where we'd vacationed several times. Located at the southernmost part of the US, a mere ninety miles from Cuba, The Reach overlooked the ocean. On January 17, we wed on the resort's pier to the sounds of crashing waves and chirping gulls. It was just the two of us and a justice of the peace. We had a very nice dinner at a beachfront restaurant next door to the resort, watching the restaurant owner's golden retriever play in the waves. Later in the evening, we stood on Mallory Pier, along with hundreds of others. The setting sun transformed the sky and water into bright yellows, pinks, and purples. We lingered for an hour or so, taking in the beauty. As the sun descended into the Gulf of Mexico, it felt like I'd finally escaped the chains of my childhood.

◆ ◆ ◆

My mother's health was deteriorating. In addition to her blindness and diabetes, she was now having cognitive and mental health issues.

She seemed to be becoming increasingly paranoid. Periodically, when I called, she railed about people she swore were out to get her. None of it made sense. One day she told me that my cousins, the Gould girls, had stolen the insides of her VCR.

"That's why it doesn't work!" she screamed. "Why would they do something like that?"

"Mom, are you sure Anita, Diane, and Rhoda did this?"

"Yes, Ronnie," she said curtly. "I am. Don't question me like that. I know what I am talking about!"

She was no longer the person I remembered. It was as if someone had stolen my mother and replaced her with an angry, paranoid old woman.

Lowell was experiencing his own tale of woes. He'd gone to work one day hopelessly hung over from a long night of drinking. While using machinery to transport huge pallets, he'd seriously injured a coworker. As a result, he ended up on probation at his place of employment and had to complete a remediation plan to return to work. But all this came with a big silver lining. He got sober, began attending AA meetings regularly, and offered to care for our mother full-time. He moved Mom into his two-bedroom townhouse in Newark, in the East Bay of the San Francisco Bay Area, and stored her household belongings in a rented storage unit. They became inseparable.

◆ ◆ ◆

One day I got a call from Ron Fox, a friend, colleague, and former APA president who had founded one of the first professional schools of psychology at Wright State University in Dayton, Ohio. He was also famous for his Mark Twin-like analogies, such as "that's like nailing Jell-O to a tree" or "that's like putting fog into an envelope."

"You're a damned fool, Ron; you know that?"

"I do, but what specifically are you referring to?"

"Gene Shapiro told you about the open dean position at Nova Southeastern University in Ft. Lauderdale. But you haven't put your hat in the ring."

"Ron, it's like I told Gene," I said, "I love my life in Boston. Plus, academic administration? It's not my thing."

"Come on, Ron. You have had graduate education in management with the MBA you earned while at BU, on top of your EdD. You've taken on numerous leadership positions in the APA. How could it not be your thing? You're a born leader. Plus, Nova's Center for Psychological Studies is a huge professional school of psychology situated in a highly entrepreneurial university. CPS runs a community mental health center that serves half of Broward County. We're talking 2.5 million people. With such significant resources, you could pioneer new clinical psychology training models for the twenty-first century."

"I see," I said.

He'd piqued my interest.

"Now, I should warn you. They've got some problems down there, but it's nothing you can't handle. The position is open because the founding dean of CPS, Frank DePiano, was deposed in a faculty revolt."

"Christ. Seriously?"

"Yeah, I am as serious as a heart attack. The faculty then voted the revolt leader, Michel Hersen, in as dean. But the whole thing turned into a circular firing squad because the University president then fired him. Thus, the present search for a new dean."

"Got it. It sounds a bit tenuous, don't you think?"

"It's like I said, it's nothing you can't handle. You're the man for the job. Have I talked you into it yet?"

"Maybe," I said. "But I have to talk it over with Carol."

Over the next several days, she and I aired this opportunity out, weighing the various pros and cons. As was the case when the opportunity had opened at Rutgers University almost a decade before, there was a significant downside: Carol was moving up the publishing ladder at Houghton Mifflin but needed to be in Boston to do her job. If we moved to Florida, she would be walking away from that career, essentially choosing mine over hers.

It wasn't an easy decision for us, but Carol eventually agreed to move should I be offered the position. Given how much Ron Fox had already greased the wheels, I was a shoo-in. I aced the typical obligatory campus visit, with many interviews and a presentation to the entire school. Soon I was having dinner with Nova's president, Ovid Lewis, and his wife, at their spacious Ft. Lauderdale home. As we ate, a Lionel train occasionally raced along a platform he'd constructed just below the ceiling throughout his home.

After the meal, Ovid's wife offered Carol a tour of their home. Ovid and I sat in his living room among the many curios and objets d'art stored in display cases. He offered me the position.

"How would a hundred and forty thousand dollars sound?" he asked.

I didn't say anything. I might have rolled my eyes.

"Oh, you're right. It's more like a medical school dean's job because you've got the clinic. How about a hundred and eighty?"

"Sold," I said, appreciating the fact that Ovid wound up negotiating against himself.

It took a few months, but Carol and I eventually sold our house in the Boston area, bought a new one in Plantation, a suburb of Ft. Lauderdale that was close to Nova, and moved to South Florida.

We arrived with our cats, but ahead of our belongings.

On that first night, we camped out on inflatable beds. There was a ferocious storm like neither of us had ever seen before. The sky was filled with lightning bolts. The loud cracks lasted for hours, terrifying our kitties. Adding to the torture, the low battery signal for a smoke detector kept beeping. Someone had mounted the thing near the ceiling, which was eighteen feet high. We had no ladder, so we couldn't reach it, which meant the beeping persisted all night long.

The following morning, groggy and sore, I wondered: was this an inkling of what was to come? I couldn't shake the feeling that, once again, I'd made the wrong decision.

In the weeks between my accepting the position and moving to Florida, President Lewis got pushed out of his position. The trustees ushered in a former litigator named Raymond Ferrero, Jr., who was the chairman of NSU's Board of Trustees. It wasn't the best situation, but I figured I'd make the best of it.

The atmosphere in CPS was tense and testy. I can recall during my first week how my gut tightened when I saw one faculty member, Susie Smith, who was said to have been one of the ring leaders of the revolt, deliver a memo to my associate dean, Gene Shapiro, by extending her arm through the doorway and dropping the memo on the floor, a delivery mode that conveyed hostility. Gene, who passed away in 2021 at the age of 101, was a legend in professional psychology. He was one of the group of rebellious practitioners known as the "Dirty Dozen," who during the 1980s effectively challenged the academic psychologists who had held hegemony over the governance of American Psychological Association for many decades. Gene was in his late seventies when I joined NSU. A slight man with full head of white hair, Gene played tennis with men half his age, and won more often than not. Ron Fox was also a member of the Dirty Dozen, and he agreed to serve as my organizational consultant while I was dean.

◆ ◆ ◆

Several weeks into the job, I received a visit from a man who looked and talked like a cop. He introduced himself and said he was from the US Joint Medicaid-Medicare Fraud Task Force.

"I'd like to talk to you about CPS's billing practices," he said.

"I'm happy to help," I replied, "but I just started here a few weeks ago. I'm not sure what I can tell you at this point. Maybe you can fill me in a bit on what you are looking for?"

"You've been here for only a few weeks?"

"Yes," I said, not liking his sarcastic tone.

"Well, you'll have your work cut out for you. Nova's CPS has been contracting with the state of Florida for its Community Mental Health Center, which is largely funded by federal dollars. So, millions upon millions in contracts. Let's just say I'm here to investigate fraud."

"Fraud?"

"Yes, fraud."

"What kind of fraud."

"Well, sir, the government suspects that a lot of the billing from CPS shouldn't have happened—that we shouldn't have paid you on millions of claims."

I rested my face against my palms.

Why hadn't anyone told me this?

I wondered: had I known the full extent of the problems, would I have taken the job?

Over the next several weeks, I learned that a subset of faculty members believed that DePiano had engaged in improper billings for the clinic. That's why they'd revolted. One of them had filed a *qui tam* legal action, which permitted him to sue on behalf of the United States to recover fraudulently obtained money. In addition, another faculty member, Wanda Wannamaker, had filed a separate lawsuit for various grievances concerning her treatment as a professor.

Now, some of the faculty thought I was Frank DePiano's "goon," sent in to avenge his deposing. Amazingly, even though DePiano had been pushed out as dean and was potentially implicated in fraud, he remained a close advisor to President Ferrero.

Others saw me as a "stooge" of Michel Hersen, who'd led the faculty revolt and had served a short stint as dean. Hersen had left the university shortly after being asked to step down as dean by President Lewis a few months earlier.

Our faculty meetings became scowl sessions. The thirty-five faculty members would silently file into the large conference room. The Hersen supporters crowded together on one side of the U-shaped table. The DiPiano supporters sat on the other side. With the two factions glaring at each other, my very able assistant, Diane Karol, and I sat at the bottom of the U, sometimes with other administrators sitting with us, such as the director of the clinic, or one or both of the two associate deans, trying to keep the peace.

Nova eventually settled with the government. In return for avoiding criminal prosecution, Nova agreed to pay the government back for the challenged billings by offering free services to the community for many years. Nova, like Harvard, operated on the principal of "every tub on its own bottom," meaning that the deans of each school or college had to cover their expenses and return a certain percentage of their revenue to the university. Thus, I had to find a way to fund the millions of dollars of free services.

◆ ◆ ◆

One thing you can say about South Florida is that there are a lot of people who have a lot of money, which certainly helped with fundraising. We set up an annual Humanitarian of the Year Award and presented it during an annual gala celebration. This was administered by our amazing development officer Daniela Sciarrotta, who had an effervescent personality. We selected a well-known South Florida honoree, such as Lorraine Thomas, the widow of the late Dave Thomas, the founder of Wendy's Restaurants. Then we invited the honoree's friends and family to join the host committee. Each host agreed to buy event tables to accommodate their social circles. Of course, people who were friends of the honoree, or those who aspired to be their friends, would sign up as sponsors at various levels, from silver to platinum. It wasn't exactly a pyramid scheme, but it did pull money out of people's wallets. As if that wasn't enough, we also started the event with a reception and silent auction of goods donated by local businesses.

As dean I was also responsible for bringing in grant money. Some of the faculty were active researchers, and they were awarded research grants from the National Science Foundation or the National Institute for Mental Health. In addition, I also sought federal funds that had been earmarked by one of Florida's Senators. Funded by the Edward Byrne Memorial State and Local Law Enforcement Assistance Program, Bureau of Justice Assistance, of the US Department of Justice, one of them totaled $226,166. Using these funds, we created the South Florida Medical Corrections Options Program to support the mental health needs of women in the criminal justice system.

I also gave talks in the community, such as to the Rotary Club, often about people who benefitted from our programs, such as those suffering from schizophrenia. After one of these talks, I returned to my office to receive a message from an attendee, who had a son who suffered from schizophrenia. She donated five million dollars to set up a scholarship fund for our program in serious mental illness.

But the main way I covered the settlement agreement costs was to create more academic programs. In many ways, I felt I was continually robbing Peter to pay Paul, but what choice did I have?

These included predoctoral concentrations in specialized areas of psychology such as neuropsychology, forensic psychology, health psychology, and the psychology of serious mental illness. Previously, such concentrations could only be accessed on a postdoctoral basis, through a formal postdoc or residency. The creation of these concentrations allowed faculty to focus on their areas of specialization, which won many of them over. We also developed a host of master's and specialist degree programs in counseling and school psychology and hired additional faculty in these areas to provide instruction.

The icing on the cake was our "fly-in" postdoctoral master's degree program in clinical psychopharmacology for licensed psychologists. Licensed psychologists flew to Ft. Lauderdale in the winter to participate in several weekend training sessions. Faculty in Nova's Health Professions Division taught courses in psychopharmacology. The psychiatrists from the clinic provided practicum training in prescribing psychoactive medications. Thanks to the program and others that preceded it, the Department of Defense, Bureau of Indian Affairs, and many states now permitted licensed psychologists with additional qualifications (e.g., postdoctoral masters-level training in clinical psychopharmacology) to prescribe psychoactive medications to their patients. This expanded mental health care in those jurisdictions.

These new programs positioned Nova as a leader in professional psychology for the new millennium, as Ron Fox had predicted.

All the while, President Ferrero remained suspicious of me. We never met in his office. It was always in his adjoining conference room, surrounded by stacks of folders and binders. He sat in an expensive, overstuffed chair. The rest of the chairs at the table were small, which generated the feeling of a serf visiting the king. Ferrero barked question after question, asking me what I was doing to make budget. I'd tell him about the ways I was busting my ass, about several programs I'd started that would bring in revenue, offsetting the hemorrhaging of funds of the clinic, which was a problem that I hadn't created. It didn't matter how much I did or how hard I worked. His next question was, "And what else are you doing?" It was never enough. No matter how much I prepared for the meetings, he always found a way to zero in on some weakness, leaving me feeling humiliated.

It was a mess, and I felt trapped. I hadn't created the problem but were I to leave, the problem could be blamed on me.

◆ ◆ ◆

One day, a young doctoral student, Kate Richmond, knocked on my door.

"I've read your work and want to work with you," she said.

I had several boxes of filled-out questionnaires from hundreds of people in a multicultural investigation of masculinity ideology and alexithymia, which included Black, White, Latinx, and Puerto Rican samples collected during my time at Harvard Medical School. All this data needed to be entered into a spreadsheet so we could crunch the numbers. It was an arduous task, and she agreed to take it on. We eventually published the research and Kate got second authorship.

Kate also set up a research lab named the Gender Research Team, which at its peak had eighteen members—doctoral students, master's students, and one post doc. Most were women, as the gender composition of clinical psychology programs had long been changing in favor of women. As a result, our focus broadened. In addition to masculinity, the team also studied femininity. Kate did her dissertation investigating the Femininity Ideology Scale, initially developed by colleague Carol Philpot and her students at the Florida Institute of Technology and bequeathed to us when Carol retired. We also investigated women's nontraditional sexuality. That was because the students were enthralled by *Sex and the City*, a popular TV show that portrayed women engaging in casual sex.

◆ ◆ ◆

In early 2003, Lowell informed me that our mother had been hospitalized with sepsis. The infection had started in her bladder and spread to her blood. Within days, she was gone. In many ways, I'd lost her years before her final breath. It was dementia that had robbed me of my mother. Sepsis? It killed a woman I no longer recognized.

Her funeral was held in Oxnard, where she was buried. Our relatives from Southern California attended. Lowell and I gave short impromptu eulogies.

All the while, I was moving up the ranks in APA, taking on various leadership roles and winning an election for recording secretary after completing my term as an at-large member of the Board of Directors.

Around this time, I decided to run for the APA presidency. Somehow, however, President Ferrero got wind of my intentions. During one of our grill sessions, he quipped, "I heard you are thinking of running for APA president. Don't do it." I could have asked him why he felt that way. I could have given him all the reasons I wanted to run. I could have argued that my being APA president would elevate the stature of Nova. I did none of that. I merely nodded, giving him the impression that I agreed. Later, as I returned to my office, I thought, *Fuck him. I'm running.*

I knew what I was risking. I likely would lose my job over the decision, and I didn't care. I was feeling pretty good about my chances. I'd earned recognition in psychology thanks to the work we had done at Nova. Plus, my mentor and friend Pat DeLeon (a former APA president who worked as chief of staff for the Senator Daniel K. Inouye of Hawaii) had done the research. "In all of APA's history," he said, "going back to the late 1800s, no recording secretary who ran for president has ever failed to be elected president."

My candidacy's slogan was "Make Psychology a Household Word," which spoke to the need to enhance the reception of psychological services by the public. At that time there still was a lot of stigma associated with mental illness. I also gave a subtle nod to the changing gender composition of APA by using a lot of pink in my campaign materials. They had the Barbie vibe, long before the movie came out. I also pioneered the idea of the "psychological checkup," akin to checkups done by physicians and dentists, and publicized it in a media project.

Five people ran for the top job and almost eighteen thousand members voted. The APA used ranked choice tallying, which required up to five rounds of voting. After each round the second-place votes for the losing candidates were redistributed to the remaining candidates. I won on the third round with almost ten thousand votes.

The following day, when I came into work, a giant banner was hanging from the second floor. It said, "Dean Levant Won!"

◆ ◆ ◆

Despite my stature at APA, things at Nova were deteriorating.

Periodically, Ferrero ordered me to attend meetings at the administration building with a group of lawyers. Ferrero and Tom Panza, university counsel, were both very large men and could be very intimidating.

They and the other lawyers fired questions at me, many of which I could not answer at the level of detail requested, as I wasn't allowed to bring any of my staff to the meetings and would have relied on them for that very specific information.

I found these meetings disrespectful, even humiliating, but maybe that was the point. The crowning blow was when the medical school dean complained to President Ferrero about the fly-in postdoctoral master's degree program. The medical school dean didn't think we should be training psychologists to prescribe medications. That was the job of psychiatrists, he said. Despite the program's success, President Ferrero agreed and ordered me to shut it down. I pushed back, perhaps too aggressively. Soon I was asked to step down. To encourage my compliance, I was offered a paid semester sabbatical and professorship. It gave me the time I needed to figure out my next move.

I spent the next few months searching for a new job as a dean. Serving as APA president certainly helped. During one campus visit, I overheard a group of students talking excitedly that "the president of APA is interviewing for a job here."

Eventually, the University of Akron offered me a position as dean of the Buchtel College of Arts and Sciences. Soon Carol and I were off to Northeast Ohio.

CHAPTER 16

My APA Presidency

2005

Half of my year as APA president was spent at Nova, where my schedule was very flexible, and half at Akron, where it was the opposite.

During that year I attended thirty-seven different psychology meetings and sponsored four presidential initiatives plus two additional projects. I traveled every week, sometimes twice a week, and once three times. Some of these meetings turned out to be extensive introductions to a part of the country that I knew very little about. For example, I was invited by the Mississippi Psychological Association to give a talk at their annual meeting. Katherine Nordal, who would later become the third executive director of the Practice Directorate, was my host, and she also arranged for several interesting side trips. One was to Mississippi State Hospital, one of the few in the country that had not been closed down in the era of deinstitutionalization, and one that was regarded as a high-level inpatient psychiatric facility. My observations: staff morale seemed very high, the patients seemed to be well cared for, and there was even a museum of the history of the hospital. It was quite unlike both Mendocino State Hospital, where I had stayed briefly in the 60s, and Boston State Hospital, where I did my first practicum in 1970.

The second was to Jackson State University (JSU), where I gave a more academic presentation on my work on the psychology of men and masculinity. JSU is a historically black public research university (HBCU) and is one of the largest HBCUs in the United States and the fourth largest university in Mississippi in terms of student enrollment. Furthermore, it was one of the few that housed an APA-accredited PhD program in clinical psychology. So JSU is nothing to sniff at! I will never forget how graciously I was received. In my introduction, a faculty member took pains to comment on my curriculum vitae, noting that I'd had at least one publication for every year since 1978.

Of my several presidential initiatives and projects, probably the most consequential was on evidence-based practice in psychology. APA has had a long history of competition and conflict between the science/academic and practice parts of the organization, which I have previously alluded to in describing the Dirty Dozen, a group of rebellious practitioners who rose up to challenge the academic hegemony. Just as an aside, these wars put a lot of APA members like me who considered themselves scientist-practitioners in a bind. But be that as it may, in 1995, one of APA's divisions, Clinical Psychology, had set up a task force on "Empirically Validated Treatments," that turned out to be highly divisive. They threw down the gauntlet: to be considered empirically validated a psychological treatment had to be supported by two randomized clinical trials (RCTs). This was a very high bar. Not only are RCTs very expensive and require large scale funding, typically from a federal agency, but also holding out RCTs as the sole or main criterion flew in the face of the Institute of Medicine's definition of Evidence-Based Medicine: "Evidence-based medical practice is the integration of the best research evidence with clinical expertise and patient values." Accordingly, my APA Presidential Task Force on Evidence-Based Practice in Psychology followed the Institute of Medicine's definition.

This Task Force included a diverse group of eighteen scientists and practitioners. The Task Force had brought together people who would not have been likely to attend each other's programs at the APA annual convention. They worked in mixed groups to hear and understand the multiple nuances involved in every issue. I was very impressed with how effectively the members worked to hear each other's perspectives and seek common ground. These efforts succeeded. The APA Council of Representatives at its August 2005 meeting adopted the Policy Statement on Evidence Based Practice in Psychology and received the Report of the Task Force. In addition, the Report was published in the *American Psychologist*.

The standout highlight of my term as president was giving a eulogy for Kenneth Bancroft Clark at his funeral. Dr. Clark and his wife Dr. Mamie Phipps Clark conducted research showing that Black children preferred White dolls, and that some children grew distressed when asked to say which of the dolls (Black or White) looked like them. In my estimation, this study had the most profound impact on social issues of any psychological study, ever. It was used to support the Supreme Court decision in the Brown vs. Board of Education case in 1954 that desegregated schooling. "To separate [Black children] from others of similar age and qualifications solely because of their race generates a feeling of inferiority as to their status in the community that may affect their hearts and minds in a way unlikely ever to be undone," wrote Chief Justice Earl Warren in the opinion. Kenneth Clark, who had served as APA president in 1971, had asked his son, Hilton Clark, to ensure that the sitting APA president give a eulogy at his funeral. Thus, as I was enroute from Ft. Lauderdale, Florida to Coeur d'Alene, Idaho, for a joint meeting of three state psychological associations, on what was a very long journey involving three planes and a van, I got a call from Hilton Clark, inviting me. The funeral, which was held at a historic Black church in Harlem, was attended by many prominent people, including presidential advisor Vernon Jordan, and the historian John Hope Franklin (who also gave a eulogy).

I would be remiss if I did not discuss another project that occurred on my watch, one that became highly contentious about a decade later, namely the Psychological Ethics and National Security

(PENS) Task Force. It became controversial because a group of dissident APA members fought for a decade to discredit its work, culminating in the Hoffman Report in 2015, which alleged that APA governance leaders and executive staff colluded with the US Department of Defense to weaken APA ethical standards to permit psychologists to conduct "enhanced interrogations," such as waterboarding, stress positions, sleep deprivation, and the like— all of which are tantamount to torture. The Hoffman Report has long since been debunked by multiple sources. APA is still facing litigation over it, and several APA employees who were terminated because of it won multi-million-dollar settlements.

In fact, the only psychologists ever proven to be involved with these enhanced interrogations were James Mitchell and Bruce Jessen, former Air Force psychologists who were tasked by the CIA in 2002 to establish a program of severe interrogation techniques. They were not members of the governance or staff of APA, and in fact were not even APA members.

The purpose of the PENS Task Force was to advise military psychologists from the APA Division on Military Psychology who had requested advice from the APA Board of Directors on how to adhere to the APA ethics code while they fulfilled a new role, namely that of supporting the interrogation of detainees. The PENS report correctly noted that APA's leadership agreed in advance that it is not unethical for psychologists to serve in military or intelligence settings (or in prisons and police settings, which are very similar). It never has been. Contrary to the accusations made by Hoffman, I was never a party to any conversation or email thread that discussed weakening psychological ethics or allowing psychologists to participate in enhanced interrogation techniques. If I had, I would have immediately denounced it.

Interestingly, much of the focus of the Hoffman Report was on those of us who were volunteer members of governance, rather than the paid executive staff of APA. In my thirty years of involvement in various roles, APA has always been a staff-driven organization. The matters in which I was cited as having had responsibility were all done at the behest of or on the recommendation of staff. The bottom line is that I am not embarrassed about any of the policies that I supported at the time, and I never did anything illegal or unethical. But please also understand that I am not in any way saying that I think that staff did anything wrong either. The multi-million-dollar settlements with APA employees who were terminated as a result of the Hoffman Report clearly attest to that.

I also visited the Joint Task Force at Guantanamo Bay (GTMO), where detainees were being held. I participated as the president of the American Psychological Association and was part of a group of leaders from several national health and mental health organizations as well as United States and Department of Defense Officials. My purpose in participating was to inform the participants and other individuals of APA's position against torture and cruel, inhuman, or degrading treatment. The trip afforded a unique opportunity to speak with people directly about APA's work in this area, and to clarify questions about APA's position. The trip had no "fact-finding" component.

Two members of the Behavioral Science Consultation Team (BSCTs, pronounced "biscuits"), both psychologists, were present in the initial orientation meeting, and one accompanied us for the rest of our visit. I had individual conversations with each of them. I learned that BSCTs observe interrogations from video monitors or behind one-way mirrors, consult and advise interrogations on such matters as how to establish or improve rapport and ask questions more effectively. BSCTs help interrogators who get frustrated and angry when the detainees do not provide the information they want, by offering instruction in self-control and anger-management techniques. BSCTs monitor interactions between interrogators and detainees to guard against the kind of behavioral drift that can become abusive.

One of the BSCTs who had been at GTMO only a short time told me that she had been reluctant to take the assignment because of news reports that BSCTs were engaging in unethical practices. She told me that, since being there for a couple of months, she'd had a change of attitude and stated unequivocally "I am not doing unethical things."

We visited the brand-new psychiatric wing, which offered both inpatient and outpatient services. I had a very unusual experience as we were standing at the nursing station, receiving a briefing from the psychiatrist. Behind me a voice asked "Dean Levant? Is that you?" That was the last thing I had expected to hear at GTMO! I turned to see a former doctoral student in clinical psychology from Nova Southeastern University, who was then a military psychologist. I thought to myself, *NSU's graduates sure have done a good job of getting out into the world!*

CHAPTER 17

The Best Part of Me

(2005–)

The University of Akron (UA) punches way above its weight class, so to speak, and Northeast Ohio is an undiscovered gem. How many metropolitan areas have a national park? Because of its long tire-manufacturing history, Akron earned the nickname "the Rubber Capital of the World."

The headhunters had warned: at the University of Akron, the administration and faculty got along about as harmoniously as lions fighting to lead the pride. When I arrived on the job, the University had just signed its first contract with the American Association of University Professors, the faculty union. My first task as dean was implementing that contract in my college. This involved rewriting each of the departments' guidelines for retention, promotion, and tenure, merit raises, and the naming of distinguished professors.

I had my work cut out for me.

Deans like me were middle managers, negotiating between the faculty (led by department chairs) and central administration (represented by the provost). Each new guideline went through multiple rounds of review and revision. It proved to be an extremely contentious and arduous process. No one agreed, and everyone resented the process.

In addition, the scope of the job was enormous. I supervised eighteen academic departments, twelve centers and institutes, three associate deans, and several office staff. I could not meet with all my direct reports frequently; there were just too many. Furthermore, of the eighteen academic departments, I had in-depth knowledge about one of them—psychology. I tried to school myself in these other departments by meeting with their faculty and learning about their disciplines. As the job evolved, I was working twenty-four seven and not seeing much success.

Near the end of my four-year deanship, I fired an insubordinate department chair. A huge battle ensued. As the dust settled, it seemed as if my decision had irritated pretty much everyone, including members of the administration, who opted not to renew my appointment as dean.

I could have, yet again, gone on a job search. I choose not to.

At this point, I was starting to see that the job of "dean" was impossible. No one had the skills to be good at it, at least not at a school embroiled in acrimony. I had no interest in trying yet again, at yet another school, to be the middle person between a faculty and an administration.

At the same time, the University of Akron was a Carnegie II research university on the verge of becoming Carnegie I. Its psychology department was also mighty, offering three doctoral degree programs in different specialties in psychology. The university also housed the Archives of the History of Psychology. On top of that, the current university president had an advanced degree in psychology. The place felt like home. I belonged there.

So, I returned to the faculty as a tenured professor in the department of psychology. The administration granted me a semester's leave to prepare for the role. I used the opportunity to ramp up my research program. To support my work in scale development, I audited two doctoral statistics courses, one on structural equation modeling and the other on hierarchical linear modeling, neither of which even existed when I went to grad school. Then, I set to work revising the Male Role Norms Inventory (MRNI) and developing and improving many different scales.

By fall, I started teaching several undergraduate courses. Soon, I was invited to become a core faculty member of Counseling Psychology's MA-PhD Program and given the job of directing the Department of Psychology Counseling Clinic. As a core faculty member, I could accept one or two advisees each year who were assigned to work in my lab. They started as assistant lab managers for the first year and then as lab managers in their second. Through this assignment, they worked as apprentices on my research projects and developed their ideas for their MA thesis, which often served as a launching pad for the PhD dissertation.

◆ ◆ ◆

In early July 2010, I received a call from the University of Akron police informing me that my brother, Lowell, had suffered a stroke over the Fourth of July weekend. Because he lived alone, his condition was not noticed until the morning of Tuesday, July 5, when he failed to report for work. His employer called the local police, who entered his townhome, discovered him, and arranged for him to be admitted to a hospital. By then, it was too late for effective treatment.

I flew to California to attend to him, got him admitted to a nursing home, and visited him several times over the next three months, during which time he had several hospital admissions for pneumonia. On one of these, it was discovered that he also had lung cancer.

Lowell was paralyzed on his left side but awake; However, he struggled to speak.

On the infrequent occasions he managed to say a sentence, it startled me. It was as if he briefly emerged from a deep trance only to fall back into it.

One time, as I walked into the room, he said, "And here comes

Ron, hitting a grand slam home run in Yankee Stadium!" Then he said nothing else for the entirety of the visit and even for days afterward.

As mentioned earlier, Lowell had been mentored by the poet Gary Snyder. So, I brought in Greg Brown's *The Hills of California* on a CD. In it Brown reads Gary Snyder's poem, "For All," about the wonders of Turtle Island. As the CD played, Lowell said, "Gary brought that poem just after he wrote it into our workshop and read it to universal acclamation." Then he was silent.

On another occasion, I stood next to his bed as he met with a friend. He said, "My life is over." It broke my heart.

I had durable power of attorney for Lowell's health and financial affairs. There was no hope of Lowell's recovery. Depending on the severity of his issues, he needed to be transferred from his nursing home to a hospital or from a hospital back to a nursing home. All of this required complex decisions that I felt unprepared to make. "I wish I knew what you wanted," I lamented one day as I held his hand. "I don't know if I'm doing the right thing here. I don't know how you want me to handle this. I wish you could tell me."

On top of that, Lowell had set up a revocable trust but hadn't titled all his assets to the trust. That meant endless meetings and calls with lawyers and bankers.

The stress of these circumstances caused me to suffer another depression. This time, instead of the anger turning inward, it pressed outward as irritability, anger, and aggression.

I cursed out trust officers, nurses, and hospital administrators.

Basically, I turned into my father. Again.

Knowing that I was suffering from masculine depression, I reentered therapy with a clinical social worker who practiced cognitive behavioral therapy and found a little relief.

I muddled through, and Lowell hung on for the rest of July, then August, then September.

During a visit in early October, my wife Carol suggested we tell

Lowell it was okay to let go. We knew he loved us, even if he couldn't form the words.

"Goodbye, brother," I whispered as I held his hand. "It's been a wonderful trip."

Around ten o'clock that evening, we left for the hotel. Around two thirty in the morning I got the call. He'd died. As I took note of the date, I thought Lowell would be happy. He had passed away on October 10, 2010—10/10/10. Even in his passing, he'd found a way to be poetic.

I remained depressed and angry for weeks afterward. It felt as if I'd fallen through that existential trap door that somehow sealed itself up so I couldn't escape; the door I had imagined decades before when I'd gone through the major depression.

Then, one evening, as I sat in our family room with Carol and our cats, Mickie and Keiki, the quality of the light seemed to change. Carol, the cats, and the furniture were all still there. Yet it felt as if I wasn't—not really. It was like I'd been transported into an ethereal world filled with Lowell's essence. I didn't see him. Nor did I hear his voice.

I merely felt his soft-spoken gentleness telling me that everything would be okay.

Seconds later, the room returned to normal.

Lowell's essence had departed, and so had my depression.

The anger was gone.

Caren, Carol, and I were determined to bring out a book of his best poetry. Although some of his work was included in several compilations, he'd never published his own book. Yet, as we cleared out his townhome and storage unit, we couldn't locate his poems. They were missing. We eventually found them stashed in a grocery bag in an outdoor shed, moldy, mildewed, and crawling with spiders. With the help of some of Lowell's poet friends, we put it all together and published *A Poet Drives a Truck*.

Front cover of A Poet Drives a Truck.

◆ ◆ ◆

Several years later, I received a call from Ron Fierstein, the brother of the Broadway actor, playwright, and screenwriter Harvey Fierstein.

He had an interesting proposal.

Harvey had a new musical on Broadway that, at that time, was not doing as well as he or Ron had expected. *Kinky Boots* tells the story of Charlie, who struggles to save his family's shoe factory. He pairs up with Lola, a cabaret performer and drag queen, to design and produce stilettos.

Matilda the Musical seemed to be stealing *Kinky Boots*'s thunder at the box office, and Ron had a theory as to why.

"I think it's because of the drag queens," he said. "People see it as part of queer culture. They're missing the universal themes."

"That's a shame. It's a great musical. My wife and I loved it. Still, I'm a little confused," I said, "How can I help? I'm a professor of psychology, not of marketing."

"I know, I know. I see how this might be coming out of left field for you. Bear with me. At its core, *Kinky Boots* is a story about the father-son relationship. You see, both main characters are struggling with the negative effects of their father's expectations. Charlie's father wants him to take over a shoe business, but Charlie has no interest. Simon's father wants him to be a prize fighter. But Simon is more interested in being a drag queen. You see? It's about father-son expectations. It's a universal story. Anyway, I understand you're an expert in this area."

"I am considered so," I said.

"Well, I want to draw more attention to that father-son dynamic."

"Okay, sure. But how can I do that?"

"I was thinking that our theatrical company could fund a research study on the father-son relationship. Through this research, maybe we could draw attention to the play's central theme and hopefully draw a wider audience. What do you think?"

"I can see the possibilities."

To get more insight into the play, I interviewed Harvey over the phone for an hour and learned he was influenced by Gloria Steinem's book *Revolution From Within: A Book of Self-Esteem*. Carol and I also visited New York City, had lunch with Ron and his colleagues, and saw the musical again.

As Charlie and Lola sang "Not My Father's Son," I felt as if the words had been written about my life and the lives of countless men I'd counseled over the years The lyrics spoke of how hard it was to be one's father's son, both because the father had his own plan, and because the father could not see the best part of his son.

Yes, Dad.

That was the best part of me.

If only you'd been able to see it.

AFTERWORD

I have told my life story as truthfully and accurately as I could, revealing things about my life that I am not proud of, as well as those for which I am very proud—'warts and all,' as the expression goes. Although this was a difficult and sometimes painful undertaking, I am glad that I did it, for two reasons. The more personal reason is that it has left me feeling more integrated as a person and less ashamed of my regrettable past behavior. The more generative reason is that I believe that some readers who may be struggling in their own lives might take hope from my story and find inspiration to make critical changes in their own lives.

ACKNOWLEDGEMENTS

First and foremost, I want to acknowledge my family, who gave me love and support throughout the process of writing this book: My wife and partner for life, Carol Slatter; my daughter Caren Levant and her wife, Camille Veytia; my grandsons, Adrian Shanker and Jeremy Shanker; and the many cousins with whom I continue to have sustaining relationships, particularly Diane Baines, Anita and Tom Shaw, Terry Rogoway, Craig Adler, Ted and Laurie Finkelstein, and Fern and Phil Halyard. I also want to acknowledge those who are no longer alive, who have helped me when they were: my dear mother, Wilma Idell Levant; my beloved brother, Lowell Arnold Levant; my grandparents and aunts and uncles; and two good friends—my medical school mate, Gary Bowman, and my long-time outdoor buddy, Jim Lindsley, who was always up for adventure, whether it was backpacking in the Green Mountains, cross-country skiing, running, or biking.

Additionally, I want to acknowledge my friends over so many years. This is a hazardous thing to do, because I am sure I will miss someone, so I apologize in advance for any omissions: Nancy Crowne, Marty and Fran Lebowitz, Evan and Philipa Longin, Rick Strong, Gary Brooks, Marty Belsky, Charlie Waehler, Margaret Halter, Pat DeLeon, "Dr. Bob" Resnick, Danny Wedding, Alan Entin, Elaine Rodino, Gordon Herz, Gerry Koocher, Steve Behnke, Leigh Jerome, Chris Kilmartin, Joel Wong, Doug McDonald, Norman Abeles, Joe Pleck, Kate Richmond, Marty Heesacker, Jeff Fischer, and Ryon McDermott.

I also want to acknowledge many generations of students and

colleagues, too numerous to name individually, whose relationships have sustained me over the years.

Finally, I want to thank my book coach, Alisa Bowman, my agent, Nancy Rosenfeld, and my publisher, John Koehler, for their enormous contributions to making this volume a reality.

www.ingramcontent.com/pod-product-compliance
Lightning Source LLC
La Vergne TN
LVHW091541070526
838199LV00002B/157